Ed
55

36. JUN 197

22. MAY 197

STRUGGLE WITH FORTUNE

Cardinal Newman
From the Bust by Farrell in University Church

STRUGGLE WITH FORTUNE

A MISCELLANY

For the Centenary of
The Catholic University of Ireland
1854–1954

General Editor

DR. MICHAEL TIERNEY

PRESIDENT, UNIVERSITY COLLEGE, DUBLIN

BROWNE & NOLAN LTD., DUBLIN

1954.

PUBLISHED BY UNIVERSITY COLLEGE, DUBLIN, AND PRINTED
IN THE REPUBLIC OF IRELAND BY BROWNE & NOLAN LTD.,
THE RICHVIEW PRESS, DUBLIN

PREFACE

THESE essays are, as their title indicates, a miscellaneous contribution to the Celebrations which are being held in University College, Dublin, to mark the Centenary of the opening of the Catholic University of Ireland in 1854. They make no claim to anything like historical completeness. Indeed, the history of the Catholic University of Ireland in its various transformations is so strangely complicated and in certain respects still so obscure that its writing would be a task of great difficulty and long duration.

What is attempted in the present miscellany is rather a series of sketches, illuminating, with a brightness which it is hoped will not be excessively fitful, some of the more accessible phases of the story of an institution which has played a considerable part in the history of modern Ireland. In such a presentation of such a story, anything like rigid consistency as between the various authors will hardly be expected. Each has in practice been allowed to expound his own views, and the result may at least be said to communicate some of that vitality which characterised the University and the College even in their weakest days. Opportunity has been taken through the kindness of the Director of Radio Éireann to incorporate in an Appendix three broadcast talks delivered in May and June, 1954, by the Registrar, Professor J. J. Hogan, by Dr. C. P. Curran, and by the writer of this prefatory note. It was felt that these talks, while intensifying its miscellaneous quality, might fill some of the gaps in the book.

I wish to express my warmest thanks to the Committee which helped in the preliminary organisation of the work, and especially to Professor Louis P. Roche, whose early editorial labours were an indispensable aid ; to all the contributors, with special reference to Dr. C. P. Curran,

PREFACE

Professor Patrick Semple, and Professor Mary Macken;
to the Rector of Clongowes and others, who have kindly
supplied material for illustration; to Miss Ellen Power,
Librarian of the College; and finally to the Secretary and
Printing Staff of Messrs. Browne & Nolan, who made
possible in difficult circumstances what might have seemed
at first an impossible task.

M. T.

CONTENTS

PREFACE v

"A WEARY TASK": THE STRUGGLE IN RETROSPECT 1

THE JESUIT FATHERS AND UNIVERSITY COLLEGE . 19

THE ROYAL UNIVERSITY 51

THE CATHOLIC UNIVERSITY SCHOOL OF MEDICINE
(1855–1909) 61

THE WORK OF DR. COFFEY AND DR. CONWAY
(1908–1947) 81

THE STUDENT BODY 103

CELTIC STUDIES IN THE UNIVERSITY AND THE
COLLEGE 121

WOMEN IN THE UNIVERSITY AND THE COLLEGE . 142

THE COLLEGE AND THE NATION 166

PROSPECT FOR THE FUTURE 193

APPENDIX 213

LIST OF ILLUSTRATIONS

Cardinal Newman . . . . . *Frontispiece*

Sketch of the proposed Catholic University of Ireland . . *between pages* 40-41

Certificate showing Façade of Catholic University Medical School, Cecilia Street . . . . *facing page* 64

Most Rev. Bartholomew Woodlock, D.D. „ „ 80

Most Rev. Dr. William J. Walsh . „ „ 112

Father William Delany, S.J. . . „ „ 128

Royal University, Dublin . . . „ „ 144

The Dublin Commissioners, 1908–1911 „ „ 160

Dr. Denis J. Coffey . . . . „ „ 176

Professor Eoin MacNeill . . . „ „ 192

Dr. A. W. Conway . . . . „ „ 208

"A WEARY TASK" : THE STRUGGLE IN RETROSPECT

The President of University College, Dublin

In order to understand the complicated series of events which led to the foundation of the Catholic University of Ireland, at least three factors, each in itself highly complicated, must be taken into account. The first of these factors is the peculiar reaction of the English Tory Government to Daniel O'Connell's agitation for repeal of the Union. In many ways this reaction foreshadowed the later Tory policy of " killing Home Rule with kindness." After the show-down with O'Connell at Clontarf, which ended in a Pyrrhic victory for the Government, the cause of repeal was anything but lost, as some of O'Connell's more youthful and more passionate followers believed it to be. What really postponed repeal was not O'Connell's refusal to fight a new battle of Clontarf with an unarmed host ; it was the premature senility which became evident during his imprisonment in Richmond Gaol and the measureless calamity of the Famine a few years later. That the Irish cause was by no means lost and that the English Government under its very able leader was well aware of this is made abundantly clear by Peel's policy of coming to the Irish with a Greek gift in the form of secularly controlled University Education. At the same time this policy was an interesting example of the English propensity for trying out in Ireland schemes not yet ripe or only partially ripe for introduction into England. Peel was one of the foremost exponents of the new concept of secular education with which a mild beginning had been made in England by the foundation of the University of London in 1836. To a greater degree even than the Royal University forty-three years later, London University was a mere machine for examinations. Its governing idea was of utilitarian origin and was based upon the belief that in the age of the

1

printed book formal teaching could be largely dispensed
with. In this respect the Queen's Colleges established in
Ireland by Peel's Act of 1845 were a compromise. The
Colleges, themselves strictly controlled by Dublin Castle,
were intended to provide a certain minimum of teaching,
but all their work was directed towards a great system of
examinations conducted by the Queen's University of
Ireland which was modelled on London.

Unlike the traditional Tory of the Lyndhurst type, and
in sharp opposition to the New Toryism, with which
Disraeli was later to capture the party, Peel was a devotee
of secularism and of the utilitarian principles—strangely
called liberal—in education, and Newman in 1841 had
already denounced his views on the subject in some famous
letters to *The Times*. For the student of history it is interesting to watch the working out of the chance which offered
these ideas to the Catholics of Ireland as a means of diverting
their passion for political independence. The offer had to
reckon in Ireland with two very powerful forces, one highly
articulate, the other, at that time, almost in a subconscious
or preconscious state. The first of these forces was the
Irish Hierarchy, reorganised and reintegrated since the
passing of Fitzwilliam's Emancipation Act and the foundation of Maynooth. The Hierarchy had behind it of course
the whole weight of the Western Church, then in the first
phases of what was to be one of its greatest movements of
revival. Roman policy on the problem created by Peel's
University Act was largely moulded by the Rector of the
Irish College, Paul Cullen, who in 1849 was appointed by
Pius IX Archbishop of Armagh, and whose first act on his
arrival in Ireland in 1850 was to convoke the Synod of
Thurles over which he presided as Apostolic Delegate. The
condemnation of the Queen's Colleges by the Synod was
announced in a joint Pastoral Letter on 9th September
1850, six days after the issue of the Government's Letters
Patent establishing the Queen's University in Ireland.

Far more fateful than the decision to condemn the
Queen's Colleges which had been urged on the Bishops
from as early as 1847 was the decision to take the positive

step of founding a Catholic University of Ireland. This decision was arrived at also in Rome, and the Rescript from Propaganda containing the original condemnation of the Queen's Colleges ordered also that a Catholic University should be founded in Ireland on the model of that founded—or rather refounded—by the Belgian Bishops thirteen years earlier at Louvain. This proposal was repeated by Propaganda in a second Rescript in 1848, and even before the convening of the Synod of Thurles a Committee was set up for the purpose of furthering the plan. It was this Committee which in November 1851 decided to invite Newman to accept the Rectorship. For various reasons he was not finally installed until 3rd June 1854, and the Catholic University was opened for the first time in November of the same year.

The second Irish force with which Peel's policy had to reckon was well summed up by W. K. Sullivan ten years later. Sullivan ascribed the origin of the Catholic University not to any tactical policy of opposition to " the Godless Colleges " but to an inevitable necessity arising out of the demand of 5,000,000 people for higher education. This demand was necessarily at first inarticulate and was at all times conditioned by the presence or absence of active secondary schools. Thus it is worth noting how much it was influenced at a later stage by the passing of the Irish Intermediate Education Act of 1878. The view has often been stated that the Catholic University suffered for want of a steady supply of well prepared students from Secondary Schools ; and indeed Newman himself always felt this lack and frequently discussed methods of making it good. In 1850 there were twenty-one Catholic Secondary Schools in the whole country (fifteen of them diocesan) and this number had risen to forty-eight by 1870. Sullivan's judgement indicates his belief that there was a strong if slow and obscure popular determination to secure higher education, and the action of the Catholic people of Ireland in subscribing £80,000 to the Catholic University up to 1859, and another £110,000 during the next twenty years, is as clear a proof as can be needed that the Catholics were

determined to get what they wanted. The decision of the
Bishops therefore to establish the Catholic University may
be said to have inaugurated a kind of educational policy
of self-reliance, very much on the lines of the later Sinn
Féin movement. If the results were feeble enough and
slow in accruing the fault lies not so much with the people
or the policy as with the cruel circumstances against which
both had to contend.

There were of course to be many shifts and changes in
the pattern of English policy on Irish education during the
sixty years that lay between Newman's inauguration and
the passing of the Irish Universities Act. Peel's Toryism
was to fade into Gladstonian Liberalism, which became
perhaps the most decisive single force in breaking the
English hold on Ireland. The historian may perhaps be
permitted to regret that Gladstone, who was so sympathetic
towards Newman's great rival Manning, never achieved
a juncture with the mind of Newman which was in many
respects so singularly like his own. Such a juncture, had
it occurred and had the time factor been favourable, might
well, through the provision at an earlier date of a university
system really acceptable to Irish Catholics, have largely
offset the consequences of Gladstone's heroic failure over
Home Rule. It is strange that, quintessential Oxford man
as he was, Gladstone does not seem to have really grasped
the importance of higher education in a modern community. Under Disraeli, and still more under Salisbury,
Toryism was in the end to combine with Peel's hardness ·
much of the reactionary immobility of pre-Reform days.
For Ireland its attitudes were to be almost entirely and
disastrously negative. Thus the Royal University in 1879,
in spite of the fact that its creation synchronised so closely
with the new University movement in Great Britain, was
very little more than a makeshift, which was fittingly
described by Father Delany as " at least better than
nothing." Dr. Curran has well described it as making a
ramshackle but yet workable bridge between the Catholic
University and the University College of the present day.

Shifts and changes there were to be in Ireland also,

affecting the attitude of the Hierarchy towards what they were later to describe as their " weary task " of keeping the Catholic University question alive, and affecting too the dogged semi-conscious determination of the people to settle their own problems in their own way—a determination which, because of its clash with Tory intransigence, was in the end to shatter the British Empire itself. It is unnecessary to dwell here at length upon the obscure question of the influence, so fascinating to the historian, of the various personalities of Cullen, MacHale, and Newman himself on the fortunes of the strange institution which they had jointly brought into existence at such an unpropitious moment. The present writer has perhaps already devoted sufficient emphasis to the thesis that, for all its rickety youth and slowness to mature, Newman's University was not a failure. It is probably better worth while at this point to draw attention to the curiously varied contributions made to the character of the foundling university by its distant but real connection with Louvain, by Newman's Oxford predilections and finally by the combination of Father Delany's Jesuit efficiency and the Royal University's vaguely " Redbrick " system of examinations. Each of these three influences was destined to leave an impression and even that left by the much disliked " Old Royal " has still an element of life. Newman's plan for a series of Halls of Residence, which he hoped might in time develop into Colleges of the Oxford type, was destined, not because of any inherent defect but solely under pressure of circumstance, to eventuate in the residential Jesuit University College in St. Stephen's Green ; while his Medical School alone was not only to preserve the name of his University but to play a predominant part in the growth of the Catholic medical profession in Ireland.

Other contributors to this book will tell in more detail the story of how St. Patrick's House, number 86 St. Stephen's Green, became the Jesuit University College. What the present essay is most concerned to do is to suggest that this change, like subsequent changes, was not the product of deliberate policy but of external pressures, and that, striking though it may well have seemed then and later, it merely served to mask an essential intellectual and spiritual continuity. By virtue of this persistence of an informing idea very many of the staff appointed in 1909 were the pupils of the men appointed by Newman between 1854 and 1858. Until 1883 the Catholic University could offer its students, apart from medicals, nothing beyond the essence of a higher education. Its degrees were never legally recognised, and the generous support of the Catholic poor was no effective substitute for a regular State endowment. After a couple of years of semi-interregnum, the appointment of Dr. Woodlock as Rector in 1861 seemed to give new life to the University. Thirty acres of land were bought at Drumcondra and the laying of the foundation-stone on 20th July 1862, after a muster of 200,000 people, which recalled the days of Repeal, was one of the memorable events of nineteenth-century Irish history. Dr. Woodlock seems to have had a quality comparable in some degree with that of Newman himself; but the years from 1863 to 1878 were truly lean years in the University's history. Before Dr. Woodlock retired to the Bishopric of Ardagh, negotiations had begun to bring in the Jesuit Fathers. Dr. Woodlock's transient successor was Dr. Neville, whose sustenance was provided by his appointment to a parish in the Diocese of Cork, and whose regular commutations from there to Dublin are said to have earned for him among his handful of students the nick-name " Monsignor Often-Back."

It would be a grievous mistake to assume that during its Jesuit phase, the University, now become the College, wrote off its association with Newman. Apart from the continuance on the staff of men like Casey and Arnold, there was always Cecilia Street, whose students were highly conscious of their role in Irish intellectual life, and quite capable of issuing stern reminders of their existence, if anyone indeed had really been tempted to forget it. A glance at the pages of *St. Stephen's*, the students' magazine, which from 1901–1906 did so much to enliven Father Delany's second term of office as President, will show at once how close was the link between the Medical Faculty and the Jesuit College, and how far any repudiation of Newman was from the minds of those who controlled the journal. The very first article in the first number, for example, is an article on the *Catholic University Gazette*, by no less a person than Father Joseph Darlington. *St. Stephen's*, in a time which was unpropitious enough, represented an effort at revival, and it is only to be expected that every such effort will recall the personality and the name of the founder.

Nowhere is this spirit better represented than in the Editorial for the number dated February 1906, which is worth quoting.

" The University for which we stand is one of whose prestige we may have no fear. It is not the Royal but the old Catholic University of Ireland—the University of Newman, of O'Curry, of so many distinguished and patriot Irishmen of modern times ; a University whose prestige is not of a day, not of three hundred years, but of one thousand years, for the spirit which animated it and yet animates it is the same glorious spirit which animated the scholars of ancient Ireland, which animated our fathers of the Penal Days, the love of learning for learning's sake, for Ireland's sake, and for religion's sake."

The style of this may perhaps be regarded as youthful rhetoric but the sentiment is surely significant as representing student opinion at a time when the Universities Act of 1908 was drawing close.

In his own time at Oxford Newman had made himself remarkable in the first instance as a member of a group which wished to reform the tutorial system and to restore the University Professors to what he considered their rightful place as teachers. His doctrine on this matter is bound up with the theory of Influence and Discipline which he expounds at such length in his *University Sketches*. It is noteworthy that in his Dublin venture he broke new ground in an attempt " to blend the Professorial and Tutorial Systems "—a procedure which as Dr. McGrath points out was capable of working well with a small number of students at the start of his University. On the other hand he left no one in any doubt as to his purpose of appointing as strong a professoriate as possible. " Professors *of name*, not merely able men," he told Dr. Cullen, " are absolutely necessary. It will be a great thing for the success of the institution to get professors whose names are known to the Continent, to the world." This insistence on the importance of professors may perhaps be regarded as in part a gesture towards Louvain. The same origin may be suggested both for the title of the Faculty of Arts and Letters in his draft provisions for the constitution of the University, and for many details in his curriculum. The normal age for entry was sixteen and at the end of the second year students had to submit to a public examination, the passing of which conferred the rank of Scholar. Another examination, at the end of the third year, gave the rank of Inceptor, and the examination at the end of the fourth year—corresponding to the unattainable degree—was called the Licentiate. The curriculum was divided into four groups—Christian Knowledge, Philosophy, Literature, and History. Each group contained a number of subjects and for what was called the Meritorious Licentiate each candidate had to take four subjects, one from each group. Perhaps the most noteworthy feature of this curriculum was the presence in it at every stage of tuition in Christian Knowledge. From the beginning of course the Medical School trained its students for the Licentiate of the Royal Colleges of Surgeons and Physicians, and it was the possibility of this which gave the Catholic University the nearest equivalent to official recognition for its degrees. The Faculties of Engineering and Architecture never grew beyond their initial stages, but the Medical School was destined to play a big part in the development of Catholic medical teaching, and by 1901 had come to be the largest medical school in Ireland. The Faculty of Philosophy and Letters continued to work on Newman's curriculum until the founding of the Royal University.

Clearly the great reason for handing over the control of

this Faculty to the Jesuits in 1883 was the success which Father Delany had already achieved in training students both for the examinations of London University and those of the Royal. It was the curriculum of the latter, itself modelled on that of the Queen's University and thus ultimately on that of London, which was to become dominant after 1879. A comparison of the present-day examination papers of the National University with those of the Royal will show how close is the generic link between them. Not unconnected with the comparative success of the Royal University was of course the contemporary development of the Indian and Home Civil Service which opened up great new prospects for able Irish graduates. It was the desirability—indeed almost the necessity—of exploiting these opportunities that appears to have given the Jesuits their strongest claim. The election of practically all the Professors of the Faculty to Fellowships in the Royal University served as a bridge between the old and the new, just as the election of so many Fellows of the Royal University holding Chairs in University College to Professorships in the National University was to do in 1909.

In the last of his series of articles on the Catholic University in the *Ecclesiastical Record* for 1928, Father Lambert McKenna, S.J., asserts that the taking over of University College by the Jesuit Fathers on 2nd November 1883 " may be taken as the end of the Catholic University." He himself however recognises that the Medical School must be excepted from this summing up, and the Medical School was always to remain larger in point of numbers than the College in St. Stephen's Green. It would be more just to recognise frankly that the determining factor in all these complex changes was the external one—the unwillingness of successive British Governments to give Irish Catholics what they wanted—and not any spontaneous change of policy with regard to the University on the part of the Hierarchy and their flock. The next thirty years were to demonstrate that, valuable as were the opportunities provided by the Royal University, they were very far from satisfying Irish aspirations.

Even before Lord Salisbury's " twenty years of resolute government " had come to an end with the Liberal landslide at the election of 1906, the University Question had again forced itself to the front. The Robertson Commission, which sat from 1901 to 1903, and the Fry Commission, which sat in 1906, produced Reports which cover the whole history of the question with the greatest completeness. For many years before the first of these Commissions began its work, the great Archbishop of Dublin, Dr. William Walsh, had insisted on the desirability of seeking a final solution by founding a College for Catholics within the University of Dublin. In 1904, a year after the Robertson Commission had issued its inconclusive Report, Lord Dunraven made public a proposal more or less on Dr. Walsh's lines. It was this proposal which led to the setting up of the Fry Commission by the Liberal Government. The Report of this Commission, while exceedingly valuable for the light it throws on the constitution, history and claims of Trinity College, brought the matter very little further. In January 1907, James Bryce, Liberal Chief Secretary, announced in Belfast that the Government had decided to legislate on the lines of the Dunraven scheme. This announcement finally brought matters to a head. Trinity College launched a strong movement of protest, as a result of which, and of a difference in policy between Dr. Walsh and Father Delany, it was finally decided to revert to the recommendations of the Robertson Commission of 1903. Substantially it was upon these recommendations that the National University of Ireland and its Constituent Colleges were to be organised under the Act of 1908.

The decisive nature of Father Delany's intervention at two crucial points in the history of the Irish University Question has perhaps not been sufficiently realised. The two points were the beginning and the end of the period of Jesuit administration. In 1882, when the fourteen Fellowships of the Royal University were being filled for the first time, the Senate of that body decided, at the instance of Father Delany, to concentrate all of them in the newly

constituted University College at number 86, St. Stephen's
Green. Dr. Walsh, who was at that time President of
Maynooth, favoured a policy, earlier outlined by Dr. Woodlock, under which the Catholic University was to include,
along with what was left of Newman's foundation, several
other institutions, such as Maynooth, Carlow, All Hallows,
Clonliffe, and new Colleges of university rank to be developed at Blackrock and Castleknock. In pursuance of
this policy Dr. Walsh proposed that one Royal University
Fellowship should be given to a distinguished professor at
Blackrock, Father Reffé. Although Father Delany was not
himself at this time a member of the Senate, his ability and
influence were such that he was able to secure the defeat of
Dr. Walsh's proposal. The effect of this decision was of
course to concentrate all the work of the Catholic University, except its Medical Faculty, in the new Jesuit
College. Dr. Walsh resigned from the Senate, to which he
was never afterwards to belong, whereas Father Delany
succeeded Cardinal McCabe as a member in 1885.

Father Delany's second intervention, which took place
when the substitution of a new system for the Royal University was being considered after 1900, put him once more
unwillingly in opposition to Dr. Walsh. The latter had for
many years advocated the establishment of a Catholic
College in the University of Dublin. This proposal was
opposed by Father Delany at the Robertson and the Fry
Commissions and with Dr. Healy, Archbishop of Tuam, he
was instrumental in having a unanimous resolution against
it passed in 1906 by the Senate of the Royal University.
Dr. Walsh's proposal would in all probability have had
the effect of ultimately converting Dublin University into
a predominantly Catholic institution. The joint opposition
to this proposal of Trinity College itself and of University
College, as represented by Father Delany, was probably
decisive and the consequences of the decision then taken
are still with us to-day.

The immediate success of the settlement of 1908 should
not blind the historian to its real character as a compromise,
honestly arrived at and therefore generally accepted, among

a chaos of conflicting views. It may be said that in a minor and subordinate way the Irish University Question ran parallel to the greater question of Irish self-government during the second half of the nineteenth century. Both may be said to have been fanned into new life from the embers left by O'Connell's gigantic agitation ; and it is curious to note that in the case of the University the fire-bringer should have been no other than the English Tory Prime Minister who had bested O'Connell. Whereas efforts to bring about a political settlement were protracted for so long that they came to ruin on the outbreak of the First World War, the minor question was settled by compromise in the nick of time. It may be said that University College, Dublin, in its last and most successful phase, represents, side by side with the establishment of peasant proprietorship, an enduring victory for the more moderate Irish nationalism of the nineteenth century. Of that nationalism it would be hard to find a more typical representative than the new College's first President, Dr. Denis J. Coffey. It was no wonder that the sweeping transformation brought about by the 1916 Rising should have produced difficulties and anxieties for such an institution and such a President. What is to be admired—and this is important as throwing light on the character and quality of the institution—is the comparative ease with which the difficulties and anxieties of these political earthquakes were surmounted. Nothing could better attest the organic strength of the College, its capacity to adapt itself to any possible changes in its native environment, than the fact not only of its triumphant survival but also of its continuous and almost unforeseen growth during the quarter of a century from 1909 to 1934.

The new College was indeed the result of a compromise painfully and slowly worked out. Its constitution, the nature and scope of its endowment, even the framework of its curriculum were not the product of organic growth from within, but imposed from without in response to the slowly changing dictates not of Irish but of English public opinion. Newman's Catholic University has been, and indeed still sometimes is, criticised as the effort of an

Englishman to transplant an English institution to Ireland for the benefit of English-speaking Catholics. It would seem curiously to have escaped the notice of Newman's critics that a similar—indeed a more devastating—charge could easily be framed against the National University of Ireland and its Constituent Colleges. The charge was in fact made almost immediately by Cardinal Logue who so vigorously described the new University as "a pagan bantling." Though it was designed to provide a satisfactory form of higher education for Irish Catholics, its constitution followed closely enough the model of the secular provincial universities which had grown up in England and Wales during the latter half of the nineteenth century. In theory and in outward appearance it might even be said to represent a victory for the liberalism in education which Newman in his old age claimed to have fought "for thirty, forty, fifty years," and against which his Catholic University was designed to be a bulwark.

The governing authorities of the National University and its Colleges are for the most part laymen. It is forbidden by the Act of 1908 to use its public endowment for theological or religious teaching. No religious tests are imposed on its teaching staffs, and in fact many of its most distinguished and successful professors have not belonged to the religion of the majority of the Irish people. Although the first Chancellor of the National University was the great Archbishop who had done so much to bring it into existence, its second has been the lay political leader of one of the two great parties into which the Sinn Féin movement was divided in its moment of victory. Theoretically and formally the new University College might be considered to bear a far closer resemblance to the English "Redbrick" type of secular University than Newman's Catholic University ever bore to Oxford. Yet it can more truly be said that the College provides one of the most striking examples of the Irish capacity for taking hold of English constitutional forms and devices and bending them into an unmistakably Irish shape. The enormous majority of its students, both Irish and foreign, are Catholics, and the number and vigour of their Sodalities and strictly Catholic clubs and societies bear witness to the existence among them of real intellectual and devotional vitality. The College's courses in several faculties are utilised by a large number of ecclesiastical students and religious of many types, whose presence may be said to contribute greatly to what might be called the College's personality. The absence of a theological faculty, except insofar as lectures in Catholic Theology have been provided from the beginning by the Irish Bishops for those who wish to take them in addition to their ordinary studies, makes less difference than might theoretically be expected, for the reason that ample facilities for the study of theology are readily available both in Maynooth and in numerous Dublin religious houses. In recent years the ever-present problem of systematic religious instruction for University students has begun to assume a new urgency. Newman met this problem by making Religious Knowledge one of the standard groups of subjects in which instruction was given as part of courses for his Licentiate. This cannot indeed be readily done under the present constitution of the College and University ; but there need be no doubt that a practical solution of this problem can and will be found.

From another point of view it is likely enough that the present constitution of the College would meet with Newman's warm approval. Both during his period of office as Rector of the Catholic University and on several later occasions he lost no opportunity to urge that the Catholic laity should be allowed to co-operate in the government of the University. His views on this point are nowhere more forcibly expressed than in a letter written to Mr. Fottrell in 1873 and published by Wilfrid Ward.[1] There he goes so far as to say that the absence of such co-operation was " one of the chief evils which I deplored in the management of the affairs of the University twenty years ago when I was in Ireland." The history of the new University College during the past forty-five years has clearly shown that in this, as in almost all his views,

[1] *Life of John Henry Cardinal Newman.* Volume 2, p. 397.

Newman was essentially right. The historian might even
go so far as to judge that the refusal of Cardinal Cullen to
meet Newman's wishes in this respect was one of the reasons
for the stagnation which undoubtedly did affect the Catholic
University in its earlier phase. It is curious to reflect that
what Newman so clearly recognised as a deficiency was to
be more than made up by an English Liberal statesman
after half a century had elapsed. In this particular respect
it is hardly to be argued that the Act of 1908 tipped the
balance too far on the side of lay control. The main
function of a university is on the one hand the general
education of all its students to play their part in a given
society and on the other the training of candidates for
professions requiring a high degree of intellectual attainment as well as for the higher civil service. While in a
Catholic society, such as Ireland is, it is right and natural
that general education should have a strongly Catholic
bias, this need not by any means necessitate its direct
control, and still less its financial or business administration,
by ecclesiastical authority. Newman's view was that undue
clerical control of lay higher education involves a grave
risk of ultimate conflict between clergy and laity, and
consequently danger to the interests of the Church as a
whole. There is reason to think that the change in 1909
came just in time to avert the development of this danger
in the Jesuit College. In the working out of an efficient
and frictionless method under which clergy and laity may
satisfactorily play their respective parts in Catholic higher
education, University College, Dublin, may well prove in
some respects a pioneer. Its experience at any rate has
been varied enough, and it has had much occasion to take
to heart the famous advice of the legendary parish priest
to his inexperienced curate " keep your principles intact
and act according to circumstances."

The Act of 1908, whatever be the ultimate verdict of
history upon its administrative details, at least provided
conditions sufficiently near to what had long been sought
to enable University College to enter on a phenomenal
period of growth. In retrospect it was regrettable that the

title " College," which had been adopted under duress
for the part of the Catholic University afterwards handed
over to the Jesuits, should have been perpetuated as the
name of an institution so soon destined to outgrow it.
University College, Dublin, is now larger in number of
students than such a great English University as Birmingham. The federal machinery of the National University,
for which the University of Wales undoubtedly provided
a model, performed one valuable service in conferring a
droit de cité upon Sir Robert Peel's creations in Cork and
Galway. Administratively speaking, this machinery had
long since proved rather unwieldy and only the very great
loyalty and goodwill of the three Colleges towards each
other have been able to postpone a break-down which
seems eventually inevitable. There has always been a
certain minor inconvenience peculiar to the Dublin College
in the system of nomenclature sanctioned by the Act of
1908. Just as nobody nowadays refers to the Royal University except as " The Old Royal," so it would appear
that, for the great majority of Irish citizens, University
College, Dublin, is " The National." At the same time
it has proved quite impossible to prevent foreigners from
confusing University College with that very different
institution the University of Dublin, which is of course
Trinity College under a different aspect. The origin of the
title " National University " is a little obscure. It must
have been decided on while the Act of 1908 was under
contemplation and the most probable time for this decision
was the moment when the original idea of an enlarged
Dublin University was abandoned. Several motives may
have contributed to the use of the term " National." The
description " national university " had been used in all
the preceding discussions for whatever should eventually
be the sole or principal university of the country. The first
suggested title for the new institution was *The University
of Ireland*. When *National University* was settled upon, it
must have pleased some people by the breadth and others
by the limitation it suggested.

In any case the Act of 1908 was decisive in refusing to

give legal recognition under its original title to the Catholic University of Ireland. It was decisive in other respects also. The "hands off Trinity" campaign, which was waged so energetically while the Act was being drafted, was victorious insofar as it induced the Liberal Government to leave Trinity College out of the new settlement. This victory meant that in future Trinity College was to be allowed to go its own gait and develop on its own lines. The proposal to enlarge Dublin University so as to make it in fact what its authorities at the time of the Robertson and Fry Commissions had emphatically asserted it ought to be, the national university of Ireland, was decisively rejected. This rejection amounted in fact to acceptance for Trinity of the status of a private university. At the same time, the establishment of Queen's University in Belfast might be seen in retrospect as an obscure forewarning of a policy even then largely unsuspected. Insofar as there exists an Irish University problem at the present day its outlines have been drawn by these decisions. The future will show whether they are open to modification or whether they are so rooted in the nature of Irish society as to be unalterable.

Irish controversies generally last a long time and have a way of changing their terms during their course while remaining concerned with the same fundamentals. The controversy about university education has conformed with this general rule. The struggle which began over one hundred years ago and which for its first half century seemed to consist in a succession of failures, has, during the second half century, turned in a victorious direction but under terms and in conditions quite unforeseen by those who began it. So great indeed have been the changes in external circumstances that many have failed or refused to recognise the continuity of the struggle itself. Yet the tenacity which held on for the first fifty years and the successes both qualitative and quantitative of the second half century are a vindication of Newman's effort and a fulfilment of his famous prophecy. The modern University College, altered though it is from what he might have

2

wished it to be, is none the less the harvest of Newman's sowing in what for so long seemed an infertile soil. The College has in recent years, for the first time, acquired an estate worthy of its capacities. In the physical and material sense it will take a long time and cost a great deal to build worthily on that estate. Intellectually and spiritually the future policy of the College is already laid down for it in outline. It is that it should remain faithful in all the changes of circumstance, as it has during the first century of its existence, to the idea of its founder. The College must always remember with pride that it owes its origin to the hard and little-rewarded work of one of the greatest men of nineteenth century England, whose coming to Ireland was a providential requital for secular wrongs.

THE JESUIT FATHERS AND UNIVERSITY COLLEGE

REV. PROFESSOR AUBREY GWYNN, S.J.

I

IN the autumn of 1883 the Irish Hierarchy entrusted the administration of University College to the Irish Jesuit Fathers. Father William Delany was President of University College from 1883 to 1888, and again from 1897 to 1909. His place was taken by Father Robert Carbery from 1888 to 1897. In the summer of 1909 the Jesuit Fathers handed over the administration of the College to Dr. Coffey, the first President of University College, Dublin, in its new life as a Constituent College of the National University of Ireland. I can claim to be one of the group of students who signed Dr. Coffey's roll in the first year of the new College's existence ; and I have lived for the past twenty-eight years in a community which has inherited the traditions and memories of Father Delany's College. Perhaps then I may be allowed to recall here, as best I can, some memories that have been passed from older to younger men in the past fifty years, so that to-day a more numerous generation may know something of the traditions which were ours when we first entered the College as students in the autumn of 1909.

At the outset there is a personal tribute that every Irish Jesuit would gladly pay to the memory of a priest who worked devotedly, though unsuccessfully, to maintain the high ideals of University life which Newman had sought to establish here in Dublin during the short years of his government as Rector of the Catholic University. Dr. Bartholomew Woodlock, who was later Bishop of Ardagh and Clonmacnoise (1879–94), was appointed Rector of the Catholic University in April 1861, and held that post until his elevation to the episcopate eighteen years later. In 1861 he had been for seven years President of All Hallows

19

College, which he had helped Father Hand to found in
1842. Both as President of All Hallows and as Rector of
the Catholic University, Dr. Woodlock gave of his best as
organiser and administrator; but the charge which he
received from the Irish Bishops in 1861 was very much
more difficult and discouraging than his presidency of a
College which was already becoming the centre of a nation-
wide missionary effort. Newman left Dublin for the last
time in November 1858, and the best part of three years
went by before the Bishops made up their minds to appoint
a successor. An atmosphere of failure and defeat was
inevitable during so long an interregnum, and Dr. Woodlock
never wholly succeeded in overcoming that formidable
obstacle. For a year or two it seemed that the new Rector
might succeed in bringing back life to a scheme which had
come so near to total failure. On 20th July 1862 an imposing public procession and ceremony, at which the
foundation-stone was laid of what was planned as the new
building of the Catholic University at Drumcondra, gave
the impression of new confidence and strength; and Dr.
Woodlock's surviving papers make it plain that in those
early years he sought everywhere for support and practical
co-operation. But the dead weight of government indifference, the refusal to grant any official recognition to the
degrees of the Catholic University, the lack of adequate
recruitment from Catholic secondary schools and the continued necessity of relying on the generous charity of a
hard-pressed clergy and laity for funds that were so urgently
needed, proved in the end too heavy a handicap. The last
years of Dr. Woodlock's administration were quite obviously
years of drift towards ultimate failure; but this drift was in
no way due to the Rector's lack of energy. He had done
his best under an impossible handicap, and all students of
University College owe him a real debt of gratitude. They
may be reminded that the present Aula Maxima in
Stephen's Green, though it has been recently enlarged and
improved, is still a monument to the Rector who built it
in 1878 when funds were exceedingly short.

During these last years the number of students had

dropped to little more than twenty or thirty, most of whom were resident in St. Patrick's House which came under Jesuit management in 1873. This " House " was a curious institution, which illustrates vividly the desperately inadequate buildings with which Dr. Woodlock and his staff had to be content. The students lived in the two upper stories of No. 86, whilst the ground floor and first floor were reserved for the Rector and for other official purposes. The students could only gain access to their quarters through No. 87 (now the Catholic Presbytery), using a covered passage which had been built over the entrance into the church. The two Jesuit Fathers who were in charge of St. Patrick's House lived in No. 87 ; the best known of them was Father Mathew Russell, who had founded the *Irish Monthly* in 1874 and who acted as Spiritual Director to the students from 1874 to 1880, when the Jesuit Fathers withdrew from the House.

Were it not for the need of maintaining some positive proof of the need felt by Irish Catholic students of a university that might satisfy their religious and national convictions, it is probable that the Irish Bishops would have closed the Catholic University some years before 1879. But agitation for a Catholic university was maintained, though intermittently, during all these years ; and in the spring of 1879 O'Conor Don introduced a private Bill for the foundation and endowment of a new Irish university. His bill was too frankly an effort to provide state funds for an Irish Catholic university centre to be acceptable to either the Tory government of Lord Beaconsfield or the Liberal Party under Gladstone, who was in opposition in 1879. But O'Conor Don's Bill, which was finally withdrawn, was the immediate occasion of a new attempt by Beaconsfield to settle this troublesome question. A new Royal University of Ireland, planned on the lines of that University of London which had seemed in Newman's eyes the embodiment of all those " liberal " principles he so cordially distrusted and detested, was to be the solution of the difficulty.

I must leave to Professor Semple the task of explaining

the structure of the Royal University, as it finally took shape after some three years of discussion and modification. From the point of view which concerns me here, the important thing is to understand that the Royal University of Ireland Act, which became law in the summer of 1879, opened up new prospects for the higher education of Irish Catholics. Father Delany, who was to become the President of University College in 1883, had been Rector of St. Stanislaus' College, Tullamore (commonly known as Tullabeg), from 1870 to 1880; and he had been a pioneer in the new policy of preparing his senior students for the external examinations of the University of London. The successes which he obtained in this way led others to follow his example. By 1879 it had become common for Irish schools to prepare their boys for this form of open competition by examination. The passing of the Royal University Act in 1879 meant that these boys could now be prepared for the examinations of a university which was under some form of Irish control. Blackrock College opened a special department at the " Castle " for students of this class in 1880. Its Dean, Father Reffé, quickly drew attention to the school by the striking successes which his students won in the first public examinations of the Royal University. Father Delany was moved from Tullabeg to Dublin in 1882, where he opened a small Jesuit college in Temple Street for the same purpose.

Meanwhile there had been important changes in Stephen's Green. Dr. Woodlock had become Bishop of Ardagh and Clonmacnoise in 1879, and his place as Rector of the Catholic University was taken by Dean Neville of Cork, who did his best to combine this new responsibility with his parochial and diocesan duties in Cork. Dean Neville's main duty was to act as spokesman for the Bishops in the long deliberations which followed the passing of the Royal University Act in 1879 ; but Dr. Woodlock, with Dr. William Walsh, who became President of Maynooth College in 1880, were also influential advisers in these years of transition. Interest centred chiefly on the prospect of getting some adequate, if indirect endowment for a Catholic University

College through the new scheme of fellowships in the Royal University. When the scheme was first mooted, it was expected that there would be money enough to provide for forty-eight fellowships, and Catholic hopes were correspondingly high. But Gladstone became Chancellor of the Exchequer in 1880, and his " Liberal " grant of £20,000 for the University's needs meant in practice that no more than £6,000 would be available for these fellowships. The Senate altered its plans accordingly in November 1880, and put forward a more modest scheme for thirty-two fellowships. Even this number was finally reduced to twenty-six ; and of these only half were made available for University College, Dublin, which lacked the direct state endowments that were still continued for the three Queen's Colleges.

At first the Bishops had hoped that all the money set aside for these fellowships would be made available for the unendowed College in Dublin. The Catholic University building was the natural centre of any scheme of this kind ; in 1881 it was reorganised as University College, with Dr. John Egan as its President. The Jesuit Fathers withdrew at the same time from St. Patrick's House ; and the way was open for various changes. In September 1882 Dr. Woodlock, who knew the problem as few others did from long personal experience, submitted an important memorandum to the Bishops in which he urged that the Catholic University should now be reorganised as a moral entity, in which several Catholic Colleges could be included. Recognising the need for concentration in or near Dublin, he proposed that Maynooth should provide the University's Faculty of Theology, and that Maynooth students should be prepared for the degrees of the Royal University in Arts and Philosophy. Clonliffe, Blackrock, the new Dublin Jesuit College, Castleknock, and Terenure Colleges could all be recognised as Colleges affiliated to the Catholic University ; in each of them students could be prepared for the degrees of the new Royal University. This scheme was modified by the Bishops, who added Carlow and Kilkenny to the list of affiliated Colleges ; but the teaching staffs of both Maynooth and Clonliffe were opposed to any scheme that would compel them to prepare their students for the public examinations of the Royal University. In the end these two important Colleges were excluded from the whole scheme for a reorganised Catholic University.

In addition to these troubles, the administration of University College soon ran into serious difficulties. Dr. Egan found that he had been given an impossible task, with a dwindling number of students who were now compelled to compete in public examinations with more highly organised Colleges. For some years Dr. Walsh had been urging the Bishops to entrust the Dublin College to some teaching order, and his great influence was consistently used to secure the choice of the Irish Jesuit Fathers for this important task. An informal offer was made to the Jesuit Provincial in the spring of 1882, but it was not until the autumn of 1883 that the final arrangements were made for the transfer of administration. In the same year Dean Neville resigned his charge as Rector of the Catholic University, and his place was taken by Dr. Molloy, who had made his name as a most successful popular lecturer on the Natural Sciences. With the advent of Father Delany as President of University College, Dr. Molloy's administrative duties became purely formal ; but the continued existence of his post as Rector was valuable as an external witness to the continued moral existence of the Catholic University.

II

Father William Delany was a native of Leighlin Bridge in Co. Carlow, where he was born in 1835. His father's people had been farmers in the townland of Coolnakieran, but had been evicted from their farm in 1825. John Delany, his father, set up as a baker in Leighlin Bridge, whilst three of his brothers emigrated to the United States of America. In 1833 John married Mary Brennan of Old Leighlin, and they had a family of ten children of whom only five lived beyond childhood. As a baker John Delany prospered, and his work for the relief of his neighbours during the years of the Famine was remembered with gratitude. Young William, the elder of his two sons, was then twelve years old, and he had vivid memories of distributing bread at the door of his father's bakery and of carrying bread and tins of soup to those who lay sick at home. These memories are worth recalling, for they throw an unexpected light on the early years of one who was later to be associated in so much of his educational work with the governing class in Ireland. Father Delany belongs in fact to a well-marked type of Irish ecclesiastic of the nineteenth century. Among his neighbours in Co. Carlow were the Cullens of Ballyallen, who were cousins of Cardinal Cullen; the Morans of Leighlin Bridge, whose son became Cardinal Moran; the Foleys of Old Leighlin, one of whose sons became Bishop of Kildare and Leighlin; and other families such as the Hugheses of Ballygowan and the Lyonses of Moonduff, who were noted for the number of priests and nuns to be found among their children.

In his early education as in his family life, Father William Delany had memories that must have been shared by hundreds of Irish Catholic priests in his day. He had attended the local National School at Leighlin Bridge in the early days of the National Board, and was taught there by a Mr. Conwell and a Miss Foran. When he was ten years old he gave promise of success in his studies, and was sent to the pay-school of a Mr. Lyons at Bagenalstown, where the future Cardinal Moran had recently been a pupil as well as the future scientist and professor, John Tyndall. From Bagenalstown at the age of sixteen he went to Carlow College as an ecclesiastical student under Father James Walsh, who was afterwards Bishop of Kildare and Leighlin. Two years later he was transferred to Maynooth; and it was after his first year in the class of Theology at Maynooth that he made up his mind to become a Jesuit and got in touch with the Jesuit Provincial, Father Edward Curtis. There was as yet only a Jesuit Vice-Province in Ireland, and at the moment there was no Irish novitiate. So young William Delany was sent to France, where he began his novitiate at Saint-Acheul. From there to Stonyhurst, then back to Ireland as a master at Clongowes; then for a short two years in the old half-forgotten Rome of Pio Nono; then back to Ireland in 1867; and the future President of University College was by then well set on a path which brought him eventually into touch with every practical problem of the Irish educational question.

These details may seem unnecessary, but they are instructive as showing us that the new President of University College had been in contact with most of the problems of Irish life that compelled attention in the years that are marked politically by the struggle for Home Rule under Parnell, and in ecclesiastical life by the gradual shift in personal influence from Cardinal Cullen and Dr. Moran to Archbishop Croke and Dr. Walsh. By birth and upbringing Father Delany belonged to a generation which had been taught to distrust the work of political agitators, and to concentrate on the practical tasks of education and social organisation. None the less, there lay deep in the memory of men like William Delany and his contemporaries among the Irish clergy a sense of the wrongs that had been inflicted on the people of Ireland, and a very earnest and patriotic resolve to work for the righting of those wrongs. Education was a field in which it was abundantly plain that Irish Catholics had for several generations been deprived of their natural rights ; and Father Delany seems to have made up his mind at an early date to make the reorganisation and improvement of Irish Catholic education the work which he felt himself called to undertake for the greater part of his long life. This strong sense of the need for educational work in Ireland may perhaps account for his decision to leave Maynooth in 1854 and seek admission to the Jesuit novitiate. So far as we can judge to-day, he does not seem to have had any personal contact with the Irish Jesuit Fathers before that date.

Father James Tuite was Jesuit Provincial from 1880 to 1883, and it was to him that the Irish Bishops addressed their formal invitation concerning the future of University College. That invitation was an open recognition by the Bishops of the success which had attended Father Delany's work at Tullabeg. He had been Rector of the College for ten years (1870–80), and had remained on as Prefect of Studies for another two years until 1882 when he opened his small house of studies in Temple Street. The Intermediate Act of 1878 had made a fundamental change in the position of Irish secondary schools, and Father Delany's counsel had been sought by those who were responsible for this new departure. His interest in University education was a direct result of the successes which his pupils at Tullabeg had obtained at the examinations of the London University; and he was eager to make the most of opportunities that were now offered by the new Royal University of Ireland. Dr. Walsh, who was by now the chief adviser of the Irish Bishops in these matters, had thrown the weight of his influence on the side of the Jesuit Fathers in the final choice that was made in the summer of 1883; and he welcomed the appointment of his friend Father Delany as first President of the new College. Everything seemed to promise new life and a more forward policy than had been possible during the past ten years. No less than a hundred and sixty names of students are found on the College's roll for 1883–4. To us, who have learned to count the student-body by thousands, the number seems pitifully small; but there had been little more than twenty students at the College in the preceding year, always excepting the large number of medical students who led their separate life in Cecilia Street.

Like all Presidents, past and present and (we may guess) future, Father Delany's first concern was the problem of finance. He had only one Jesuit Fellow in his community, with a salary of £400; but the name of that Fellow was Father Tom Finlay, whose worth to the new University College was not to be assessed in terms of any salary. Add to that salary another £75, which was the salary of Father James O'Carroll who had been appointed University examiner in Modern Languages; and the total of student-fees. It was not a generous endowment for a venture in higher Catholic education; and Father Delany found himself without books in his library and without any adequate scientific equipment. It was wholly characteristic of the man that he began by buying the books and ordering some small equipment for what did service as a scientific laboratory. His librarian was Father Denis Murphy, whose name is still remembered as a scholar who did useful antiquarian work in Irish history of the seventeenth century. Father Murphy held no post under the Royal University, but he was appointed bursar and librarian of the small community. " I am bursar and librarian," he used to say at community recreation ; " but I haven't a penny in my pocket nor a book in my library." The books of the Catholic University had been packed in cases and sent, first to Clonliffe, then to Maynooth. Those who have examined them in detail since their return to University College in 1909 will agree, I think, that they were not the kind of books that either student or professor would have found useful in the routine work of teaching for the examinations of the Royal University.

This urgent need of funds to meet immediate expenses which could not be avoided gave its full meaning to a sharp dispute on matters of high policy within the first few months of Father Delany's presidency. Dr. Walsh had never believed that the Royal University Act, as interpreted by the Senate which had been debating its functions and organisation for the past three years, was a suitable scheme for Irish Catholics. He was still attached to his own project, which was also supported by Dr. Woodlock, of a Catholic University existing as no more than a moral entity into which several Catholic colleges could be incorporated as opportunity arose. To foster this scheme he proposed that the small number of fellowships, each worth £400, which were available for the indirect endowment of a Catholic college or colleges as salaries for University professors, should be divided among several colleges, not concentrated in one Dublin college. The claims of St. Malachy's, Belfast, had often been urged ; and it is very much to Father Delany's credit that he was willing to accept this special claim in recognition of the exceptional difficulties which the Catholics of Belfast had to face. But this proposal fell through, and Father Delany took alarm when he found that Dr. Walsh and Dr. Woodlock were about to propose a scheme in which at least one fellowship should be given to Blackrock College, with the intention of considering the claims of other colleges in the near future.

Carlow and Kilkenny, no less than Castleknock and Terenure and perhaps Clonliffe, were all possible claimants of
fellowships under this scheme.

Father Delany had other plans ; and he was supported
in these plans not only by a large majority of the Senate
of the Royal University but also by some at least of the
Irish Bishops, including very notably Archbishop Croke of
Cashel. In his view failure was inevitable if the small sum
made available for this kind of indirect endowment was to
be scattered among several colleges. Inevitably, some of
these fellowships had to be given in bare justice to survivors
from the first years of the Catholic University : men like
Stewart and Ornsby, who had staked their careers on the
success of the Catholic University, but who had now passed
the age at which they were useful members of a teaching
staff. Father Delany was eager to increase the number of
his Jesuit Fellows, for the very simple reason that he could
use their salaries for the general purposes of the College.
He began with one Jesuit Fellow in 1883 ; two more were
to be added at an election held in January 1884, thereby
bringing the sum available from this source to the modest
figure of £1,200 per annum. But Dr. Walsh gave notice
that he would propose Father Reffé for one of these fellowships ; and he was supported by Dr. Woodlock and (after
some hesitation) by the Archbishop of Dublin, Cardinal
MacCabe. Father Delany was asked to withdraw the name
of one of his Jesuit candidates ; but he declined to do so,
and his decision was backed by a large majority of the
Senators who voted in the election. Dr. Walsh and Dr.
Woodlock resigned from the Senate of the University in
protest against this decision, and Father Delany was left
to carry on his work without the active support of two men
who had hitherto been among his best friends.

Looking back on this ancient dispute from a distance
of seventy years it is easy to understand that strong human
feelings were aroused on both sides of the controversy ; but
it is also easy to understand why Father Delany felt bound
to take the stand which in his view made all the difference
between success and failure. Humanly speaking, we may

well ask ourselves whether we should now be celebrating
the centenary of the Catholic University in 1954, if Dr.
Walsh's proposal had been preferred to Father Delany's
policy of concentration. There had been a long tradition
of failure and disappointment in the attempt to give life
to the Catholic University which the Irish Bishops had
entrusted to Dr. Newman in 1854. A policy which scattered wholly inadequate sums of money among several
Catholic colleges, in Dublin or near Dublin or all over the
country, was not likely to commend itself to men who were
faced with the immediate practical problems of administration ; and the strong support which Father Delany received
in the Senate made it plain that those who had given most
thought to these problems felt that he was right. But it is
pleasant to think that time has wrought changes here, as
in so many other once contentious problems. To-day our
Faculties of Arts and Philosophy owe much to the presence
and influence of a large body of students from the College
which has taken the place of Blackrock College as a house
of studies for senior students ; and Clonliffe, Castleknock
and Terenure have all given of their best to the life of
University College under its new administration.

III

Father Delany was the moving spirit during the two
terms of his presidency at University College, but he was
never more than the leader of a team which, though small,
did not lack talent. His first colleague was also his most
distinguished, if we are to count distinction by long service
rendered to the College and the country over a period of
more than fifty years. Father Tom Finlay was a native
of Co. Cavan, and his brother Father Peter—who was
later to be prominent as Jesuit theologian and director of
souls at Milltown Park—shared for a time a fellowship in
Metaphysics which was nominally allocated to Father Tom.
A later generation has been so accustomed to think of
Father Finlay as an economist and an active supporter
of Plunkett's movement for the reform of Irish agriculture
that his earlier career as a professor of Philosophy has long

since been forgotten. But those who are interested in the history of Irish university education will remember the exceptionally able evidence which Father Finlay gave before the Privy Council on questions that arose concerning the status of Scholastic Philosophy as an academic subject in the early years of the Queen's University in Belfast; and he never lost his interest in the problems of Catholic philosophy. None the less, Father Finlay was never the type of academic philosopher who finds it difficult to cope with the problems of everyday life. His own energy and enterprise in these early years were quite astonishing. Though a Fellow of the Royal University from 1883 onwards, he was not resident in Stephen's Green until 1887. During the five years 1882–87 he was Rector of Belvedere College, where he left his mark both in buildings and in the organisation of the school. He and Father Peter founded a monthly review, the *Lyceum*, in 1889. Father Tom took an active part in its production from 1889–94, and acted as sole editor of the *New Ireland Review*, which took the *Lyceum's* place in 1894 and was continued until February 1911. Its place was taken by *Studies* in 1912. His interest in practical social problems was clear to all from the first; but this interest was actively stimulated by his first contact with Sir Horace Plunkett in 1889. From that date onwards his work for the Irish Co-operative Movement took him far afield through the country as a whole; and it was natural that, as his interests had shifted, so he should exchange his fellowship in Metaphysics for a fellowship in Political Economy, when that chair fell vacant in 1900.

Father Tom Finlay was more than an exceptionally able, versatile and energetic colleague. He was also, all through his life, a most loyal friend; and Father Delany had no more loyal supporter in those controversies and difficulties that must always mark the progress of any educational institution. As early as 1881 he had been sent to help Father Delany as Assistant Prefect of Studies at Tullabeg, and he had been with him in the temporary experiment of a Jesuit house of studies in Temple Street. As the years went by, his position in University College was hardly less

important than that of the President himself, and his
influence on the abler type of student was immensely
stimulating. In the end Father Tom Finlay became almost
a legend; and in his later years he could thoroughly enjoy
an opportunity of producing some unexpected memory
from the past. At his first interview with Sir Horace
Plunkett in 1889 he had impressed that much-travelled
social reformer by his knowledge at first hand of German
agricultural organisation, which had attracted his attention as a young Jesuit student at Maria-Laach just after
the Franco-Prussian war. Many years later I was witness
of a dialogue in which a distinguished American Jesuit,
who was then Rector of the Gregorian University at Rome,
expressed his interest on hearing that Father Tom was
himself a past student of the Gregoriana. "And when
were you last in Rome? " came the gracious question. "At
the Vatican Council " was the quick reply; and we were
reminded that Father Tom had been a young student in
Rome during the eventful year 1869–70.

Two other Jesuit Fellows were added to the staff in
1884 : Robert Curtis, who taught Mathematics for several
years, though his health made it impossible for him to be
ordained to the priesthood; and Father Gerard Manly
Hopkins, whose election in January 1884 gave University
College an association, not understood in his lifetime, with
modern English poetry. Father Hopkins came to the
College as a professor of Ancient Classics, and held that
post until his death in 1889. His career as a teacher had
not been successful in the English Jesuit schools, and those
who remembered his lectures in Dublin seem to be agreed
in their verdict that he was quite unable to impart the
knowledge which he had gained at Oxford as a pupil of
Nettleship and Jowett. In his official letter of recommendation Nettleship spoke of Hopkins as " one of the
cleverest and most original men at Oxford in his time ",
and praised " his great care and accuracy, and a curiously
delicate perception in the use and criticism of language ".
The raw young students who attended his classes in Dublin
were little accustomed to such fine distinctions, and there

is a legend—true or false, I do not know—that on one famous day they persuaded their professor to lie on the floor and let them drag him round the table by the heels so as to illustrate Hector's fate at Troy. This is not the place to assess the part that University College played in developing the genius of a poet whose most impressive sonnets were composed in the small room allotted to him in what is now Newman House. We may not have had a successful professor of Classics in those five years ; but the name of Gerard Manly Hopkins, in association with the names of John Henry Newman and James Joyce, makes Newman House a spot with literary traditions and memories that are not easily equalled elsewhere.

Neither Father Denis Murphy nor Father James O'Carroll held fellowships under the Royal University ; but they were both in residence, and gave to the College a tradition of learning, one in Irish history, the other by his unusually wide range of familiarity with the languages of Europe. To these names must be added the name of Edmund Hogan, who was on the teaching staff of University College for the year 1884–85, and then again from 1888 onwards. As compared with Father Delany and Father Tom Finlay, we have here a man whose main interest lay in the careful and loving study of the Irish language and Irish traditions. A native of " the Cove of Cork " to quote Douglas Hyde's words (to be more precise, he was born on the island at Clonmel), Father Hogan was born in 1831 and died in 1917. On his death Hyde saluted him as a " connecting link with the era of O'Donovan and O'Curry . . . a pioneer in many fields of Irish history, philology and topography." Like Father Hopkins, Edmund Hogan was not the man for an ordinary class, and his teaching activity was at its best with a single student in an untidy bedroom. But the most distinguished of the scholars whom he trained has left us an admirable account of Father Hogan's teaching methods, and I need make no excuse for citing here Eoin MacNeill's tribute to his master in Celtic studies :

" In the summer of 1890 I spent a fortnight in the Aran Islands, and came back to Dublin full of the pur-

pose of extending my knowledge of Irish. I made enquiry
at University College about instruction there, and was
referred to Father Hogan. He received me genially, and
when I explained to him that I only wished to study
Irish under direction and not for any special academic
goal, he gave me to understand that he raised no objection and invited me to come straightway and study under
him. Being in the Four Courts by day, I used to come
to his room in the evenings as often as he could allow.
After some months, from being a student I became what
might almost be called my professor's apprentice. I was
making gradual headway in Middle and Old Irish.
Father Hogan always had something in hand for publication, and he brought me right into his own work and into
almost every part of it. As much as possible, he handed
over to me parts of his work to do and threw me on my
own resources for the doing of it. . . . In these tasks
I found the greatest pleasure, not more because they
were congenial than from being associated with so kindly
a teacher and director."

Eoin MacNeill goes on to tell how Father Hogan made
his gifted apprentice do all the spade-work for an edition
that he was then preparing of *Cath Ruis na Rig*. " In this
way I got my first introduction to ancient manuscripts and
their technique. I had also to prepare the first draft of the
English translation and of the Vocabulary, and to supply
a good deal of material for the introduction and annotations.
Finally I had to correct the proofs." His part in this work
of collaboration was so successful that Father Hogan soon
insisted that his young student-apprentice should prepare
an edition in his own right. " He knew better than I did
then that the publication of creditable work is the most
effective Degree that can be conferred on a student. It
was like the antique custom of giving arms to a youth, and
my feeling about it was not quite heroic." But Father
Hogan insisted ; three Middle-Irish poems were chosen ;
this time MacNeill was left entirely to his own resources ;
the edition was accepted for publication by the Royal Irish
Academy, and was well received. "Amateurish as it was,

the appearance of this essay in scholarship as a booklet seemed to bring me into another world. I had gone out among the giants." How many of our professors in Father Hogan's day (or since) have had equal success in this highest test of the teacher's craft?

Another notable figure in the early years of the new College was Father Jacques Mallac, a French Jesuit priest who had been brought in to strengthen the teaching in Philosophy. Father Mallac was an ardent Thomist, while neither Father Tom nor Father Peter Finlay could be classed as more than nominal Thomists in so far as they accepted St. Thomas as the most authoritative Doctor of the Schools. There ensued a stimulating interchange of criticisms and counter-attacks, which men of an older generation like Professor Magennis in Dublin and Professor Howley in Galway used often to describe in conversation, and to which both men—and others among their contemporaries—seem to have owed a good deal of their personal interest in the problems of Scholastic Philosophy. Father Mallac taught Philosophy here in University College from 1884 to 1890, when he was recalled to France where he died soon afterwards. To judge by the collection of French classics which he left behind him in the Jesuit library, formerly at Newman House and now in Leeson Street, he must have been a royalist in politics and a disciple of Louis Veuillot. He and Father Finlay belonged to two very different schools of thought, and those who still believe that a Jesuit community is disciplined to think on a given straight line may perhaps learn something from this half-forgotten chapter in the history of University College.

But the two Jesuit professors who, next to Father Delany and Father Finlay, were most conspicuous in the life of the College after the first few years were undoubtedly two English convert priests : Father Joseph Darlington and Father Henry Browne. Father Darlington had been born in Wigan in 1850, and Father Browne in Birmingham in 1853. Both men had been to Oxford, and Father Darlington had been for a short time an Anglican clergyman. Father Browne had read himself into the Catholic Church before he had completed his course at Oxford, and joined the Irish Jesuit Province in 1877. Father Darlington, after a winter spent on the Rhineland in a vain endeavour to fight off the doubts that had begun to trouble him, was received into the Catholic Church in 1878 and came to Ireland as tutor to a Catholic family. In 1880 he entered the Irish Jesuit novitiate, and as early as 1885 we find his name entered as a member of the Jesuit staff at University College, teaching Latin and Greek and acting as Assistant Prefect of Studies. He remained for two years in that capacity ; then did a short course of Theology at Milltown Park, and came back to University College as Dean of Studies and University examiner in English Literature in 1890. For the next nineteen years he was, perhaps more than any other member of the small community, the linchpin of what was at times a somewhat ramshackle conveyance. Many long years later, when Father Darlington was recovering from a serious illness, I found him one day in reminiscent mood. He began to look back on these early years, and thanked God for the opportunity that had been given him of doing what he could to forward and sustain the work which Newman had come to establish here in Ireland. Father Darlington's eager good will, his patent desire to help every one in any way he could, his keen interest in the daily life of the students and in particular of any student who was in any kind of trouble, his sense of humour when faced with what seemed to be an insuperable difficulty, above all his genuine devotion to what he had undertaken as an apostolic work : these are some of the qualities which account for the host of stories that had gathered about his name by the end of the old Jesuit College and the transfer to the new. Father Darlington was close on sixty years of age when the transfer was made, and he was dropped from the list of professors in the National University to make way for younger men. But he continued to work for the welfare and comfort of the students in University Hall. Even in his last years, when memory and intellect were beginning to fail, it was both edifying and pathetic to watch the eagerness with which he clung to any work that might keep him still in contact with the young men of a new generation. Meanwhile he had become a keen disciple of Sinn Féin ; and it was he, with his characteristic sense of humour, who suggested what some of us thought a perfect title for the volume that was published in 1930 as *A Page of Irish History*. Father Darlington was quite clear in his own mind that the proper title was and should have been : *Whigs on the Green*.

Father Henry Browne was in some ways the very opposite of Father Darlington, though both men were fast friends throughout life. Nobody was ever quite sure why Father Browne made up his mind to enter the Irish instead of the English Jesuit Province ; and there was never any doubt as to his own nationality. Nor was Father Browne in any sense a typical Oxford scholar. He had nothing of that " curiously delicate perception " which Nettleship had found and praised in Gerard Manly Hopkins : indeed Father Browne could sometimes startle his class by some unexpected indifference to the meaning or beauty of a Greek word. But he had in abundance an enthusiasm for the Classics as a standard by which all scholarship ought rightly to be judged, and his own personal interests lay in what (before 1914) he was fond of calling the *Realien* of classical scholarship. The discoveries of Schliemann at Troy and Mycenae, the later discoveries of Sir Arthur Evans in Crete (and these had an added value since they had been made and interpreted by an Englishman), the problem of Greek music, the dating of Greek coins, the development of Greek sculpture and architecture, the new light which came in his lifetime on the history of Greek thought and political life in the Hellenistic age : these were the problems which attracted him in succession, each new enthusiasm replacing but not quite obliterating some earlier interest. Father Browne was a propagandist by nature, and his pen was always at the service of the Classics when he sensed danger from the scientific trends of modern education. He was in contact with many leading classical scholars of England, and was a familiar figure at meetings of the Hellenic Society. Not content with these personal contacts, he made up his mind to found an Irish Classical Association for which he enlisted support from Maynooth and Trinity College as well as from the three Colleges of the National University and the leading Irish secondary schools. For him life was a battle on behalf of old and well-established values, and he was at all times successful in communicating a good deal of his own enthusiasm to his class in University College. With little or no ear for music, he would chant to us a Greek choral ode ; though musical purists might well express surprise at this rendering of an unknown music, he did at least bring home to his class that these odes had been written to be sung on a stage, not studied with the help of a grammar and a dictionary. And Father Browne had another excellent quality as professor. He took an active interest in the personal problems of his students, and was always quick to advance their interests. For many years he was Director of the Students' Sodality, which met in those far-off days in what was then the Domestic Chapel and is now the Salon in 85 Stephen's Green.

Two other Jesuit names came to the fore in the last years of the old College : Father George O'Neill, who was Professor of English Language in the new University College, having taught English Literature for some years in Father Delany's College ; and Father Michael Egan, who was a Fellow of the Royal University and then became the well-loved colleague of Henry McWeeney and Arthur Conway as Lecturer in Mathematics under the new administration. But it is time to turn from this long list of Jesuit names, and recall some memories of the Catholic laymen who did so much to give the old College its prestige and to make easy the transition from old to new in 1909–10.

IV

The first name on this roll of honour must surely be John Casey, whose reputation as a mathematician was equalled by the respect he had won as a man prepared to make great sacrifices for what he held to be Catholic principle. Born at Kilbehenny, near Mitchelstown, he was

educated at the local national school and afterwards at a
pay-school in Mitchelstown. For some years he taught as
a schoolmaster, then was for a time headmaster of the
model school at Kilkenny. In 1858 Dr. Salmon persuaded
him to come to Trinity College as a student of mathematics,
and he took his B.A. Degree there in 1862. For the next
ten years he taught in Kingstown School, but his reputation
as a mathematician was by now so well established that in
1875 the authorities of Trinity College offered to appoint
him to a special chair of Mathematics at a salary of £400.
Cardinal Cullen heard of this offer and put pressure on
Casey to take a post, with a very much smaller and less
secure salary, at the Catholic University. After some
hesitation—for Casey knew well the extent of the sacrifice
he was making—he accepted the Cardinal's offer and taught
Mathematics in the Catholic University until 1882, when
he became a Fellow in Mathematics of the new Royal
University. During the year 1882–3 Father Delany secured
Casey's services as a tutor for his young men at Temple
Street, and Casey was perhaps the only one of those taken
over by the new Jesuit College in 1883 who could be counted
an efficient teacher of his subject. Father Darlington, who
attended his class in Spherical Trigonometry in 1884–5, has
left us an amusing picture of his methods as a teacher.
" When he entered the room we saw the tall and well-built
figure of a quiet and simple man. We felt that being in
his company was more like being with a child than an
elderly man ; his voice was pleasing, his words cultured—
and very humorous. We sat all round him in a cluster,
and the first thing he did was to bring out of his pocket a
potato with a knife, and he commenced operations by
cutting it into cubes. He then said that since his boyhood
many devices had been invented to teach spherical trigonometry, but he had found nothing better than the potato
which had been presented to himself in some country
school." It sounds childish and foolish ; but the plain fact
remains that Casey's text-books of Mathematics, which were
widely esteemed in England as in Ireland, were published
here in Dublin during these same years between 1880 and

1889. His death in January 1891 was indeed the end of a long chapter in the history of Irish education ; and Casey had taught both his colleagues and students a lesson which could be understood even by those who knew nothing of Mathematics.

Very different was Thomas Arnold, Matthew Arnold's younger brother, who has told the story of his chequered career in *Passages from a Wandering Life*, a book of reminiscences which he published in 1900, the last year of his long life. As a young man Arnold—who had known Wordsworth and Southey at home, and who was a friend of Clough—had gone to seek his fortune in Australia and New Zealand. There he had, after some disappointments, secured a position as inspector of schools in Tasmania, then known as Van Diemen's Land. He married the granddaughter of a former Governor of Van Diemen's Land, and his standing in the colony seemed to be well assured. But Arnold had been troubled for some time by doubts as to his religious convictions, and in 1856 he was received into the Catholic Church by Bishop Willson of Hobart. Local feelings were stirred by this action, and Arnold came home with his wife and children. Newman was still Rector of the Catholic University, and he was glad to secure the services of a convert who was also a scholar. From 1856 to 1862 Arnold was Professor of English Literature here in Dublin ; but Newman's departure was a severe personal loss, and he was glad to accept the offer of a post as senior classical master at the Birmingham Oratory School in 1862. Even here he found no peace of mind, for he was one of the converts whom Acton was drawing towards his party of Liberal Catholicism. In 1865 he left the Oratory School and ceased to call himself a Catholic. He settled at Oxford where he made a name for himself as a competent editor of Old and Middle English texts. He was a candidate for the chair of Anglo-Saxon in the University of Oxford in 1876 when he suddenly made known his intention of seeking reconciliation with the Catholic Church. The decision was made in time to injure his chance of election, and in 1882 Arnold was glad to return to Dublin as a Fellow of the new Royal

Sketch of the proposed Catholic University of Irela

n Stone of which was laid in Drumcondra in 1862

University. For the next eighteen years he taught English Literature in University College, but his active literary work had come to an end. One of his former students can still remember a forlorn old man, sitting in an uncomfortable class-room and lamenting that this should have been the fate of Matthew Arnold's brother !

Another link with the days of Newman, though he belonged to a younger generation, was George Sigerson, who completed his medical studies at the Medical School of the Catholic University in 1859–60, but took his M.D. in Queen's University. Sigerson's teaching career belongs really to the Medical School at Cecilia Street, where he was appointed a professor in 1865 ; but his name appears on the staff of University College as Lecturer and Examiner in Biology for the year 1883–84. He was still a familiar figure at what is now Newman House in the first years of the National University, where he lectured to a large class, mainly composed of First Medicals. To us, who watched some of the more unusual proceedings from the garden at the back of Newman House, the class-room sometimes gave the impression of a bear-garden ; but Sigerson was by then the Grand Old Man of Anglo-Irish letters, whose *Bards of the Gael and Gall* (published in 1897) was a classic of its kind. He had been born near Strabane as far back as 1836, and was in his ninetieth year when he died in Dublin early in 1925. After his death Douglas Hyde wrote of him : " Born and reared near Strabane, but with a Kerry ancestry, educated partly in Galway, and partly in Cork, and later in Paris (in close touch with the Irish there), he typified all that was best and broadest and sanest in our race." But he is quick to add that Sigerson " always boasted that he came from the old Norse "—a fact that he was sure to stress if, as a young student, you ventured to attend his weekly evenings in a house that was full of miniatures and engravings and curios of every kind.

One or two other names that appear on that first lecture list of 1884 recall familiar figures of thirty years later. Mgr. Molloy appears on the list as Professor of Physics, but a tutor is added who did in fact almost all the teaching work : Joseph McGrath, B.A. (Lond.). Joseph McGrath and Hughes Dowling had been encouraged to act as private tutors in Mathematics and Science during the transitional period just before the arrival of Father Delany's new staff ; and they were both retained as most useful members of that staff for the next ten years or so. Joseph McGrath was a neighbour and connection of Father Delany, being himself a native of Bagenalstown ; and he had been a boy under Father Delany at Tullabeg. In 1892 he ceased to act as tutor in Mathematics and Science, and was appointed as one of the two Secretaries of the Royal University, his colleague being Dr. (afterwards Sir James) Creed Meredith, round whose name students of more than one generation have built a whole legend of amusing stories. The appointment of two Secretaries was inevitable in an institution like the Royal University, where a delicate balance was everywhere maintained between Protestant and Catholic. Meredith was a stout Protestant, and Sir Joseph McGrath (to give him the title with which we were familiar in the early days of the National University) was a stout Catholic, who did more than one man's work in the slow task of maintaining the routine administration of the Royal University. When the National University began to function in 1909, it was inevitable that Sir Joseph McGrath should be appointed the first Registrar of the new University ; and to him is due in large part the efficient administration which we have long since come to expect from the central office in Merrion Square.

The names of Hughes Dowling and McGrath bring us to a generation that got its first opportunity under Father Delany's new administration. With the death of Casey in 1891, his pupil and worthy successor, Henry McWeeney, succeeded to the chair of Mathematics ; and I think there would be universal agreement that no single professor of the new College commanded at all times more respect and confidence and genuine affection than Professor McWeeney. In his later years, when he had come to be one of the senior professors of University College, he gave the impression of qualities such as one has always been taught to expect from a High Court judge : a rare sense of justice and fair-play, a very human enjoyment of the day's work and the day's pleasures, a delightful sense of humour—and (but here I speak as one that has not understanding) a gift for clear exposition and the skill of an artist in the mysterious regions of Pure Mathematics. I do not know whether his best years were in the old College, or in the later years when he was so often Dr. Coffey's faithful counsellor and friend ; but few men have done as much for the welfare and prestige of University College, and it is sad to think that his name is now for so many no more than a faint memory from the past.

Arthur Conway was younger than Henry McWeeney, and I must leave to another contributor the task of assessing his great work for the College as Professor, Registrar and President. But for us who were students in the first years of the College or junior members of the staff in later years, the two names are inseparable ; they stand for solid achievement in their own academic field of work, but also for those human qualities that have created so strong a sense of family loyalty among the members of our staff over so many long years of growth and unexpected expansion.

Another name comes easily to the mind when one thinks of Henry McWeeney and Arthur Conway. These two were typical Catholic students and professors, men who were characteristic of the Irish people that had so long been held back from the full opportunity of higher education. John M'Clelland was of northern Presbyterian stock and he came to University College from the Cavendish Laboratory in Cambridge. His appointment dates only from 1903, and his best work as the true founder of our Faculty of Science was done in the new College. But it is surely characteristic of the traditions that have been inherited from the old College that this somewhat stern Presbyterian (and I choose my words deliberately, having sat for a year in M'Clelland's First Arts Class) felt himself at home as one of the team that took over from the Jesuit Fathers in 1909, and that I have never heard any of them speak in anything but the highest terms of the work that he did both for the College and for its students.

Another name that must be mentioned here is that of John Bacon, who was appointed Professor of English Literature in 1901 in succession to Father Darlington, who in that year took Father Finlay's place as Professor of Metaphysics. John Bacon was a nephew of Father Delany, whose sister had married Mr. William Bacon of Carlow : we may add that another nephew, Father Michael Maher, S.J., gained high distinction in these same years as a Professor of Psychology in the Jesuit house of studies at Stonyhurst, and was the author of a text-book of psychology which had a high reputation in its day. John Bacon held the chair of English Literature until 1909, when he accepted an appointment as first Secretary and Bursar of University College, Dublin, and also Supervisor of Examinations. As has happened more than once in the history of every University, administrative talents were revealed by this change of work which were to prove of almost inestimable value to the College in the years that lay ahead. For the rapid growth in our student-population and the multiplication of courses and subjects and diplomas and degrees created a long series of practical problems that might well have got out of hand, if someone with less business capacity or less strong will had been in charge of the College's main office. Dr. Coffey, Dr. Conway, Mr. Bacon : for many years these three names stood for the three offices of President, Registrar and Secretary of the new College ; and it was plain to all that they stood also for a team that was conscious of a common purpose and a common tradition.

V

Father Delany's first term of office as President came to an end in 1888, after five years of courageous and farsighted administration. But they were years that were cramped at all times by the need of adequate funds, and Father Delany was not the man to let the lack of money stand in his way when he felt that something needed to be done. His attitude towards the problem of cash, and his willingness to incur debts that he felt sure would be repaid once success had been assured, were characteristic of his policy, both in Tullabeg and in University College ; but his views were not shared by all who watched his energetic policy with some alarm. Hence the change that was made in 1888. Father Delany was removed from the President's office to Gardiner Street church, where he quickly won a new reputation as preacher and confessor and director of souls. His place in University College was taken by Father Robert Carbery, a man who shared many of Father Delany's educational ideals, but who could be counted on to do nothing rash or improvident. Some of those who were students of the College between 1888 and 1897, when Father Delany returned for a second and longer period of office, remember the contrast which was apparent in the day-to-day work of the College under the two Jesuit Presidents. Student-debates were avoided by Father Carbery, publicity of every kind was disliked ; books were read, lectures were given, examinations were passed, salaries were paid ; but there were many who felt that the spring had gone out of the year. There was no interruption in the work of the College, as I have tried to describe it ; but the return of Father Delany in 1897 made an immediate and visible change in the daily life of the College. The " L. and H.", which had been allowed to lapse, was revived ; a students' magazine, *St. Stephen's*, was started in 1901 ; and the Academy of St. Thomas, in which many of the ablest students took an active part, was started in the same year. Father Delany's second period of office lasted for twelve full years (1897–1909), and found its fitting end in the successful campaign for the establishment of a National University, openly designed to give Irish Catholics a fuller opportunity of higher education in Colleges that were planned for their needs.

I do not propose to attempt here any detailed account of the many controversies, public and domestic, that marked this second period of Father Delany's presidency. The country as a whole was being stirred to new life. The celebrations for the centenary of 1798 ; the founding of the Gaelic League ; the work of the Irish Co-operative Movement ; the new literary movement that was centred round the Abbey Theatre in Dublin ; the political campaigns for Home Rule under the leadership of John Redmond ; the first signs of a new national consciousness as fostered by Arthur Griffith in the Sinn Féin movement ; these were all symptoms of a new life that would not be denied. Father Delany was far from being out of sympathy with many of these movements, though he himself belonged to an older and more cautious generation in all that concerned public policy. When the Gaelic League organised its first public procession through the streets of Dublin, Father Delany walked in person at the head of his students ; when the School of Irish Learning was begun here in Dublin, with Kuno Meyer as its most active figure, Father Delany could always be counted on for a subscription or a substantial grant towards a prize or scholarship ; and he invited men like John MacNeill and P. H. Pearse to lecture on Irish in the evening extension classes which were a notable feature of his administration in the last years of the old College. But his own personal interests were still centred on the campaign for a final and satisfactory solution of the Irish University question, and his pre-occupation with the ebb and flow of English party politics in relation to this particular problem brought him further and further away from the more advanced ideas of a new generation.

The ten years that preceded the passing of the Irish Universities Act in 1908 were filled with a long series of proposals and counter-proposals and often passionate controversies on this subject, which have not yet found their historian. Father Delany, as was inevitable, took a prominent part in these controversies. He gave important evidence before the Robertson Commission in 1902 ; he insisted on the need for a separate University for Irish Catholics, in opposition to those who were working for a Catholic College within the University of Dublin ; he opposed Bryce's scheme in 1907 on which Catholic opinion was divided, and which came to nothing in the end ; and he did as much as any man to help Birrell in framing the

Bill which took final shape in the Act of 1908. Once again, as in 1884, Father Delany found himself in opposition to Archbishop Walsh on a matter of public policy. The Archbishop, who had rendered an immense service to the cause by his constant reiteration of Catholic claims throughout the twenty-five years that lie between 1883 and 1908, was convinced that the most dignified and adequate solution of this thorny problem was a completely Catholic College within an enlarged University of Dublin. It is all the more pleasant to recall that in 1904 the Archbishop took an opportunity of paying public and most generous tribute to Father Delany's work. The occasion was the tenth anniversary of the Students' Sodality, which had been founded in the old chapel of University College. The Archbishop's words that day were so generous and so unexpectedly warm in their praise that Father Delany was for a time at a loss to find words to express his thanks; and it is plain from his surviving papers that he was in close touch with the Archbishop in all the controversies and negotiations of the next few years. The two men had not worked side by side in every issue and they held different views; but they were at all times conscious of working for a common cause, and both knew that on the main issues of principle they were completely at one.

Father Delany was seventy-three years old when what was for him final victory came with the passing of Birrell's Act in 1908. He knew, as others knew, that the new University was in essence a compromise, but he believed it to be the best that could be obtained or expected as things were in the days of Asquith's Liberal Government. His views were shared by most of those who had taken an active interest in the University question; but Father Delany's government of the College ran into serious trouble in 1905 and 1906. The students—and who can blame them?—had for many years resented the custom which was observed each year at the Conferring of Degrees by the Royal University, that " God save the King " should be played on the organ at the end of the ceremony. In 1905 a successful ruse on the part of the students enabled them to block the approach to the organ, and the anthem was not played that day. In 1906 extra precautions were taken by Creed Meredith, who was mainly responsible for this aspect of the work of the Royal University, and a public demonstration was avoided—much to the indignation of those students who were refused admission to the Hall. What was done at Earlsfort Terrace was not the concern of Father Delany and his College on Stephen's Green ; and the President made no secret of the fact that in his view the playing of the British national anthem was needlessly provocative. None the less he was acutely conscious of the need to gain English goodwill at a time when the prospect of settling the University question seemed more than usually favourable ; and he himself had been brought up in a tradition of loyalty to the Crown. A series of minor incidents, which he handled badly, put him more and more in opposition to the student-body ; and he ended by making the grave mistake of summoning the police to prevent the students from staging a demonstration in the College buildings. It was the kind of mistake that students neither forgive nor forget, and its immediate effect was that for the next three years, the last of his presidency, Father Delany lost in large measure the trust and respect which had been his for so long. It was his further misfortune that these same years saw the struggle for women's full share in higher education come to a climax. Here again, though he made some concessions under pressure, the President's instincts and training were against a change that younger men were demanding on behalf of the women. The story of this dispute, and the part played by Sheehy-Skeffington who resigned his position as Assistant Registrar of the College sooner than accept Father Delany's policy, has been told elsewhere. It helped to make Father Delany's last years of government more difficult.

When the Act of 1908 had been passed and the new National University was about to take over from the " Royal " in 1909, Father Delany found himself suddenly caught up in a violent controversy that stirred the whole country on the question of " Essential Irish "—to use a phrase that has long since been forgotten. Once again he found himself in opposition to the demands of a new generation, though here he might fairly plead that, in so far as the demand concerned the quality of higher education, he had some competence to judge. He was not afraid of unpopularity, and made himself the leader of those who resisted the attempt to impose a knowledge of the Irish language as a compulsory subject for Matriculation. In vain he appealed to his own previous interest in the teaching of Irish as proof that he was no enemy of the language : he was plainly taken aback by the vehemence of public feeling, and in the end he was defeated. The question was in fact no longer a question of higher education. It had become the symbol of a nation's wish to assert its individuality, and the Gaelic League won its first clear victory on this issue. How far that victory has been justified from a purely educational standpoint is a question which is perhaps as disputed to-day as it was forty years ago.

Looking back on these old controversies we can see that the last years of the old College's existence were years of intense political and intellectual activity ; and it is only right that this book should include some memories of one who was himself the contemporary and friend of many who were prominent in the student-life of that gifted and most voluble generation. It has surely been their bad luck that many who have never visited Dublin, and who know nothing of the country or its history, should believe that they know all that there is to know of student-life in the old College from Joyce's vivid descriptions in his *Portrait of an Artist*. Perhaps I may be allowed to quote here the comment of one who was Joyce's contemporary, and who was for many years a well-loved figure in the new College. Writing in the summer of 1909 Arthur Clery paid a moving tribute to his *Alma Mater* in an essay on " The Passing of University College," which was printed in the *Leader* of those days. When this essay was reprinted in 1930 as a contribution to the Jesuit volume of reminiscence, *A Page of Irish History*, Professor Clery (as he then was) added a brief comment on Joyce's pen-picture. In

4

his essay he had written that "the new movement [the Gaelic League], by giving us students an ideal, raised the tone of our lives, and an exceptionally high moral standard prevailed among us." To this passage he added a footnote in 1930 : "Readers of Mr. James Joyce will get a different impression, but this is the actual fact. Among the students of the College about this time were—P. H. Pearse, T. M. Kettle, F. Sheehy-Skeffington. Joyce is true as far as he goes, but confining himself to one small knot of medical students, he gives a wrong impression of the whole."

One last word may be said of the President who had ruled the College for so many years, and who had himself fostered so many of the activities and interests which, in the final phase, escaped him or began to turn against him. Father Delany had never any doubts as to the temporary character of the administration which he and his fellow-Jesuits were asked to take over in 1883. When he was giving his evidence before the Robertson Commission in 1902, one of the commissioners asked him this question : "In view of any permanent arrangement that may be made, do you advocate the continuance of the College as it exists at present under the management of the Jesuit Fathers?" To this question Father Delany gave a clear answer : "Certainly not : such an arrangement would be entirely inadmissible. In the first place, no endowment, however generous, could make of the institution in St. Stephen's Green a suitable University College ; in the next place I consider that in the new institution there should be room for all the best intellects of the country—the best man winning, whether priest or layman. It should be National in its constitution, and be governed by a body thoroughly representative of the whole Catholic people."

Those are generous words, and I think it may fairly be claimed that Father Delany forecast fifty years ago what has since been taking shape beneath our eyes. I think also that in making his statement, Father Delany was consciously and deliberately following the tradition which he had received from the first Rector of the Catholic University of Ireland.

THE ROYAL UNIVERSITY

PROFESSOR PATRICK SEMPLE

THE Act of Parliament which established the Royal University in 1879 was, with all its shortcomings, the first official measure which recognised the grievances of Irish Catholics in the matter of university education. The grave grounds for criticism which attached to it in its first form were gradually abated, if not altogether removed, during the discussions and negotiations of the next three years, and the university may be said to have begun its working life in 1882. The first positive step taken was the establishment at the beginning of 1881 of the Senate which was henceforward its governing body. The university was an examining, not a teaching, institution, on the analogy of the University of London ; but the Senate, which was composed of equal numbers of Catholics and Protestants, was empowered, by an exceedingly important amendment of the Bill, to appoint a number of Fellows who were to be not merely the examiners but also teaching Professors. The Queen's University had been abolished in 1879, but its three constituent colleges were left intact. There were now to be twenty-six Fellows of the new university, of whom twelve were assigned to the Queen's Colleges, one to the Presbyterian Magee College in Derry, and the remaining thirteen to a Catholic college or colleges capable of teaching at a university standard. The headquarters of the Catholic University in St. Stephen's Green had lately been put by the Bishops under the charge of the Jesuit Fathers, and had already begun to be known as University College. It seemed clear that this should be the Catholic institution to make use of the Royal University Act. Its outstanding rival was Blackrock College, no less successful in secondary education. Dr. Walsh, President of Maynooth College (afterwards Archbishop of Dublin), who was one of the leading Catholic Senators,

strongly favoured Blackrock, and thought that some at
least of the Fellowships should be established there ; but
the general feeling was that all the Fellowships should be
concentrated in one place ; and when ultimately he was
defeated, on proposing Father Reffé of Blackrock for a
Fellowship, he resigned from the Senate. He had never
been very enthusiastic about the Royal University, and
he never afterwards showed any public interest in it. He
lived to see his views largely realised in the National
University, in the establishment of which he took a leading
part and of which he was the first Chancellor.

The Fellows were the examining and teaching body.
They were appointed, at first for seven, later for five, years,
but could be reappointed when this period expired and
usually were—not invariably however. They were paid a
salary of £400 a year—not over-generous, even according
to the standards of that time ; but only the Fellows who
taught in the unendowed college in Dublin received this
sum in full. Those who belonged to the Queen's Colleges
received such amount as brought up their college salary
to £400. They lectured in the colleges to which they were
attached. They met three times a year in Dublin to
arrange the papers for the ensuing examinations and settle
the distribution of work ; and also to fix the courses for
the coming year, which were changed from time to time.
There was no autonomy among the colleges in this respect ;
all read the same work. The first meeting was usually in
April. Each subject had its own committee. For example,
each of the six examiners in classics read out the list of
questions which he proposed for the examination ; they
were discussed by his colleagues and approved or amended ;
so that each paper in its final form had the sanction of the
whole group. The examinations were in June. The
answers were read and marked, and the results had the
agreement of at least two examiners—for honour papers,
generally of all. Then a meeting of all the examiners of
all subjects concerned, presided over by one of the secretaries of the university, heard all the marks read and
decided the fate of each candidate. A meeting similar to

that earlier in the year settled the papers for the autumn examinations held in September. For these the same procedure was followed, and here the awards of highest standing, (B.A. Honours and M.A.) were made. This brought the ordinary examining work of the year to an end, for the Arts Faculty at all events. There were four examinations altogether, held at intervals of a year, namely Matriculation, First University, or First Arts, as it was usually called, Second University, and B.A., and the standard was a minimum of 30% for pass, 60% for second class honours, 70% for first class honours. As for the higher grades, the small number who proceeded to the M.A. degree could do so after the lapse of a year from the B.A. The Doctorates (D.Litt. and D.Ph.) could not be completed till three years after B.A., and were very exacting in their requirements.

What has been said above describes, perhaps in too much detail, the examination procedure for the Arts Faculty. The other Faculties (Science, Medicine, etc.) had, of course, their own rules and methods, but the same general principles applied. One defect insisted on by some of the members of the Robertson Commission, the lack of extern examiners, was perhaps more specious than substantial. In fact, any candidate's paper was read by at least one examiner, usually by more than one, in addition to the particular professor under whom he had worked, and in the case of the very numerous candidates who did not belong to any of the colleges and were strictly outsiders, all the examiners were in effect externs. It is probable that the provisions for a uniform standard were more effective than those of our present system. The Pass students from outside would probably have had most reason for complaint, but I have never heard that they did complain. The examiners in Metaphysics, Ethics, and History of Philosophy for the Degree, unlike their colleagues, sat together ; one of their number read aloud the candidate's answer, and all then discussed it and fixed their award. It took some time perhaps but must have been very effective. It did not please their senior secretary, Sir

James Meredith, who had a general superintendence of the
conduct of the examinations, and suspected that examiners
occasionally enlivened the monotony by conversation on
things in general ; but his hints at hurrying up the proceedings were quietly ignored—and he had no right to
intrude while the examiners were in session.

Associated with the examinations were a few—a very
few—scholarships and prizes established by private benefactors, and a certain number of exhibitions. There were
also entrance scholarships, for which a special examination
was held annually in Dublin : twelve in number, ranging
in value from £40 to £20. To three of them (in modern
languages) a condition was attached that the candidate
must be a natural-born subject of the crown. A gold
medal was awarded at the M.A. examinations, but only
for special distinction and on the special recommendation
of the examiners ; and there were two other gold medals,
one for the best English verse composition, one for the best
Latin verse composition. The subject each year was
named by the Senate—in the last year of the University
(1909), " Clonmacnoise " for English, " Marathon " for
Latin—and the candidate must be an undergraduate or a
graduate of not more than one year's standing. The
standard of performance was in general excellent, and the
voluntary competition was a better arrangement than that
in vogue at the Intermediate Examinations where Latin
verse was practically forced on candidates who hoped to
make a good figure. The two outstanding distinctions
were the Studentship and the Junior Fellowship. The
Studentships were awarded annually and tenable for three
years and were worth £100 a year. They were five in
number, one in classics, one in Mathematical Science, one
in Mental and Moral Science, one in Irish Language and
Literature, and one in History and Political Economy.
The standard was that of the M.A. Degree and the competitor must obtain that degree ; if he already held it he
must be under twenty-six years of age. Better was the
Junior Fellowship, £200 a year, tenable for four years.
Three were offered each year, the subjects being changed

annually, so that in fact there was a Junior Fellowship only every second year in a particular group of subjects. The candidate had to be a graduate of not less than two years' standing. The holding of the Junior Fellowship carried with it one obligation, (the Studentship had none) : the holder had to assist in examinations, being in fact in the same position for the time being as the Fellows, except that he did not lecture. There was no such obligation to travel or to study in either the Studentship or Fellowship as there is in the present Travelling Studentship. The Fellows were assisted not only by the Junior Fellows, but also by a number of examiners who were appointed by the Senate. These did not take part in the setting of the papers, but helped in marking them, under the direction of the Fellows. They held office for a year only, but could be reappointed indefinitely.

All awards, results, and recommendations had to be referred to, and confirmed by, the Senate, who were the ruling body of the university. They met several times a year in the building in Earlsfort Terrace, on part of whose site the present University College building stands. It was erected first for an exhibition of arts, industries, and manufactures in 1865 ; a second exhibition of a similar kind was promoted there in 1872 by a Guinness family. It was afterwards in the hands of the Board of Works and was transferred finally to the Royal University to be its headquarters and working home, the Board of Works taking on itself the care and control of the fabric. It was an unimpressive structure, facing Earlsfort Terrace, its features on that side being a long glass-covered verandah—which students at examination times found pleasant as a refuge in bad weather—and, on top, three statues of more than human size, Hibernia in the centre, Industry, and Commerce. The statues were, I believe, the work of a Belgian sculptor ; when the façade was demolished to make way for the present building, they were taken down and consigned to the back premises in lonely exile, leaning against a wall, where they were not so long ago, and may be still. One further distinctive mark ; there was a clocktower at the end of the façade nearest Stephen's Green. This was also taken down, and, minus the clock-dial and its works, re-erected at the College of Science in Merrion Street, as a rather grandiose chimney for its heating system. Inside the Royal University building there were several large halls which were used for examinations, and on the first floor were the offices of the university and a large chamber where the Senate met. At the head the Chancellor was enthroned, or his principal deputy if he were absent, flanked by the secretaries. Around were the chairs of the Senators, mostly arranged in pairs ; which gave rise to the story, true or false, that, as the Senators were in equal numbers Catholics and Protestants, they were similarly paired off. For the rest of the building, which was very solid, it had been intended that it should be altogether removed to make way for the present college ; but the outbreak of the 1914–18 war and other serious difficulties prevented the execution of more than a part of this plan. Thus a large part of the older building remains, some of it in ruins but a great portion still in use. In the space between Hatch Street and the south end of the main building, there was a group of well-constructed laboratories, over which the curator, Dr. Adeney, presided. These, which even in outward appearance were a pleasant contrast to the unattractive aspect of the main building, are still intact and have for a number of years been used by the Medical School and other departments of the present college. In fact they have been in use as they never were in the old days, when they were used only for examination purposes. No teaching or lecturing was ever done in the Royal University buildings. Here at least the university justified its repute as a purely examining university. It was the same with the Library. A large and well chosen selection of books was to be found in a long hall upstairs, still in use as our Arts Library ; but only the Professors and Examiners had access to them, and even they only when they came together to set papers or decide results. Then the requisite furniture appeared. At other times the hall was bare and empty save for the bookcases round the walls, which were generally locked. True, one will find in the old calendars full and elaborate regulations for the use of, and borrowing from, the Library, but I am afraid these meant nothing ; certainly they were never put in practice. As for students, they were not thought of. The National Library was their place of refuge, and their obligations to it were deep and lasting.

The older generation of Dublin citizens were well acquainted with one part of the Royal University building —the Great Hall. It occupied a large space on the ground floor, was nobly proportioned, and was the scene of all conferrings of degrees and other occasions of high ceremony. But as these did not represent many engagements in the course of the year, the Senate often lent the hall for the use of the citizens, especially for concerts and music and sometimes for assemblies on matters of public interest. The concerts of Feis Ceoil in its earlier years were held there. There was really no other such hall in Dublin ; and when, with the demise of the Royal University, it was withdrawn from public use the loss was deeply felt and even resented ; and as no other building has ever appeared to fill its place the musical world still regrets it. The great conferring of degrees was at the end of September or beginning of October. The Senators took their places in their robes of state on the great platform with its seats rising in tiers, the Chancellor high in their midst, the secretaries at the sides, the recipients of the degrees in due order on the floor below, each in his or her appropriate gown and hood, their admiring families at the sides or in the fine galleries which have now disappeared. The Chancellor always felt bound to deliver an address. It was at the last meeting of the kind in 1909 that the last Chancellor, Lord Castletown of Upper Ossory, made known to the public what had hitherto been uncertain, that the new institution would be called the National University. At the lower end of the hall were gathered the general body of students, ready to express their views, approving or otherwise, as each new graduate, summoned by the sonorous voice of the Senior Secretary, went up for due recognition. It was

all in fact very much as it still is, or was till lately. The
singing and "barracking," if noisy, was generally good-
natured, and there was on the whole very little rowdyism.
Even at the worst there never were such scenes as seem
quite usual in other universities, in Scotland and elsewhere.
The Great Hall after many years of neglect has now been
restored to its old-time function, but without galleries it
is a mere shadow of what it once was.

Convocation remains to be mentioned. Women were
not admitted to be members, why I do not know, but they
did not miss much, for it was a rather futile body. It met
in Dublin once or twice yearly, but for some reason the
members who attended were mostly from the North, and
they were mostly men of mature age. The Dublin or
southern members and the younger graduates for the most
part failed to appear, again it would be hard to explain
why. Convocation, however, discussed its business seriously
and sent up its proposals or protests, as the case might be,
to the Senate, but nothing much seemed to result. One
gentleman, in this case a Dublin man, who should have
known better for he lived not far away, had a standing
complaint that members of Convocation were not admitted
to the grounds of the university. "He had never even
seen them"—with good reason, for they did not exist.
The grounds he meant were what at the present day are
called the Iveagh Gardens. They are of course situated
immediately behind the university building, but they never
were in possession of the Royal University.

The Royal University was recognised from the beginning
as an institution which by its very nature could not be
permanent. Its faults were obvious and no effort was ever
made to conceal or palliate them, yet like many threatened
things it contrived to live a long time—for thirty years.
It is easy to complain that it was an examining, not a
teaching, university, and that it was not residential. The
reply to the first complaint is that it was not entirely true.
A great number of its graduates passed its examinations
without attending any of its colleges or going through any
of its courses of study ; but its Fellows, who were also its

examiners, did lecture, and their students, who gained many of the highest places at the examinations, could not be regarded as the products of a mere examining system. The second complaint, impressive enough sixty or seventy years ago, makes little impression now. None of the modern universities are residential. However desirable residence may be, modern conceptions evidently do not favour it, and it can no longer be regarded as an essential. And as for the examining system, while we recognise its weaknesses, it must be admitted that it gave many students a chance of gaining good degrees whom circumstances barred from attending the lectures of the Fellows. This applies particularly to women students. The Royal University, was, I believe, the second university in the British Isles which admitted women to degrees at all, and we know how well the great women's colleges in Ireland, North and South, profited by the permission.

If we put aside these familiar complaints, let us look at the really serious shortcomings. The university was never generously endowed. Its Fellows and Examiners were not very well paid. The libraries, laboratories, scientific equipment, fell far short of what a university required. And what the government failed to offer was not made up by private benefactions as in other countries. I must make an exception of Belfast, whose wealthy citizens have always shown their appreciation of the institution, then a college, now a university, which has flourished in their midst.

Then there were serious faults in the method of administration. The ruling body was the Senate, all of whose members were nominated by the government. So too were the Chancellor and Vice-Chancellor ; and the Fellows appointed by the Senate and deriving their authority from it, were thus indirectly government nominees. No working or teaching Fellow or Examiner could be a member of the Senate. This was a fault common to all the educational boards set up in this country by the British government. No intermediate teacher or national teacher could be a member of the Intermediate Board or National Board. In the latter case, towards the end of its existence, two teachers were admitted, but both had retired from active work. Seemingly the official mind was convinced that such persons would be biassed and prejudiced in their own favour or in favour of their friends. Therefore there was a hiatus, as it were, between the governing body and the teaching body, with only imperfect and limited points of contact. I mean no insult to the Senators, whom individually all rightly honoured and admired, but in the last resort it was the government that ruled ; and least of all had the professorial and examining staff power of control. Yet no group of men deserved more consideration than the teachers and examiners. Meeting only twice or three times a year, coming from the opposite regions of Ireland, differing in religion, probably in politics, no ground of dissension or ill feeling ever showed itself among them. All were the best of friends. When the University came to an end, the inevitable break-up of their association was regretted by all.

Whatever else was to be said of the Royal University, nothing could ever be said truthfully against its standards and the quality of its degrees. Its papers were carefully prepared, its results given with care and meticulous examination ; no suspicion of bias could be charged against it. The candidate, man, or woman, who got a good degree from it could hold his own against any competitor, and deserve any success he might obtain. With its defects of organisation the Royal University could not be maintained permanently. It had to give place to another, better endowed, free from government control, at liberty to expand without interference, better in every way. But we must not let " better " crush " good " under foot. The Royal University with all its faults was good ; let that be its epitaph.

THE CATHOLIC UNIVERSITY SCHOOL
OF MEDICINE (1855-1909)

Professor William Doolin

It is easy, we all know, to be wise after the event. It is less easy, after a century crowded as none before it with scientific development, to focus one's backward vision accurately in the effort to visualise the odds which Newman had faced in establishing his Catholic University School of Medicine and Surgery in a city by-street, and to realise the degree of courage which had sustained him in bringing his task to successful accomplishment.

So far as our present imperfect records have allowed, the story of the establishment and the opening years of the School at Cecilia Street has been told elsewhere.[1] For those unfamiliar with the facts as we know them to-day, a brief summary may here be advisable. Newman had purchased a suitable building—the old school of the Apothecaries' Hall; it contained, however, no equipment worthy of the name. He had secured the services of three teachers—Ellis in surgery, Hayden and Cryan in anatomy —men whose capacity had already been proven in the established " private " schools in Dublin. He had no funds wherewith to pay them other than the donations collected weekly for his purpose at the church doors after Sunday Mass : a government still strongly anti-Catholic would afford his University neither its formal recognition nor one penny of public money with which to facilitate " denominational " education. With so uncertain a prospect of success, the leading Catholic physician in Dublin—Dominic Corrigan, whose reputation had already spread far beyond these shores—fearing for his own professional advancement, had declined to take part in his project : the title of his School notwithstanding, Newman had found no Professor of Medicine. An alternative choice

[1] *Studies*, June, 1953.

had been suggested to him, but it was the name of a man too far on in years for so hazardous a venture. Newman required men imbued with his own courage and confidence. Even in expressing his appreciation of Ellis's skill in having secured the Apothecaries' premises in Cecilia Street for his School, Newman somewhat impatiently described him as one " with little idea of making ventures."

The opposition from the established medical schools appeared truly formidable. In Dublin, the extra-collegiate schools, popularly, but not properly, known as the " private " schools—Ledwich (1836), Carmichael (1826), and Dublin (Hargrave, 1832)—accounted in 1855 for a combined total of 279 pupils. The School of the Royal College of Surgeons, with its roll of 129 students, far exceeded in attraction that of the School of Physic at Trinity College, with its muster of 43 entrants, while the schools in the Queen's Colleges at Belfast (81), Cork (63) and Galway (22), despite the stigma of " godless " teaching, returned a combined total of 166 entrants in that year.

One apparent oversight on our Founder's part yet remains unexplained. In the first half of the century Dublin's repute as a centre of medical teaching stood high upon two pedestals : the teaching of anatomy and the system of bedside teaching within the hospital wards introduced by Graves and Stokes. In Ellis and Hayden Newman had secured for his staff at the School two men who had already made their mark in other schools as teachers of anatomy : their reputation in this regard was more than creditable. That he was fully alive to the intrinsic value of the close association of a University School of Medicine with the staff of a teaching hospital is revealed in his second Report to the Bishops, presented in October, 1856, in which he drew their Lordships' attention to the close integration of the School of Physic with Sir Patrick Dun's Hospital, and of the Surgeons' School with the City of Dublin Hospital at Baggot Street. We know that the suggestion had been made to him that he should make some such approach to the authorities of St. Vincent's Hospital : it was at the time the only hospital in the city under Catholic direction and had the further advantage of its situation on Stephen's Green, in close proximity to the University. But there is no record extant in either School or Hospital to show that he ever followed up the suggestion. Not improbably, with a multitude of more pressing matters requiring immediate solution on his mind, he had left this to one side for later investigation.

The School was formally opened on 2nd November, 1855, with the delivery of an Inaugural Address by Ellis, as Dean of the Medical Faculty. Thirty-six pupils started their dissections at Cecilia Street under the guidance of Hayden and Cryan without any guarantee that their courses of instruction would entitle them to enter for the professional examinations of any of the chartered licensing corporations. For teachers and taught alike, the venture was a pure gamble.

Audentes Fortuna iuvat. Between August and October, 1856, the Council of the College of Surgeons extended its recognition to the lectures " delivered in the Cecilia Street School of Medicine." By this time, too, a young man, Richard Lyons, a Cork-born graduate of Trinity, not yet thirty years of age, back from service with the armies in the Crimea, had been found to fill the vacant chair of Medicine. With his appointment, two others had been made—McDermott, to teach materia medica, and Stephen McSwiney for medical jurisprudence. W. K. Sullivan, appointed earlier in the year to the chair of chemistry, lectured, not in the School, but at St. Stephen's Green.

Ellis, when taking up his new duties as Dean and Professor of Surgery in the Catholic University Medical School, had already reached an age at which most men to-day would be thinking of retirement. Born in 1792, the son of a Wicklow farmer, he had been sent to Dublin in the year of Waterloo to be indentured as a surgeon. (The centuries-old system of apprenticeship was not abandoned till the 1840's.) In 1820, he had obtained his Letters Testimonial from the College of Surgeons, soon thereafter becoming attached to St. Mary's Hospital on Ormond Quay, there to begin a life of active teaching, first of anatomy and later of surgery, faithfully pursued for more than forty years.

During the early years of the century, in which the need for surgeons in the armies of Pitt and Wellington was urgent, nearly eight hundred young Irishmen had obtained a certificate in the College of Surgeons qualifying them for army service.   Mindful of John Hunter's earlier taunt that " it was scarcely necessary for a man to be a surgeon to practise in the army," the War Office stipulated that candidates for a commission " must have had hospital experience."   Many of the so-called Dublin hospitals of these years were mere lodging-houses containing a few beds, rented or purchased by ambitious teachers ;   the instruction there given was sufficient to comply with the letter of the regulation.   The main subject of teaching there afforded, however, was anatomy.

Ellis's reputation as a teacher grew rapidly ;   within a few years he was invited to join the staff of the best known of these schools, that of John Kirby.   This school had been opened by Kirby (1808) in a stable at the rere of a small house close by Mercer's Hospital.   The landlady was a laundress, whose signboard over her front door bore the words :   " Mangling done here."   The Dublin wits could not resist the implication, gleefully declaring that the legend on the door did duty for landlady and tenant alike. At the end of the year, Kirby transferred his premises to a house in Peter Street (opposite the present Adelaide Hospital), there conforming with the requirements of the Army Board by installing two beds, his " hospital " being dedicated to the patronage of SS. Peter and Bridget.

We must not regard these private schools of a century ago with too supercilious an eye.   We are looking at foundations.   Anatomy—the knowledge of " that vile instrument, man's body "—was then in all centres the basic subject for students of physic and surgery, and the private school flourished in London and in Edinburgh as in Dublin.   References in the London journals of the period to the superiority of Dublin teaching were frequent,

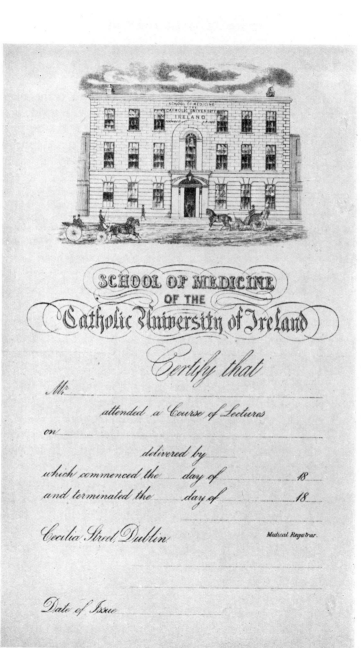

Certificate showing façade of Catholic University Medical School,
Cecilia Street

and the teachers in all these schools were, as had been John Hunter and Astley Cooper, men engaged in active practice. To few was it given to leave their name attached to individual discovery, thereby gaining an eponymous fame such as that of a Colles, an Alcock, a Houston—now sadly, and (in the writer's opinion) mistakenly, neglected ; but Ellis, Hayden, Cryan—even the doubter, Corrigan— had won their spurs as teachers in one or other of these now forgotten schools. Of them, Kirby's was the most successful and the most popular, and there Ellis had taught anatomy till his appointment in 1837 as Professor of Surgery in the newly opened School of the Apothecaries. By this time, he had joined the surgical staff of Jervis Street Hospital, where he had Corrigan as his senior colleague. In 1850 he had been elected President of the College of Surgeons, and, with Corrigan, consultant to the College at Maynooth. He was now the leading Catholic surgeon in Ireland, and as such had been brought to Newman's attention on the latter's first arrival in Ireland.

A modest and retiring man, Ellis has left no *literas scriptas* on which to assess his status as a surgeon. The Dublin journals of his day, the *Medical Press* and the *Journal of Medical Science*, have been searched in vain for any article from his pen, but by a happy chance the writer was last year entrusted by Dr. Macnamara, of Corofin, with a precious heirloom—the notebook filled by his grand-uncle with an almost verbatim report of Ellis's lectures delivered at the School in the winter session of '59–'60. From this fading ink and the carefully written pages filled nearly a century ago one can so easily conjure up the vision of the earnest student committing to paper by candle-light in his Dublin lodgings the fruits of his teacher's knowledge. These pages reveal the conscientious teacher, anxious to convey to his class what he had learned from authority rather than from personal observation. The names of Dease, Colles, Porter, recur on almost every page ; they were the men from whose hands the slender torch of surgical knowledge had been passed to him.

The passing of the Medical Act (1858) tightened the

5

shackles placed upon the infant School of Medicine. The
Irish corporations nominated by statute to issue diplomas,
possession of which entitled the holders to have their names
entered upon the *Medical Register*, were the Queen's and
Dublin Universities, the Royal Colleges of Physicians and
Surgeons, and the Apothecaries' Hall. Degrees conferred
by the Catholic University of Ireland were ignored, its
courses of study not " recognised "—save by the Irish
Surgeons and Apothecaries. Although a few years earlier,
in far Quebec, the Catholic University of Laval had been
incorporated (1854) by Royal Charter of Queen Victoria,
and the Cardinal Archbishop of Quebec appointed as her
Royal Visitor, the Government's attitude towards higher
education nearer home remained rigidly anti-Catholic.
" The poor Papists in Stephen's Green would not get
from the public funds what would glaze a broken pane of
glass "—such was the disappointed reflection of his Grace
of Cashel.

Yet as the years went by it became increasingly apparent
that the youths taught in Newman's School and entered
on the *Register* with the Letters Testimonial of the College
of Surgeons could hold their own with any in the spheres
of service open to them. The quality of the teaching there
received was steadily making its mark on the decreasing
lists of students entering the schools in Cork and Galway,
their endowments notwithstanding. How valuable these
endowments were we find revealed in the columns of
Hansard. On a vote in the House for the funds of the Queen's
University in '59 a Scottish member rose to comment that
"at the examinations for the preceding year there were
21 examiners, and 48 pupils were examined. That seemed
an inordinate amount of sack to a pennyworth of bread."
But grosser extravagance yet remained to be disclosed :
out of the 48 pupils examined, 12 had been awarded gold
medals, and £240 distributed among them in money
prizes. This was too much for Scots thrift. " The amount
of prizes distributed to the pupils," the honourable member
indignantly declared, " was utterly disproportionate to
their numbers."

Despite the depression which had been the inevitable aftermath of the Famine years, the calculated neglect of government and the strong counter-attraction of the bursaries at the Queen's Colleges, the numbers attending the School slowly but steadily grew. By 1860–61, the roll had passed the 100 mark ; by the close of the century its numbers had nearly trebled.[1] In 1861 a new Catholic hospital, the Mater Misericordiae, was opened on the north side of the city. From the day of its opening, its staff has always been closely associated with the School. Ellis was appointed senior surgeon, taking with him Henry Tyrrell, who had been Newman's first Demonstrator of Anatomy and Ellis's assistant at Jervis Street Hospital. Tyrrell, having obtained his Fellowship of the College of Surgeons in 1863, was to succeed his old master as Professor of Surgery on his death in 1867. With Ellis went, too, Hayden, Newman's first Professor of Anatomy, as physician to the Hospital. His appointment marks a distinct break with Dublin tradition. The Dublin anatomists had hitherto all been practising surgeons ; Hayden was the first anatomist to turn to the gentler art of physic ; his successor at the School, Robert Cryan, followed suit by joining the medical staff at St. Vincent's. Their joint service in Cecilia Street had covered a spell of twenty-five years (1856–1881). On Cryan's death there entered on the scene as Professor of Anatomy a young assistant physician to the Mater, Christopher Nixon, who was destined to play a long and influential part in the expansion of the School's activities.

We may pass rapidly over the content of the teaching which these men had to offer their pupils in these early years. By the '60s, while in Paris Claude Bernard and Magendie had already laid the foundation-stone of experimental physiology, and in Berlin Virchow's *Cellularpathologie* (1858) had blazed the trail for the pathologist of the future, clinical medicine—in which we include its humble handmaid, surgery—was still an observational art based upon anatomy, its practitioners

[1] Dr. Birmingham's evidence : Report of Robertson Commission (1901).

blind to the contributions which physics and chemistry
had to make to the development of their art. Its science
Magendie had roundly declared to be *une science entièrement
à faire*. From Vienna Dietl had echoed the Frenchman's
scornful verdict with the statement that "so long as
medicine is art, there will be no science ; so long as there
are successful physicians, there will be no scientific
physicians." It was even more true of Dublin and of
London. Intellectually, their leaders were still living in
the eighteenth century : the physician, ruling supreme
in the professional hierarchy, regarded his colleagues in
hospital, the upstart surgeon and the lowly apothecary, as
necessary adjuncts to his art. The Medical Act had
placed them all on the same legal footing, subject to a
common disciplinary code, but they shared no common
intellectual meeting-ground. Each group held to its
individual Society, medical or surgical ; of these Dublin
Societies,[1] the Pathological was the most vigorous, even
though the majority of the communications made there
were mere deductions from anatomical observation.
"Truth," Locke tells us, "scarce ever carried it by vote
anywhere on its first appearance," and although Joseph
Lister had made the first meeting of the British Medical
Association in Dublin (1867) the occasion to demonstrate
that Pasteur's microscope had revealed the bacterial
cause of disease and that he had found the counter-
stroke, it took many painful years before his gospel of the
antiseptic principle was accepted by his Dublin or London
colleagues.

While, under the *aegis* of the Surgeons' College, "the
School" was growing steadily in numbers, things were
going sadly otherwise with the rest of the Catholic University
on St. Stephen's Green. By the early '80s, there were
scarcely a score of pupils in Newman's old classrooms ;
his professors were face to face with virtual bankruptcy.
With the establishment of the Royal University of Ireland

[1] Nearly thirty years later, the fusion of these Dublin Medical Societies
brought about the foundation of the Royal Academy of Medicine in Ireland
(1882), an example followed in London later by the establishment of the Royal
Society of Medicine (1907).

(1879), the Queen's University was abolished, its three Colleges in Belfast, Cork and Galway made independent. To gain the benefit of the new University's degrees and fellowships, the Catholic University, with the exception of the Medical School, was turned into a college— University College, Dublin ; and this in 1883 was placed under the management of the Society of Jesus, with Father Delany as President. Now, for the first time, University degrees in Medicine were open to students of our Medical School. To its classrooms came in increasing numbers through the two decades following young men who, under the Intermediate system, had been adequately prepared —as the entrants for Newman's courses in Philosophy and Letters had not been—to avail themselves of all that a university syllabus had to offer them. Not all students of the School took the Royal degree, for which preliminary graduation in Arts was essential ; many continued to sit for the Surgeons' Licentiate. From their ranks came the teachers who, in the opening years of the twentieth century were to lift their School to its greatest heights.

A School of Medicine is not merely a place where instruction is given ; it is, properly regarded, an association for the advancement, by both research and teaching, of a science or a group of allied sciences. Abroad, through this troubled half-century of Irish politics, the work of Pasteur, Virchow, Koch and others was revolutionising the whole body of practical medicine and surgery. In Dublin, the official schools had ceased to be productive of new ideas, their teachers content to follow where, for a brief spell, under Graves and Stokes, Dublin teaching had led the van.

At Cecilia Street, we have seen, Christopher Nixon had succeeded to the Chair of Anatomy. Alone amongst British universities, the Royal insisted upon a course in Ophthalmology for its M.B. degree ; here another young Mater man, Charles Coppinger, was appointed to give the lectures. Later, Nixon passed to him the lectures in Physiology, which subject hitherto had always been taught pari passu with Anatomy. (Certain " advanced " schools to-day, one notes with interest, are reverting to the older combined method of teaching). From his chair at Edinburgh, Sir William Turner ruled the world of British anatomists, training up a group of young assistants to adopt its teaching as a wholetime profession. The first of these, Daniel Cunningham, came to the school of the R.C.S.I., lately augmented by the addition of the Ledwich and Carmichael Schools, there to stay for a year before transferring to the Chair at T.C.D. (1883). Having awaited the appearance of someone to take up a similar post in Cecilia Street, Nixon vacated his Chair of Anatomy to Ambrose Birmingham, as soon as the latter had graduated " first of First Honours " in the Final M.B. examination of the R.U.I. in June, 1886. Within a few months of graduation, Birmingham set out on his lifework. Nixon was appointed Dean of the Faculty, and later Professor of Medicine on the death of Lyons, and with Birmingham as his Registrar managed the School with efficiency and success. In 1892 the authorities of the Catholic University had the School incorporated under the Educational Endowments Act of 1886.

Whether as Professor or as Registrar, Birmingham's zeal and energy were inspiring. He had, too, the gift of friendship. With his two colleagues in Dublin, Cunningham (T.C.D.) and Frazer (R.C.S.I.), he was soon on the best of terms. To his duties at the School they added those of the Secretaryship of the newly founded Section of Anatomy and Physiology at the Academy, through whose annual *Transactions* his own original work became more widely known, thus leading to his appointment as External Examiner at Cambridge. When the first edition of Cunningham's *Textbook*, dedicated to his old Master, Turner, appeared in 1902, Birmingham's section on *The Digestive System* was greeted by the critics as an outstanding contribution to the literature of his subject. While working on this, he had prepared the notes for a dissecting *Manual*, illustrated by his own hand, to appear in three volumes ; only the first of these did, in fact, appear. It was the handbook used by generations of Cecilians who had never

seen him *oculis suis* : worn out by his exertions, still in his
early forties, he passed away too soon (1904), the victim
of a premature arteriosclerosis. His lifework had helped
to restore Dublin's reputation as a centre of anatomical
study to the place it had occupied when his century was
opening. His successor, E. P. McLoughlin, carried on
his tradition for forty years, and is happily still with us.

Nixon held the Chair of Medicine till his death in 1914.
In the closing years of the Royal University, this portly,
elderly gentleman of impeccable courtesy was done grave
injustice by a group of disorderly students inflamed by the
political atmosphere of the period. They little knew that
the Sir Christopher Nixon whom they publicly taunted
had been for more than twenty-five years one of the
staunchest advocates of university education for Catholics,
and that his influence as Dean had been the mainspring
in the development of the School on its scientific side.
He had vacated the Chair of Anatomy directly he had
found a younger man of promise who would, as full-time
occupant, bring its teaching to a level with that of other
schools. He had consolidated the Lectureship in Physiology
(later elevated to a full Professorship), for an even more
brilliant student, Denis Coffey. Sensitive to the advance
which would accrue to clinical teaching by the introduction
of scientific methods in the hospital wards, he had persuaded
the authorities at the Mater Hospital to undertake a new
venture in Dublin medicine by the establishment of a
laboratory for clinical pathology. The offer of a salaried
appointment at the Mater induced Edmond McWeeney to
take up pathology as a speciality. From the Senate, hard
pressed for funds, Nixon secured the establishment of a
Studentship in Pathology, worth £400. All this before
1892 ! Much of that " drive " had disappeared from his
teaching as he lectured to us in the November of his days,
but to those who hearkened to the slow measure of his
speech he was a sound, if slightly " prosy " teacher, and to
all the most patient and considerate of examiners.

By October, 1905, " the School " was making ready to
celebrate its Golden Jubilee. These men, from Ellis to

Nixon, had nursed it through its infant and adolescent phases, despite all obstacles. The once contemned " private " school, small in numbers and unrecognised by public authority, now, with nearly 300 pupils on its roll, stood fourth in size on the list of " recognised " schools in the United Kingdom. For the quality of its teaching the General Medical Council's Visitor, the Crown's representative for Scotland on the Council, had vouched in his last report : "Any man who got the diploma of the R.U.I. was a man who had been effectually taught and examined."

Why, I have often wondered, do so many surviving Cecilians refer to that institution in which they graduated as " the *old* Royal " ? It had come in as an interpolation between " the Catholic " of Newman's Rectorship and " the National," of which I, *juvenis fortunatus*, was the first graduate to sign its virgin roll. Its course had lasted barely thirty years, years of frustration and disappointment, cold years to so many young men and women who had passed out with its degrees and Honours into a work-a-day world, but with the conviction—often expressed to me years long after—that somehow they had felt cheated in their youth : they had known no " university life." For the word, as applied to the R.U.I., was a misnomer. It was a mere examining machine, it taught nobody. For the aloof, abstract creation that it had been they could feel no spark of pride or affection ; their loyalties, as they voiced their individual feelings, were reserved for " the College," or " the School," or " the Hospital," in which last institution the " medicals " alone had enjoyed some experience of a residential term.

In the School as first I knew it, the students followed two courses : some two-thirds of our number, disliking the compulsory course in Arts required for the " Royal " degree, continued, as their forerunners had done, to take the Licence of the Conjoint Colleges ; the smaller number counted it the wiser course to secure a University degree. "Surgeons' men " took all their first year subjects at Cecilia Street ; those entering for " the Royal " came to " 86." In the second year both were to fuse in " the

School," where in the political divisions of the time they were as one in their arrogant claim that they alone—the Medicals—were true " Newman's men " : the rest of his University had suffered by its transformation to a Jesuit College. It was ever the failing of youth " greatly to find quarrel in a straw."

At " 86," we were to meet the last surviving link with the early years of the School—our Professor of Biology, the venerable Dr. George Sigerson. Slow of gait and stooped of figure, with his great mane of silver-white hair and carefully tended moustache and beard, he looked every inch a descendant of the Vikings of old—a Sigur's son. Born in Strabane (1836), he had graduated in the Queen's University, travelling afterwards to France to study with Duchenne of Boulogne and Charcot at Paris. The great Darwin himself, we were told, had proposed him for Fellowship of the Linnaean Society, and he was an intimate friend of Douglas Hyde. To one fresh and impressionable student, I fear, he was the more romantic a figure, not for his associations with Newman or Hyde, but for his quiet statement that he had known the immortal Sarah Bernhardt in her youth, as he listened with a tolerant smile to my juvenile ravings, who had seen her once— from the high altitude of the " gods " in the Gaiety Theatre !

McClelland took us for Physics, and Hugh Ryan for Chemistry. Men of comparable brilliance both, yet how differently they handled the restless young colts whom they had to teach ! One stern look from McClelland's eye, as he paused in mid-sentence, would quell the fidget or the whisperer ; Ryan, his sandy moustache dyed an ever-deepening brown from his endless cigarettes, just " suffered " the antics of the unruly back-benchers in the class. What agony of soul it must have been to these men to spend their mornings in the sheer drudgery of this elementary teaching in rooms bare of all equipment save blackboard and benches. In retrospect, one can imagine their sense of bitter frustration as their thoughts travelled back to the laboratories they had left—Thomson's at Cambridge, Emil Fischer's in Berlin—where each had won

high honours in the happy pursuit of original work. Round
the corner, in Earlsfort Terrace, was equipment valued at
£20,000 held fast under lock and key for fifty weeks in
the year, but not to be used in research : it was " University
property," there " for examination purposes only." The
niggardly waste of it all !

For a Dubliner-born, the transition next autumn was
frankly depressing. Even from the shell of Whaley's old
mansion one had felt some sense of continuity with the
Georgian architecture of a capital city. Across the Green
in the sunshine of the May and June mornings we had
sped between trees and flowers to the National Library
after lectures, lingering awhile on the steps outside to listen
to Paddy Little or Sarsfield Kerrigan engaged in grave
dispute with all the solemnity of Athenian philosophers
in bygone centuries. But " the School," hidden away
at the bottom of a city by-street, bore all the outward
signs of " shabby gentility." At the time of its incorporation in 1892, £3,000 had been spent in decorating
it ; but it had seen no painters since. Its windows
uncleaned, the grey plaster flaking off its walls, the dark
hall within filled with the noise and clatter of strange
students thronging round the notice-boards—was this
where one was going to spend the next four years ?

Above, there were two lecture theatres, dark and air-
less, built originally to accommodate 100 to 120 students ;
more than twice that number now crowded daily into
the benches to listen to teachers who often, for lack of
floor-space, had to duplicate their classes. Only in the
dissecting room, on the top floor, was there a sense of space.
From older hands we learned that " this place is run on
the students' fees." And so it was. According to Mgr.
Molloy's evidence before the Fry Commission in 1906,
the School's total annual income from endowment after
its incorporation in 1892 was £55. It received no funds
from public sources ; the State had never paid one penny
towards its maintenance or equipment. These expenses
had to be met before the professors' salaries were paid.
Insensibly, we came to notice that the great men who

came down from their hospitals to lecture on the clinical subjects *drove* down—but the whole-time teacher, whose day was spent in a succession of classes, came on foot. There seemed little incentive here to a life devoted to science.

Of the dozen or so men through whose hands we passed in the next four years, three in particular stand out in my mind as having exerted the most formative influence upon our generation.

The name of Denis Coffey is now so closely woven into the fabric of University College that it is difficult to draw the picture of the young Professor who guided our first footsteps in Physiology half a century ago. One's first impression was of his shyness. It was a far from unfriendly quality, for he had the readiest smile and the gentlest laugh of any, teacher or student, within those mouldering walls. In him we found a man who, although he had won every possible academic distinction on his own way through College, was yet the most approachable member of the staff, who was never at a loss for any student's name or record, so that to the general body he was known as " the students' Professor "—in which capacity the back-sliders saw the best of him. He was the busiest personality in our cramped community, often lecturing twice and three times in a day in addition to constant laboratory work ; he never seemed to leave the premises, yet always could find time to attend or take the chair at committee meetings concerning the welfare or the recreations of the youth in the School. He was quite *the* most selfless individual whom we had ever met. The purpose of our earlier subjects had often been obscure to us as we made them up ; Dr. Coffey taught us to see in physiology the application of those subjects—biology, physics, chemistry—to the study of medicine, so that later we were to realise that the pathology of the laboratory or the clinic was really the physiology of the sick man. Outside the class-room, he taught us more : from his richly stored mind, well informed on all subjects—history, classics, philosophy, travel—we learned, almost unconsciously, that the future of Ireland

—*our* future—was the subject nearest to his heart, and that the scientific education of Irish youth was essential to her —and our—progress and prosperity. In all this he never preached, but his sincerity and conviction were apparent to all.

To Coffey, medicine was biology, and physiology an ever-widening branch of that science, capable of almost infinite expansion. To take part in that expansion, he had devoted all his early vacations to post-graduate study abroad—first Louvain, then Munich, Leipzig, Madrid. But as the Professor whose every day was crowded with other duties, the scientist was lost in the teacher—for him, original research had to go by the board. In the first issue of a short-lived periodical—*The Irish University Advocate* (1904–05)—he has left a contribution on " The Place of Medicine in a Modern University " which well repays reading to-day. It was a profession of faith, and a veritable *cri du cœur*. His College stands to-day his monument and his reward.

The R.U.I. had held its first entrance examination in November, 1881. In that batch of entrants was a young Dubliner whose father, a prominent journalist, had sent him for his secondary education to the Collège de St. Bertin at St. Omer. Entering " first of first " on matriculation, the young McWeeney thereafter pursued concurrently a brilliant course in both Arts and Medicine, to wind up with two Studentships—the one in modern languages, the other in pathology—a feat unique in the University's records. With his gift of tongues and his scientific ability, his post-graduate course lay clear before him : a year with Rokitanski at Vienna, a second with Koch, then supreme in the world of bacteriology, at Berlin, brought him home to Dublin where the chair of Pathology and Bacteriology awaited him—the first chair in these young sciences to be established in any University in Britain or Ireland. From his " lab.," tucked away in a small room on the top floor of the School, a stream of communications to the Section of Pathology year by year enriched the *Transactions* of the Academy, mostly on bacteriological work. The war in South Africa had demonstrated that bacteria could be more lethal than bullets ; in London, Almroth Wright—a fighting Irishman —was making clear to the world the preventive powers of inoculation against typhoid, even as ten years earlier v. Behring had demonstrated the value of anti-serum in diphtheria. To listen to McWeeney's exposition of these triumphs of scientific medicine was little short of fascinating. As a lecturer he was brilliant, clear, humorous, and with a most amusing hesitation in his speech, which we believed he could control, keeping it, as it were, hovering while we waited expectant for the operative words. To us youngsters, who had now begun our hospital attendance, he was the immediate link in our bipartite courses, for, holding a full-time post in the School, he was attached to a hospital.

Between him and McArdle there was a close bond of friendship. Even as a student I had had the good fortune of dining in both their homes, returning to regale my mother with the doings and the conversations of these men —the stars in my limited juvenile firmament. There I first watched them playing Bridge, then just coming into fashion as a polite evening's relaxation. At the table, I could observe the essential difference between the two characters : McWeeney, the scientist, carefully calculating his possible tricks, McArdle by comparison reckless, playing on the principle of " clear it or smash it," perfectly happy if he won the last !

For McArdle, my feelings then were little short of hero-worship. I had been his patient in the year before I started medicine ; I was his resident pupil at Vincent's and later, when his house-surgeon, was to act as " best man " at his second wedding. My recollection of his teaching is so closely associated with both School and hospital that it is impossible now to disentangle the elements of each. Looking back, I believe he was at his best in the hospital ward or in the operating theatre. He had had no such training in the *principia* of science as had the others of whom I have just written. " Mac " was, in sober truth, a self-taught man, virtually the last of the old school of Dublin's surgeon-anatomists. In his teaching he was factual, incisive, authoritative—all that the student going for his Final wanted a teacher to be ; he gave us *facts*, and gave them with a force and drive that was unforgettable. Years later, after his death, I found how he had learned, as he came to surgery in the first years of acceptance of Lister's gospel, of the antiseptic system. Mrs. McArdle had asked me to go through his books, and to keep such as might be useful to me. There I found complete series of English, French and German periodicals of the '80s and '90s ; " Mac " knew not a word of French or German, but the first Mrs. McArdle had been a good linguist, and there, interleaving these journals, in her fine convent-taught handwriting, were admirable *précis* of hundreds of papers on surgery. How those two must have worked together as " Mac " fought his way up from the bottom of the ladder !

Fully conscious of the deficiencies in his own early education—he had qualified from Cecilia Street in the Surgeons' School in the year before the R.U.I. was established—the cause of " the School " had no stronger supporter than he through these last years of " the old Royal," whose M.Ch., *honoris causa*, had been conferred upon him " for services rendered."

To us, who were his students, he seemed the most vital personality in the School. How often did we not hear the phrase, " It's a great thing to be alive ! " fall from his lips. Gascon by temperament, he made enemies ; he was forceful, assertive, a " bonny fighter " in the good cause, but by patients and students alike he was almost worshipped for his courage, his generosity, his good humour.

> *Certains mortels ont le don de répandre*
> *Bonheur et joie où se portent leurs pas.*

" Mac " was of that delectable company.

.   .   .   .   .   .

In this oblique biographical approach to history one could not single out for mention each individual's contribution to the common struggle. As the narration has been a personal one, the writer will (he hopes) be forgiven for having made his own selection. The *leit-motiv* throughout has been that of courage in face of all difficulties. It was a courage inspired by Faith : they asked not to see the full outcome of their joint effort—which is not yet. " It is enough for me," Newman once said, " but to begin." His courage, his faith, inspired these men to whose accomplishment allusion has been made ; in their places stand to-day the pupils who have succeeded them, to travel yet further on the road he planned, mindful of their memory, as was Pericles of his Athenian dead :

" For the whole earth is the sepulchre of famous men ; and their story is not graven only on stone above their native earth, but lives on, woven into the stuff of other men's lives."

PROFESSORIAL STAFF
CATHOLIC UNIVERSITY SCHOOL OF MEDICINE
1855—1909.

Anatomy :	1855. Thomas Hayden.
	1865. Robert Cryan.
	1881. Christopher Nixon.
	1886. Ambrose Birmingham.
	1905. Edward P. McLoughlin.
Chemistry :	1855. W. K. Sullivan.
	1873. John Campbell.
	1899. Hugh Ryan.
Surgery :	1855. Andrew Ellis.
	1867. Henry Tyrrell.
	1879. Patrick Hayes.
	1904. John S. McArdle.
Medicine :	1856. Richard Lyons.
	1887. Christopher Nixon.
Materia Medica :	1856. Robert McDermott.
	1859. Francis B. Quinlan.
	1901. Martin Dempsey.

Medical Jurisprudence : 1856. Stephen McSwiney.

Midwifery :	1859. John A. Byrne.
	1891. Alfred Smith.

Botany & Zoology : 1861. George Sigerson.

Ophthalmology :	1881. Charles Coppinger.
	1883. Denis Redmond.
	1901. Louis Werner.
Physiology :	1883. Charles Coppinger.
	1893. Denis J. Coffey.

Pathology & Bacteriology : 1891. Edmond J. McWeeney.

Hygiene :	1892. Anthony Roche.
	1908. James N. Meenan.

Most Rev. Bartholomew Woodlock, D.D.
Rector, Catholic University of Ireland
1861–1879

THE WORK OF DR. COFFEY AND DR. CONWAY
1908–1947

PROFESSOR J. J. HOGAN

UNIVERSITY COLLEGE, DUBLIN, as established by Mr. Birrell's Act and by Royal Charter, 1908, was the final attempt of the United Kingdom to provide acceptably for the higher education of Irish Catholics in their capital city. It followed upon a long series of projects and foundations either not viable or doomed by their conditions to be second-rate and temporary. This latest arrangement, as we shall see, had serious faults; but it was good enough to give scope to the first President's wonderful zeal and prudence, working with a devoted staff upon fine and plentiful material—the youth of a resurgent nation.

Denis Joseph Coffey[1] was born in Tralee in 1864. Graduating from the Catholic University Medical School, he won the Biology Studentship in 1889, and went to do advanced work in Louvain, Madrid and Leipzig. Professor of Physiology at the Medical School from 1893, he became Dr. Ambrose Birmingham's chief lieutenant; and on his death in 1905 succeeded him as Dean and effective head of the institution. He was admired as a scientist, a teacher, and as one whose good influence on students went far beyond their professional training. No mere specialist, he read widely, particularly in history and above all in Irish history. He was marked out by his general ability and distinction, as well as by the office he held, for an important place in

---

[1] Except where it is stated otherwise, Dr. Coffey's words are quoted from his annual *Reports* to the Governing Body. These quotations, and figures from the *Reports*, are given by permission of the Governing Body, U.C.D. The Royal Commission on University Education in Ireland, outside Trinity College, Dublin (1901; Final Report, 1903) will be referred to as the *Robertson Commission*. The Royal Commission on Trinity College, Dublin, and the University of Dublin (1906; Final Report, 1907) will be referred to as the *Fry Commission*.

81

whatever new university system might be created. He gave remarkable evidence before the Robertson Commission in 1901, and in 1906 he was a member of the Fry Commission. In 1908, at the age of 44, he was named in Parliament as first President of the new College; he held office until 1940, when he was 76.

Dr. Coffey's first preference, like that of the Irish Bishops, had been for a State-endowed Catholic University in Dublin; but it was certain that British opinion and powerful interests in Ireland would never permit this. His second preference was for something more practicable— a new college in an enlarged Dublin University, congenial to Catholics in its general atmosphere as Trinity was to Episcopalian Protestants. This solution had been proposed by Gladstone in 1873; it was acceptable to the Bishops, and was strongly favoured by Dr. William Walsh, Archbishop of Dublin; and it was recommended by the majority (Baron Palles, Coffey, Douglas Hyde, Raleigh of Oxford, Jackson of Cambridge) of the Fry Commissioners. Such a scheme avoided the serious disadvantages of having two universities in one city; it offered to the new foundation the help of the older one's traditions and prestige; and it seemed that the State could hardly give a mean endowment to the second College when the first was, in Gladstone's phrase, " the richest College in the world." Mr. Bryce was preparing to legislate on the majority report when he was succeeded by Mr. Birrell, who preferred a line of less resistance—a federal National University, with a Dublin College based on the old University College and the Catholic University of Ireland Medical School—leaving Dublin University and Trinity College undisturbed.[1]

The new College was quite evidently an immense ad-

[1] A minority of the Commission had observed that " To compel an ancient and proud corporation into a close and continuing union, repugnant to the strong feeling of its members, must, at best, be a dangerous experiment."

It should be said that a section of Catholic opinion did not altogether like the Bryce scheme, which undoubtedly had its own disadvantages, and was better pleased with what Mr. Birrell eventually gave us. This was the view of Father Delany, who had almost created the old University College, and thereby proved that a real university for Irish Catholics was possible. Father Delany was Birrell's adviser on many points; both their names merit our honour and gratitude.

vance. Its constitution, and the appointments to its chairs,
showed it to be a place where Catholic students with a
national outlook—" the old inhabitants of the island "—
could feel at home. It had more than seven times as much
money from the State as the old University College
had (indirectly) enjoyed ; the old Medical School had
lived on fees alone. There was the framework of a full
university—a pretty full range of faculties, to which more
could be added, in place of the Arts and Medicine alone
of the two former institutions.

The shortcomings were stated in a letter of Archbishop
Walsh to Mr. Birrell. The Archbishop thought the National
University scheme good enough to accept the Chancellor-
ship. But he told Birrell that it was second-best to " one
that would give us equality with T.C.D. in point of
University status, v.g., a second college scheme in the
University of Dublin." " But supposing," the Archbishop
went on, " that as regards status in the world of learning
we have to submit to our fate as representatives of a con-
quered and subject race, our next look-out is, are we to have
equality in *anything* in the scheme. This depends most of
all on the amount of money we are to get. I take T.C.D.
Are we to get as much as it has from public sources ? Or
I take T.C.D. and Belfast. Are we to get as much as
these two Protestant colleges and universities will get ?
If so we have equality in one substantial point. If not,
not."[3] The Archbishop made a third strong objection—
there was, despite the recommendation of the majority of
the Commissioners, no provision for the residence of
students. All three of his points were grave, as time has
shown. But the initial financial injustice was the one that

[3] The Archbishop had long been accused of wanting to plunder Trinity.
This, from a Unionist journal of 1885, reads curiously in 1954 : " The Royal
University will do very well in its handsome quarters in Earlsfort Terrace,
and Trinity College need not be ejected from the buildings of which it has
made such good use. It will be time enough to throw sheep's eyes at them
when the Archbishop gets his Parnellite Parliament in College Green. When
that goal is reached Trinity College and many other good things besides will
have to go by the board." The Parnellite Parliament has been sitting for a
generation, Trinity is happily undisturbed—and University College is doing
what it can in handsome but all too narrow quarters (a façade and a corridor)
in Earlsfort Terrace. Our revolution was mild.

bore most heavily during Dr. Coffey's period.[1] For, of
course, there was in fact no sort of financial equality.
University College was started with an annual endowment of £32,000, which, when students' fees were added
to it,[2] amounted to about half the income of Trinity
College. That initial endowment was never changed in
essence until after Dr. Coffey's time, despite the enormous
growth of the College ; it was only supplemented by
increases to meet the fall in the value of money, and (on
the transfer of the College of Science) by an amount with
an equivalent obligation. Even more grave was—as it
still is—the fixing of our grant for buildings and equipment
at £110,000. That implied that we must be a very tight
little college, in the shadow of Trinity's magnificence and
of a State College of Science whose buildings, to cost immediately twice our sum and ultimately far more, were
already rising. The figure of £110,000 has cramped and
checked the College to this day. No fresh grant for building
has been obtained in the whole forty-six years ; though
we have received the College of Science buildings and been
recouped for the wartime revision of our original building
contract and for expenditure on temporary buildings and
adaptations.

Dr. Coffey was a man who had little personal interest
in money, and perhaps at first no great skill in dealing with
it. But this was probably the greatest battle he had to
fight, and he fought it well. In nothing is his heroic devotion better shown than in his thirty years' tugging together
the ends that could not meet. Under conditions that
recalled the hedge-schools of the centuries of Irish disability,
he nurtured the spirit of a true university ; not allowing
the starkest poverty in space and resources to prevent an

[1] The point about residence will be touched on later. That concerning
status and name made it harder for us to gain recognition outside Ireland.
Anything remarkable done by us tended to be misattributed ; so late as 1950
the *Osservatore Romano*, in its obituary of Dr. Conway, called him *professore
emerito di Fisica matematica all' Università di Dublino*.

[2] Our whole income has been made up of grant and fees. Large private
benefactions were not to be expected in this country ; but we owe to Lord
Iveagh the valuable gift of the Earlsfort site.

Members of the Irish Party protested against the figure of £32,000, and
there seems to have been a chance that it might be made £45,000.

immense general success. In the circumstances, the success had to be limited and flawed. Short-sighted people, as is their wont, frequently blamed him for the flaws and limitations, while taking the success as a matter of course.

Probably, if peace and Union had lasted, the expansion of the College would have been met, as was promised, by bigger grants and a bigger endowment. Dr. Walsh thought that a start must be made somehow, and that each successive ministry, in quest of " sops for the Irish," would supplement the inadequate establishment. A different principle might have operated, even under Westminster—the tendency to assume that what is once settled is settled for good, and that if an autonomous institution cannot fend for itself it must be owing to mismanagement. In any case, the time for "sops for the Irish " from Westminster was almost over ; the European war was at hand, to be followed by the Irish revolution and civil war. Irish Governments should not be overmuch blamed for our subsequent difficulties. The United Kingdom dissolved before it had more than begun, rather meanly, to provide what its best statesmen had long acknowledged to be owing to Ireland—a proper university for the majority of its people. What the resources of the United Kingdom could have done easily, perhaps over an extended period, was more than could be achieved at once by a small new State, engaged first in civil war and reconstruction, and then in schemes of more obvious and immediate public interest than the creation of a university can ever be.

Things were tight even before the war, partly because the College was buying permanent equipment and libraries out of income. In one matter Dr. Coffey and the Governors thought they ought to take a risk, rather than submit to the pettiness implied in the capital grant of £110,000. They planned a College which should cost £220,000 to build and equip ; a quadrangle with a central block ; fairly ample for 800 students, it would reasonably house 1,000. Half the scheme was put in hands, and the grant would meet this ; the other half, if no further grant was made, would be built out of savings, or on credit, or somehow. Two sides of the quadrangle were finished in 1919, at a cost inflated by wartime prices to £155,000; so that we had less than half the buildings designed for 800 to 1,000 students, with 1,147 students to be packed into them, and a crushing overdraft. Even then, Dr. Coffey for a while struggled against fate; he thought a third wing *must* be built, grant or no grant. To-day, after thirty-five years, nothing of the original plan has been added to the half quadrangle of 1919, and it seems certain that nothing ever will. The *desiderata* of the 1901 Commissioners may perhaps ere long be satisfied—that "what is done for the Irish Roman Catholics must be done on an adequate and impressive scale," "that in the dignity of the buildings . . . and the equipment of the establishment, the institution should command respect and inspire enthusiasm"—but now that the College has passed the 3,500 mark these *desiderata* can scarcely be satisfied on the narrow Earlsfort site.[1]

In the immediate post-war years the numbers shot up; in 1920–21 we had 1,327, and expenditure exceeded income by £6,000. Dr. Coffey reported his failure to get from the new University Grants Committee " resources adequate to the size and importance of the College," though it was already as big " as all but one or two of the modern universities of England." " The present position is indeed intolerable," he says, though habitually an avoider of strong words; and he concludes, " we look forward with confidence to the new era about to open for our country." No relief could be expected in 1921–22. Dr. Coffey had to be content with pointing out that while all universities had suffered, our case was the worst; we had been caught

[1] Robertson Commission, Final Report, p. 34. Baron Palles, Dr. Coffey, and Dr. Hyde, in their Note appended to the Fry Commission Report, quoted the above and added the following : " Were there any marked difference between the dignity of the buildings of Trinity College and those of the new College, it would serve to prevent the Roman Catholics of Ireland being convinced that the principle of equality upon which they have throughout insisted had been admitted and acted upon. Were this so, a sense of long-felt injustice would continue. The feeling of unrest would not be laid—a sense of inferiority would exist in those connected with the new College, and thus the consummation so devoutly to be wished for, a final settlement, would not have been reached."

by the war unbuilt and unequipped, and with us numbers had grown more than anywhere else. Bigger numbers, of course, brought more in fees ; but a university cannot be run on fees ; their increase is quickly cancelled, and more than cancelled, by additional teaching and other charges. Large dependence on fees is dangerous, because a fall in numbers immediately brings down the revenue but does not make possible a quick reduction in expenditure. This had set in by 1922–23, creating a position " of acute hardship." Ironically enough, the University Grants Committee, useless to us while we were within its field, became useful now that we were cut off from it. Dr. Coffey in 1924–25 writes that the annual endowments of British universities have been permanently adjusted, and quotes the opinion of the Committee that " a modern civic university " requires an income of at least £150,000 a year ; ours was well below half of that.

The arrangement of 1926, giving us the College of Science and an annual grant of slightly less than its running cost, was the first important effort of the Irish State to meet our claims. We obtained immensely valuable space and equipment for science, and the only school of Mechanical and Electrical Engineering in the country. This transfer, and that of the Albert Agricultural College at the same time, confirmed beyond doubt our place as the principal university institution of the country. But on the financial side there seems to have been a miscalculation, made in good faith on both sides. We gained no new revenue for general purposes, though we needed it badly. It was thought that such revenue would be gradually released, as we extinguished offices duplicated between the two institutions. Had our numbers, slowly falling for some years, become settled at 1,200, it might have worked out so.[1] But by 1929–30 we had more than 1,500, and by 1933–34, 2,000. All the College of Science teaching offices

[1] 1926 is often spoken of as the golden moment when the College could have pressed harder and received much more. But this is to be wise after the event. We got a very great deal to go on with. Who could see that 1926 was so soon to be followed by the world economic crisis and new difficulties at home ? The 1926 arrangement, incidentally, provided for a financial review after five years.

were still required ; and the College floated, till the end of Dr. Coffey's time and beyond it, only upon the rising product of fees. By 1931 he had to report that we were struggling harder than at any time in the past sixteen years. " In proportion to such numbers (1,684) the College is worked with a smaller staff and lower general expenditure than any similar institution in Great Britain." Two undertakings, the erection of a small medical building to replace the ruinous Cecilia Street, and the purchase of the grounds at Belfield, bulk large in the Reports of these years ; they were necessary, and they cost what now seem paltry sums, but at the time they caused great anxiety and hardship, as we had to try to pay for them out of income. But Dr. Coffey, watching the College starve and the overdraft mount up, had always a brave word. In 1917 he had written " Not to-day nor in the immediate future can all of its (the College's) possibilities come into view." And years later : " there is at least the deep satisfaction that there is always growth " ; " there is no fear of the future."

In 1937–38, Dr. Coffey's second-last year, a simple comparative figure will sum up the conditions he had battled against and managed to keep from being disastrous ; in that year the average income per student of five English provincial universities and the University of Wales—none of them wastefully run—was £159 ; ours was £55. How was so much done on so little ? How was anything done at all ?

Before we attempt an answer, let us consider another great difficulty which beset the College during the Coffey period. Political anxieties and dangers were hardly less than those arising from finance, and they were to some extent linked together.

A strong Nationalist, Dr. Coffey was at the same time a believer in gradual and peaceful transformation.[1] But

[1] He was moderate but not lukewarm. His nationalism was deep and organic, it grew out of his intimate knowledge of the people, places and history of Ireland. He had been a Gaelic Leaguer of the early days, and, though linguistic facility was not one of his gifts, he knew the language in some ways better than many who spoke it more fluently. He knew the Sinn Féin leaders and agreed with them on some points. Even to the appeal to force his attitude was not that of narrow condemnation. Many remember

from 1914 onwards, a College much too young to have developed any degree of apartness from its environment was swept by all the storms. At first the general readiness of the country to fight the war along with the British Empire was pretty strong in the College ; by 1915 at least 230 of our staff, graduates and students were in the British forces ; by the end of 1916, 450 had volunteered. But the opposite current ran powerfully ; and in 1916, while one of our staff was killed in British uniform on the French front, another was executed by the British in Dublin, and many, staff and students, were in internment camps. Soon the College was overwhelmingly Sinn Féin in sentiment, and was supplying some of its strongest elements to the active side of the movement. Until the truce in 1921 there was constant danger that the College might be closed by authority or wrecked in some retaliatory fury. Coffey's coolness and discretion on dangerous occasions has become legendary ; but luck was also necessary, and it was on his side. Then followed the civil war, which, while it postponed any financial help from a native government, divided our students sharply and dangerously. The civil war atmosphere abated very slowly. Then, in 1932, came our first change of government ; and at that immature period of our independent history a change of government meant little less than a revolution. Our staff in the main favoured the losing side, to whose government the College had supplied many of its leading men. Relations with the new government were therefore, through our fault as much as theirs, rather delicate. Dr. Coffey met the situation with tact and patience. He succeeded in convincing all our statesmen that, though he might have his own views, he genuinely desired to be fair to all and to keep the College out of politics. He steered us through many crises, from 1914 onwards, almost to the happy position which, one may say, has now been attained ; that the College is a national institution and as such stands aside from party.

the true feeling of his speech at the unveiling of the memorial to Kevin Barry, the 18-year-old student who was taken prisoner in an ambush and summarily hanged.

It is proper to add that in the days when party feeling ran high, the head of the government, who was also Chancellor of the University, at all times exerted his great influence for moderation and unity.

One answer to the question, how so much success was won against such odds, is the fine quality of the first staff. Since Newman's time there had been a sort of underground preparation, growing more intense in the days of the Jesuit College, for the future university. Enough of good men would probably have been available earlier, if the opportunity had come ; it is certain that they were ready in sufficient numbers in 1909. Our first staff were good scholars and excellent teachers. In general ability and in character they were the very pick of the country. It was a gallant and a hopeful enterprise, attractive to able and generous men. Looking at it from another point of view, what else, at a time when there were not many openings for a Catholic Irishman in his own country, could be compared with a chair in the new University ? In 1910 the prospects before that staff must have seemed bright. But when the troubles gathered that were to outlast their time, they showed their powers of adaptability and endurance. They took overwork as their routine, and accepted a pecuniary return that at best was not more than modest.

The foundation staff included A. W. Conway, Registrar from the beginning and later to be President ; H. C. McWeeney, a fine mathematician who seemed the perfect type of the teaching professor ; Robert Donovan, Professor of English, whose ordinary speech was perfect prose, and who in other times would have been prominent as a statesman ; Father Corcoran, Professor of Education, one of our most forceful personalities ; W. Magennis, equally distinguished in literature and philosophy ; Father H. Browne, Professor of Greek, an Oxonian who had come to the Jesuit College in the distant wake of Newman ; George Sigerson, poet and Professor of Zoology, a living legend, who had entered the Catholic University just as Newman left it ; John McClelland, physicist, a Northern Presbyterian who had worked happily in the Jesuit College ;

J. W. Bacon, a man of letters who transformed himself into
a first-class administrator ; John MacNeill and O. J.
Bergin, leaders of scholarship in the early language and
history of Ireland ; Douglas Hyde, who had fought
valiantly for a just solution of the University question as
well as for the revival of the Irish language and who was
to close a great career as first President of Ireland ; Father
Finlay, founder of our School of Economics ; Hugh Ryan,
a very honourable name in Chemistry ; J. M. O'Sullivan,
a philosopher turned historian, later to divide his great
gifts between study and statesmanship ; Mary Hayden,
who both as a teacher and an academic personality justified
the full equality given to women in the College. All of
these have gone, but we rejoice to have still with us others
of not less distinction—five of them actively teaching, after
forty-five years : Professors E. P. McLoughlin, P. Semple,
Monsignor Shine, M. F. Egan, S.J., Mary M. Macken,
Monsignor P. Boylan, P. F. Purcell, J. Bayley Butler,
J. Lloyd Jones, J. J. Dowling. Future staffs may equal
some of these in scholarship, and perhaps surpass some of
them ; harder to match will be their all-round ability,
character and devotion.

Between the original staff and the President there was
a close bond. He held them in very deep affection ; we
can sense the emotion with which he records the passing
of men like Bacon, Donovan, McWeeney—" the greatest
personal loss since the foundation of the College." But he
was in a certain way solitary and aloof, nothing like *primus
inter pares* even with the most senior of them ; they were,
like the rest of us, his children rather than brothers. That
was how they felt it themselves. They knew that he knew
them through and through, and that he expected a great
deal of them ; but also that he would be lenient with any
failure other than disloyalty to the College.

During Dr. Coffey's time the number of chairs rose
from 35 to 55, of lectureships from 13 to 33 ; assistants and
demonstrators, very few at first, became a large body.
Half of the original chairs were filled again under him ;
and very many junior teachers, professors and lecturers of

the future, were chosen. The selection was very largely his work, and he did it well. Ever on the watch, rarely erring in his judgement of men, he would put mere undergraduates on the track of academic careers. He worked upon certain definite principles, though he could not in all instances perfectly realise them, owing to the poverty of the College and the suddenness with which new staff was often required. He believed that we must normally take our staff from our own graduates. We were new, and had a tradition to make ; there were no other institutions quite like ours ; and our own appointments were, for the time at any rate, the only openings that could encourage our graduates to devote their lives to study. To keep an isolated College open to the main currents of scholarship, he endeavoured to ensure that those who were to teach here should spend some years at a university outside Ireland, and return with a higher degree.

Another reason why so much could be achieved in the face of such difficulties was of course the students, their quality and their number. As there had been an underground preparation of staff, so had there been of students ; a solid middle class had grown up in the country, and we had had good Catholic secondary schools for a long time. From the first, our students were good enough, in character, ability, and preparation, for any university. They gave inspiration and confidence to a staff that might else have been discouraged ; and they complained hardly at all of the very little we could do for them.

As the numbers grew, we could in most ways do less for them ; there was less to go round. The students' classrooms, libraries, laboratories were overcrowded and ill-supplied, their clubs ill-provided, their Union non-existent. Lodgings, in a city of rapidly-growing population, were either overcrowded or very expensive ; a serious matter, as our hostels were few and small and most of our students came from the country. But in spite of all, the numbers had a heartening effect which was felt by everybody. They showed the essential greatness of an institution that was outwardly petty ; they made us national and representative, they stimulated competition and provided a richer life. The students may be said to have made the College when, by their irresistible pressure, they forced it into a greatness unforeseen and not provided for by the State—and even somewhat embarrassing to it.

Consider what the growing numbers meant.[1] In all countries university numbers have risen since 1910, partly through the more democratic ordering of society, partly through the need of more elaborate training in various professions. With us these forces operated, but not these alone. The old Irish race, partially excluded from higher education till now, was swift to see and take its opportunity. A generation entered *en masse* into the heritage of learning from which, though as eager and as apt for it as any people, their forbears had been shut out. Students came from all over the country, as they have never done to any other institution ; less than a third of them from Dublin and its environs, hardly less than two-thirds from the four provinces.[2]

Those who in 1906 were opposed to a generous solution of the University question advanced some reasons that by now look foolish, as well as some that were from a certain point of view sound enough. They deprecated the notion that any large number of Irish Catholics should be educated, because " the great Catholic majority mainly consists of poor and ignorant peasants " ; they spoke of the " misplaced charity " of " attracting the unfortunate sons of labourers to a university." But our thousands of students were not brought to us by any misplaced charity. Their

[1] Some figures have already been given, but it may be well to recall them here. In the first normal year, 1910–11, we had 695—somewhat more than the combined numbers of the Jesuit College and the Medical School. We passed the thousand in 1916–17 and reached 1,332 in 1919–20 ; thereafter there was a fall, going to 1,154 in 1926–27. But in 1929–30 we were above 1,500, clearly and permanently ahead of all other Irish universities and colleges. In 1933–34 we passed 2,000, and in 1939–40, Dr. Coffey's last year, were at 2,398. The 3,000 mark was passed in 1944–45 ; and, one may add, that of 3,500 in this present year. As maximum numbers have been fixed for the professional faculties, recent growth has been chiefly in Arts and Science.

[2] In 1920–21, 28 per cent. came from homes within 30 miles of Dublin. Later the proportion of Dublin students tended to rise ; in 1939–40 it was 37 per cent. ; but in 1951–52 it was down again to 31 per cent.

parents paid for them, or they paid for themselves by winning scholarships. Our proportion of assisted students has never been too high; it is now very far below that of any British university.[1]

More intelligent was the objector of 1906 who, knowing that knowledge is power, said that the foundation of such a College as ours would cause " grave danger, at no distant date, to the peace of the country." In truth, a reading of the Fry Commission papers to-day must convince anyone that there could hardly have been a real solution of the University question without a political revolution, gradual or violent, as the cause or the consequence. The crowding of students to University College, Dublin, meant the making of a new Ireland. The young revolutionaries of one day were shortly to be members of governments, heads of departments of State, judges, technicians, organisers of new industries. The brains of modern Ireland were forged, under difficulties but swiftly and just in time, in the College.

There were those, within and without the College, who murmured that we ought to restrict our numbers; it would lessen the difficulties of space and finance; and would it not be better to give something really good to a select few ? Such unreal arguments carried no weight, least of all with the President. The students were there, it was our duty to take them so long as we could fit them in; where else should they go ? Dr. Coffey believed that, even at the end of his time, the permeation of the country by the College was far from complete. Nor was he moved by the argument that so many graduates could not earn a living ; most of them did, though some had to wait ; and of course people may fail to earn a living whether they are graduates or not. Nor lastly was he deterred by accusations that we

[1] The Irish Universities Act of 1908, which founded the College, empowered the County Councils to found scholarships, and most of our assisted students are the beneficiaries of this system. The number is somewhat above 200 ; in 1918–19, at its highest, it was 272. From 1914 to 1920, County Scholars made up between 20 per cent. and 25 per cent. of our total numbers, and the scholarships gave the College something of an indirect endowment in those difficult years. In 1944–45 a smaller number of Scholars made just over 7 per cent. of our much greater total numbers. Between County and College scholarships we have now about 10 per cent. of assisted students, which contrasts strikingly with the post-war 80 per cent. in British universities.

educated for export; he knew that we educated for Ireland, though some graduates might in the event need or choose to go elsewhere.

Time has shown the rightness of the instinct that brought students in masses to the new College. The history of the Engineering School is particularly striking in this respect; starting from nothing, it grew to greatness and became indispensable to the country well within the tenure of its first professor, P. F. Purcell. For a long time there were few engineering openings in Ireland; most of the graduates had to emigrate or become teachers of mathematics or science. Yet they came. If we had at some point restricted our intake of engineering students to the number then certainly required in Ireland, the effect would have been disastrous. Supply preceded demand, but as the supply grew the demand caught up with it, or more than caught up; at present, though the School is above the 300 mark, there are often not enough graduate engineers to go round.[1] Of roughly 1,000 engineers graduating between 1930–31 and 1951–52, just 80% are known to be working at home, and only 14% known to be outside Ireland. A very similar picture could be drawn of the Commerce Faculty. In general, it is to be said that the proportion of our graduates who leave Ireland permanently or for the greater part of their lives is smaller than has often been supposed, and that it is decreasing. The main emigrant groups are missionaries, doctors, and women secondary teachers.[2]

Dr. Coffey's relationship with the students was unique, and an important binding force against all centrifugal tendencies. He knew every one of them and never forgot them. He was like a remote ancestor to them all, or an old Irish genealogist; he considered each individual in the light of his family name and district, and looked for

[1] Newman, who realised a century ago that the Catholic University must play its part in a social revolution, already laid down the principle that " the supply must be before the demand, though not before the need." (*My Campaign in Ireland*, p. 370).

[2] The Medical School, which for a long time made up nearly half the College numerically, is now relatively small, and its emigrant proportion has greatly fallen.

hereditary and traditional qualities. Among this immense family he moved continually, though it cannot be said that he exactly put students at their ease. His name was always in their mouths, because he *was* the College, and if they had anything to complain of, *Coffey* was to blame. But much stronger was their reverence and affection. In any sort of trouble they always found their way to him, and never in vain ; there survives a whole legend of services done by him for students, of the most varied kinds and often the least to be expected of the President of a College. Discipline was, as it still is, almost wholly spontaneous. It was never bad, though up to 1930 there was a certain wildness which has since disappeared. Dr. Coffey rarely thought it necessary to punish a student. He almost seemed to hold that " the student is always right " ; but in the cases where others thought him dangerously lax, his forbearance nearly always turned out to have been wise.

Three matters remain to be treated in this account of the first President—his handling of the religious side of the College, his attitude towards advanced work, and his administrative methods.

Few things were so much misunderstood or misrepresented at the time of the Fry Commission as the intentions of Irish Catholics in regard to the religious aspect of the proposed Dublin College. It was spoken of as " a medieval college," certain to be dominated by the Bishops and so fettered in its teaching that it would be a crime to join it in one university with another college, in which science was free and professors were chosen on their academic merit. In vain had Archbishop Walsh written that the Bishops required no religious tests, that they did not think it reasonable, a university being principally a place of secular teaching, that there should be a preponderance of ecclesiastics in the Governing Body. Time has proved that the fears and suspicions of 1907 were entirely groundless ; our teaching and investigations are under no restraints. But Dr. Coffey took care, as the constitution of the College of course permitted him to do, that the Catholic life of the great majority of the students should be an intimate concern of the College ; he fostered and organised it, and gave powerful example by his presence at all religious exercises. He brought a succession of Catholic scholars and scientists from abroad to lecture here. On all important occasions, such as the Dublin Eucharistic Congress of 1932, he saw to it that the College should show itself publicly to be " the representative university institution of the largest community among the Irish people." He valued the arrangement by which the students of Clonliffe College take their course in Philosophy at the College, with its ultimate effect that all the clergy of the Dublin Diocese will be our graduates ; and he rejoiced when, one after another, the religious orders of men and women sent their young members to us—giving us, incidentally, an Arts faculty of a size and quality unusual in modern universities. He followed with deep interest the careers of Catholic missionaries trained in the College ; and in due time welcomed the pupils they sent us from their schools overseas. Under his direction, the College, without infringing the letter or the spirit of its constitution, became a Catholic university in a way peculiar to itself ; and brought at least some of Newman's prophecies to fulfilment.

To research and publication, the advancement of learning, I have heard it said that Dr. Coffey was indifferent ; and that he thought of a university as little more than a place of undergraduate teaching, a glorified secondary and technical school. This accusation was certainly unjust. He had a deep respect for the advancement of knowledge ; he had himself made a real beginning as a researcher in physiology. But the College was understaffed, and teaching was the prime necessity. It did not hurt Dr. Coffey to see men capable of original work abandon the prospect of it for the sake of their teaching, as it would have hurt him to see them neglect their teaching. For the time, we had to be mainly the higher—very much higher—secondary and technical school ; it was the half-way stage, we had previously had secondary schools and nothing more ; later on, if we now successfully laid the groundwork of a

7

university, we should have the superstructure as well. Of
course, some splendid research work was done in Dr. Coffey's
time, particularly in Celtic studies and science ; and a lot
of good occasional work was done by some of our busiest
teachers. If Dr. Coffey seemed to notice it all rather little,
it was because his mind was on the main task, in which
failure would not be recompensed by the brilliant successes
of any investigator.[1]

To speak of Dr. Coffey's administration brings us close
to his personality and his greatness. No personal portrait
can be attempted here.[2] The greatness of the man was
felt by all who knew him, but it was not and is not easy to
define. He had not the gift of so ordering and expressing
his thought as to illuminate and convince an audience,
though they might feel that he understood the matter and
was right ; and he has left no remarkable memoranda of
principle and policy. The chief confirmation of his greatness lies in facts not words ; he took the whole responsibility of an immensely difficult enterprise on his shoulders,
and the enterprise succeeded. That the College we know
to-day should have been built up without Dr. Coffey is
unthinkable.

He did a vast amount himself. This was partly for
simple and obvious reasons. All presidents of colleges must
do a great deal. The President of our College must do a
very great deal, because it is, and has long been, practically
a university with the administrative machinery of a small
college—only two senior officers besides the President, and
only one of these full-time. If he is to delegate much, it
must be to professors already very fully occupied in teaching.
Again, it is plain principle that in any crisis the captain
remains on the bridge ; and there were few intervals of
easy steering in those thirty-two years.

But Dr. Coffey kept things to himself and made his
government of the College mysterious to an extent beyond

---

[1] Research in the College suffered not only from the demands of teaching,
but also of course from the lack of space, equipment, and of a great or even
a good library.
[2] See biographical articles by Mary M. Macken and J. M. O'Sullivan,
Studies, 1940 and 1945.

anything required by those conditions. He rejected common efficiency and ordinary business methods ; he did not answer letters as they came, if at all ; it was difficult to see him, though he was always in the College, and when you saw him he would talk about anything but the business you came upon. He had what seemed a morbid dislike to having people ask for things or make suggestions, appearing to regard all propositions as *prima facie* dangerous or unnecessary. Yet he neglected nothing ; the unanswered letters were not forgotten, the suggestions that nettled him sometimes became his own line of action, and the requests he would not allow to be worded were sometimes granted later on, unasked. He wanted time, and he was ready to pay a lot for it, in efficiency and in his own comfort.

It is probable that the main reason why he delegated so little was that he acted not upon clearly elaborated plans, whose execution could be entrusted to a subordinate, but upon an instinctive tact, which only operated when the moment for action had come. The difficulty of the times, when a false step might mean disaster, must have increased an inborn caution and subtlety. Blunter men could not understand, and often found it hard to co-operate ; they thought he was fumbling, when he was feeling his way. Those who understood him best were often baffled, though their confidence remained unshaken ; they would be heard to say, " I wonder what he meant by that," " I wonder why he took that line." One of his main principles was that he—that is, the College—could not afford head-on collisions, and to avoid them he would wait patiently for a situation to clear or opposition to grow weary—or he would yield, tactically, what on a short view seemed to be (but never was) the whole position. For all the indirectness of his methods, he never finally shirked a decision or gave way on an important principle ; and he could be, when a rare occasion called for it, startlingly prompt and downright. Rectitude and courage were fundamental in him.

A sensitive man, somewhat frail, and one who could never put the College out of his mind for a moment, the weight of anxieties must have been a heavy one ; he surely felt it a good deal. Yet though he was hard pressed at times, he was certainly not an unhappy man. He was serving a great work, and he could see that it was not failing in his hands ; and his mind was fixed upon larger issues still, so that he viewed even the College *sub specie aeternitatis*. Besides, there was the zest of skilful play and keen fighting ; and he must have quietly enjoyed his many victories, though he was far too charitable to indulge in any sort of triumph.

With Dr. Coffey's retirement the first chapter of our history may be said to have closed. It may be summed up like this. Owing to incredulity, imperfect sympathy and active jealousy on the part of those who had authority and influence, the College which was bound to become the principal university institution of Ireland was begun on far too small a scale ; the remedy of this defect was postponed by war and political stress, and by the proportions to which delay itself swelled the cost of the remedy ; the irresistible crowding in of students burst the narrow bounds set to the development of the institution ; an admirable body of teachers coped with this expansion, so that it did not eventuate in chaos and an abandonment of academic standards ; and a great President met every emergency— selfless, undaunted, and infinitely resourceful.

The second presidency was much shorter than the first, and hardly made a complete chapter. It was a period of transition, wherein, while the struggles already described went on and even grew more intense, new elements of strength and new possibilities of development, together with a fuller public recognition, began to appear.

Dr. Arthur Conway, Professor of Mathematical Physics and Registrar since 1909, came to the Presidency in 1940, somewhat late in life, and held it until 1947.[1] Born in 1875, he had graduated in Mathematics from the old College, spent three years in Oxford (both reading and rowing well), and taught in the old College from 1901 until its transformation. A scientist of the highest distinction, he became quite early a Fellow of the Royal Society, and was

[1] Dr. Coffey died in 1945, Dr. Conway in 1950.

later on a member of the Pontifical Academy of Sciences. Even as President he kept in the forefront of mathematical studies, and found time for relaxations like golf and cross-word puzzles (of the hardest sort) ; such things gave him a valuable detachment, a fresh and free mind. It must have been hard to be Dr. Coffey's successor, but Dr. Conway took over in a most natural and easy way, and from the start did things in his own fashion. The President was now accessible, and things ran on the lines of ordinary efficiency. Seeing that no individual could any longer carry all the tasks that his predecessor had borne, he began at once to delegate some of them. The office of Registrar now became more important than Dr. Coffey had allowed it to be ; its new holder, the late Professor J. J. Nolan, undertook several major tasks, and introduced a new clarity into our administration. The Faculties, working under their Deans, now for the first time became administrative realities. The President attended to such diverse problems as social amenities for students and research by members of the staff ; the President's Reports became far more general in scope, less preoccupied with the single question of finance. The provision of proper College buildings, which Dr. Coffey had had to give up in despair, was again made a live issue. Dr. Conway was clearly fitted to lead the College in a second great epoch of its existence—one of relaxed tension and general expansion. As it turned out, he could only prepare the ground for such an epoch—for what we are now seeing under his successor. His own time was to be one of greater tension and narrower restriction than perhaps any we have lived through.

As wartime conditions developed, the strains that Dr. Coffey had already declared to be " intolerable " were greatly increased, and the College was brought to " a state of grim and unrelieved penury." The annual endowment, never more than barely sufficient, sank lower and lower in real value ; the overdraft grew to a dangerous figure. Meanwhile, student numbers were rising more steeply than ever before ; we added just a thousand between 1940–41 and 1946–47. Overcrowding became far worse than before ; more staff was badly wanted, but we could afford little in this way, being unable to pay the staff we had. The income per student, even with the reduced value of money, fell to its lowest figure.[1] Dr. Conway fought against these troubles as manfully as his predecessor had done. He set up a committee by which a full statistical survey of the College and its needs was prepared ; this survey was of great value in gaining relief from the State as soon as was possible after the war ; and it forms the groundwork of all our later planning. Dr. Conway made more than one attempt, frustrated by the lack of money, to purchase building sites ; and he began the reconditioning of the ruinous Old Buildings from which we have since gained important temporary relief. When our new buildings have gone up, it will be remembered that it was under his leadership that we abandoned the idea of completing the original small-scale quadrangle, and began to plan for something far bigger and on wider ground. This is perhaps symbolical of the second presidency ; a time of stress and temporary discouragement, but one in which the seeds of a better future were sown.

[1] Comparing 1944–45 with 1910–11, the students had multiplied by more than 4, the endowment by a little over $2\frac{1}{2}$, the product of fees by nearly 9. Income per student was considerably less in nominal value than in 1910–11 ; it was perhaps about one third in real value.

THE STUDENT BODY

James N. Meenan, M.A.

THERE is a school of thought which holds that a university need not possess students. It is unlikely that Dr. Newman would have agreed; probably he would have said that a university would look rather foolish without them. Certainly he would have agreed that a survey of the hundred years since the Catholic University was founded should include some account of the student body. In a famous passage in the *Idea of a University* he said :

" When a multitude of young men, keen, open-hearted, sympathetic, and observant, as young men are, come together and freely mix with each other, they are sure to learn one from another even if there be no one to teach them ; . . . they gain for themselves new ideas and views, fresh matter of thought, and distinct principles of judging and acting, day by day. . . . I am but saying that that youthful community will constitute a whole, it will embody a specific idea, it will furnish principles of thought and action. It will give birth to a living teaching, which in course of time will take the shape of a self-perpetuating tradition, or a *genius loci*, as it is sometimes called ; which haunts the home where it has been born, and which imbues and forms, more or less, and one by one, every individual who is successively brought under its shadow. . . ."

In all its vicissitudes, it has been a generous tradition of University College that no small part, perhaps the most important part, of its training lies outside its lecture rooms. But it must be admitted that there is little formal unity in the history of a student body which, in the last hundred years, has lived under three universities and during that time has had some six or more separate centres of study. It is difficult to reconcile in the same frame the life of students in the Catholic University of the 1850's with the customs of " 86 " and Cecilia Street in the 1890's and both in their turn with the present day. There have been too many changes of political thinking and social habit. Even the simple change of scale presents its difficulties and hinders while it heightens the contrast between the Catholic University with its thirty to forty students and University College with just one hundred times as many to-day.

To our mind, student life was curiously unorganised in that patriarchic society in Harcourt Street where the Rector carved under-done mutton for his thirty students. True, there was already the L. & H. which in those days added the title of "Aesthetical "—a boast discreetly dropped long since. But, beyond these specialised activities, life was curiously haphazard. We hear of boating on the Liffey, swimming at the Pigeon House and hunting in Meath. There is still rowing (which is not at all the same thing as boating) on the Liffey : there is still swimming ; but the third pastime brings us up short. True, within the last decade we have seen a professor whose gown half-hid his hunting-kit, but it is unlikely that he was followed to the meet by many of his students. These hunting types, and those other students who went to " some race-meeting " (profitably it seems, since they dined in town and did not come in until twelve), were a source of some anxiety. The Rector did his best to keep his boys at home by providing a billiard table—full-sized, as his correspondence makes clear. One would not have thought that the Billiard Clubs of later days could trace so respectable an ancestry. Not indeed, that the various dissipations of the city were open to students who lodged with the Catholic University : in the 1860's the doors were locked at 7 p.m. and no one got out without the deposit of half-a-crown, forfeit if he was not back by ten o'clock. The medical students in Cecilia Street, many of whom were not so confined, had greater freedom to embellish the carefully built up reputation of medical schools everywhere. It is possibly by some instinctive memory of such curfew that successive students' magazines, however zealous for clubs or gowns, have been chary of residential quarters.

Thus, in the earlier decades of the College there were students rather than a student body. Not so many students at that : when the University Bill was before Parliament in 1873 there was some question whether there were seven students or forty-three. However numerous, students then had not that degree of uniformity which comes from a common background of school education. Most of the schools from which the College now draws its students were established by the 1870's, but their curricula varied— varied so much that they sent up " gentlemen who have yet to learn such elementary truths as that Jerusalem is not in Africa, that the Helots did not live on the shores of the Red Sea, and that the patriarch Job lived and died before the Babylonish captivity " ; truths now so self-evident, one hopes, that they have been forgotten through sheer familiarity. Secondary education was not standard-ised until the Intermediate Education Act of 1878 ; soon after, as a matter of policy, the prize-winners were sent to University College. It is not a coincidence that it is then that College life becomes more recognisable to modern eyes ; that student activity becomes more organised ; and that the apostolic succession of Auditors of the L. & H. becomes more constant, if not yet enriched by the short but sinister list of anti-popes. On the sporting side, it should be remembered that football, in any of its branches, did not emerge in modern form until the 1870's and 1880's. Athletics and boxing were still, in Ireland, for individuals rather than for teams. Neither tennis nor golf had yet been introduced to the country.

And so the earlier decades of the hundred years must be passed over in favour of the better-authenticated (or more written-over) six decades since the golden age of the later 1890's. There may well have been Auditors more puissant than any of whom we have record, footballers or athletes more skilled than any we have seen ; but their names have not survived, *carent quia vate sacro*. Later ages have not lacked their historians : there have been some groups who not only wrote about each other while at College but continued to do so for a generation after.

To-day, it seems, one's mere presence in College in the days of Joyce has become a major source of dollar income. But the glamour of having been a young man at the same time as the artist is not solely dependent on that : the closing years of the century saw a burst of student activity which eclipsed all that we know of what went before. Moreover, these are the first generations of students who made their mark on national history ; these are the generations whose names appear in the events of fifteen to twenty years later. There were, of course, others who preceded them in College whose contribution was as important ; but from now onwards one can point to groups rather than to individuals.

These matters may be studied in the pages of *St. Stephen's*, the student magazine which first appeared on June 1st, 1901. The date was symbolic, on that day in 1854 Newman had published the first issue of his *Catholic University Gazette*. But there was to be a difference, consciously and unconsciously summed up by Father Darlington's comment in *St. Stephen's* that in the *Gazette* " the students and their doings do not appear at all but in our venture everything will be either by them or for them or through them."

By our degenerate standards, the most remarkable thing about *St. Stephen's* is that it appeared regularly for over six years, sinking at last in the stormy L. & H. rows of 1907. The second most remarkable thing is the high level of its contents, which the later *National Student* has only at times equalled in any of its so numerous resurrections. In those days perhaps students (and the authorities) of University College felt themselves to be on their best behaviour in a sense only paralleled in the years after the foundation of the National University in 1908. For *St. Stephen's*, the University question (that invaluable stand-by for Auditors in search of an Inaugural) was still undecided : it was still necessary to prove that the need for Catholic university education was not met either by Dublin University or by the Queen's Colleges. For the same reason it was desirable not to upset the Hierarchy, the British Government or the Irish Party—bodies which themselves had not yet reached any clear decision on the matter. And so, much space was devoted to showing the good examination record of the College in competition with its better subsidised rivals, to stating the Catholic point of view at a time when scientific fashion ran heavily in the other direction, and to examining the university systems of countries such as Austria which might provide guidance for Ireland.

Some of this, it must be admitted, makes heavy reading to-day; for many students it must have been heavy reading then. It is only in the light of what came later that interest attaches to the references to Joyce's contribution on Mangan or to the advertisements of lectures on Irish history and literature by Eoin MacNeill and Patrick Pearse. The majority of students perhaps turned away from the university system of the still Dual Monarchy to the notes that told of the goings-on, very discreet, in the ladies' hostels, of the doings in Cecilia Street and of the fitful activities of the new clubs.

At that time, as it seems to-day, student life was at once both united and separated. The medical lectures were given in Cecilia Street, the arts lectures in " 86 "; until the time of the new College, the lady students received their lectures in the seclusion of the halls. Only an occasional lady student, at that time, brought blushes to professional cheeks by her presence in medical classes. The links were not many; principally the L. & H. and the National Library (between them constituting College life for so many generations of students) and some clubs and societies. Dances there were not : no lady was out at night. But those who did gather in " 86 " were perhaps more closely knit than any succeeding generation. There were comparatively few students; not many more than the smallest Faculty holds to-day; many of them had been at the same school. The same people were to be seen and heard in all the societies, on the committee here, in opposition there; their activities in the L. & H. joined with discussions in the St. Thomas Aquinas Study Group and both, no doubt, with the Choral Union. That body in its turn, the forerunner of the Musical Society, gave

itself ample scope : it held a special concert to help the
funds of the Soccer Club. The L. & H. was then firmly
in the grip of the law school from which came eight of the
nine auditors of the period. Consequently it indulged in
what is still a favourite College activity and revised its
constitution, for the third time since 1857. The process
did not do it much good, for in the next year, 1905, we
read that " it seems hopelessly on the decline." As much,
no doubt, was said before : it has certainly been said often
since, rarely so forcefully as by the *National Student* of 1919
which asserted that the society " was sinking into a dis-
honoured grave." Other societies made their appearance—
the Légion Française in 1902, followed by the Cumann
Gaedealach which applied itself without delay to the
propriety of taxing bachelors.

The clubs too begin to fill out and be something more
than transient phantoms. The Soccer Club, the senior of
all, dates from 1895 ; its seniority being helped by the fact
that not all Irish schools had yet realised that Rugby had
displaced Soccer in social precedence. But easy recruitment was not without its dangers as we learn from a plain-
tive note which informed students that the club was open
to them all and was not, as appeared to be thought, confined to Clongownians—a pardonable mistake, to judge by
previous contributions. The Rugby Club was not yet
born, but the Hospitals Cup was already in existence and a
note recording a victory of Vincent's over the Mater in a
" hard and sternly-contested " game prophesies that the
winners may get the Cup on the condition, emphasised
with sinister italics, " *if they keep in training*." There was
still no Athletic Club, but a Hurling Club was founded in
Cecilia Street in 1900—and founded all over again in 1905.
Proposals for a Gaelic Football Club obtained no response ;
on the contrary the tide ran the other way and a Hockey
Club was founded in 1905. This aroused the protests of
The Leader, then and later a stern critic of any back-sliding
into West Britonism, but it might have saved its breath—
the club soon succumbed under the weight of two committees at the same time. To assist all these enterprises,

an Athletic Union had been formed some years before but
it collapsed, leaving behind a mass of debts and a discouraging memory. And other themes, well-worn fifty years
later, now make their appearance. An L. & H. reading
room was opened in 1902 but soon shut again, so firmly
that *St. Stephen's* suggested it as a new proposal in 1905.
In that year too, the establishment of a University Club
was suggested—perhaps not for the first time even then.

And so the scene is in many ways not so remote from
ours. But there are differences ; perhaps not all in ex-
ternals. To the reader of *St. Stephen's* it seems a settled life.
The L. & H., still barred against lady students, could settle
down to debate if the British occupation of India had been
justified by its results, some of the speakers intending to
assist in the administration of the Raj. Along the Green,
in the ladies' halls, a paper on " Francis Thompson "—
the Rev. G. O'Neill, S.J. to propose the vote of thanks,
the Rev. F. G. Watters, S.M. to second it—level discussions
drowned by the rattle of the Clonskea tram as it lurched,
its yellow signs tossing, over the points by Byron's. Down
in the Dolphin the law and medical professors dined their
students and, in the intervals between musical contributions, were toasted by them. A pleasant life, it seems,
certainly more peaceful than any generation of students
was to know for twenty years to come.

In the early years of the century the Royal University
seemed to be an unconscionable time a-dying. A new
approach to the University question was promised re-
peatedly, and as often delayed while discontent not only
against the University but against those who held its
highest offices grew. Conferrings in those days were far
more lively than they now are ; indeed it is within comparatively recent days that they have become so dull.
Fifty years ago, no such function was complete without a
rendering of " Sweet Rosie O'Grady " and other appropriate airs. But, as so often happens, what was not to be
sung was far more important than what was ; and in 1904
the Conferring was abandoned long before it was time to
play " God Save the King." Next year things were still

better ordered : the gallery with which the Great Hall
was then furnished was occupied and the organ seized.
There was much legal correspondence between the Senate
and the students held responsible. From this the only
tangible result was that the Chancellor resigned while the
students remained unscathed by so much academic lightning
and press comments on "Jesuit hooligans."

The L. & H. was not so lucky. In 1905 it passed a
resolution of congratulation to the heroes who routed the
Senate. That perhaps was only to be expected : the
Society has passed more subversive motions in its time.
This one, however, was ordered by authority (which had
still to walk warily) to be removed from the minute book.
This was not done and in the following year, 1906, the
quarrel deepened when the President of the College was
censured for calling in police to disperse the students after
the Conferring. This time, the President sent down the
Auditor, deprived him of the auditorship and expelled him
from the Society. He and his supporters, refused the use
of any room in " 86," retired to Avignon ; to be more
exact, Cruise O'Brien held his Inaugural in the Antient
Concert Rooms in Pearse (then Brunswick) Street. To
attempt to summarise further would be unfair to both
sides in the schism : one thing that is certain is that the
minute book disappeared so completely that it has never
since come to light and has remained as lost as any book
of Livy. But, as in the contemporary case of the Crown
Jewels, there are the most interesting theories about its
present whereabouts.

The split was healed although its effects lived on for
some years and Cruise O'Brien's chief supporter, John
Ronayne, returned to divide the year 1911–12 with Patrick
McGilligan after the most famous of all elections. But in
the interval, the Society had capitulated to change and
admitted lady students to membership. Since then, Auditors have felt sure of a safe majority in private business
but their predecessors who reigned in more masculine days
are still ready to talk like so many Catos, and at appropriate
length, of the degeneration of modern times.

At long last, the new University Act was passed and the new University College was saluted by the appearance in May, 1910, of the first *National Student*. Its title was more obvious than that of the short-lived *Hermes* which appeared after *St. Stephen's* had sunk under a Presidential thunderbolt. But, then and later, any editor short of a topic could find his leader in a discussion of the relative importance of adjective and noun. Here again, as nine years earlier, there was a strain of responsibility. The new University had to justify itself, it had to apply itself to the task of moulding the new State—then to be created by a measure of Home Rule at no far distant date. There was much talk, in place of Austrian universities, of what Stein and Hardenberg had done for Prussia a century before. At times, it is true, there was some feeling of inadequacy. " Remove the Medical School from University College," asked one contributor, "and what have you left? A miniature Maynooth with a handful of lay students." But the College was stoutly defended and *The Leader*, still critical of the new dispensation, was somewhat unfairly compared (unfavourably) with " Horatio Bottomley's English penny dirty." And running through all controversies, there is a feeling of hope and freshness and a new start in which everything would become possible. The new College was to be suitably housed " somewhere in the suburbs and in its own playing-fields " ; the Medical School was " to be out of Cecilia Street in six months " (even that minor change took just twenty years). For the rest, there was to be a proper students' room, a students' union ; above all, a university tradition was to be created. " It's something new in Universities," said Manders to Bernard in *The Wasted Island*, " The National's new. It may be a bit shoddy, but we might make something of it." Readers of Eimar O'Duffy's novel can still recapture the spirit of those days and, if they read the first and more outspoken edition, judge if some schools still produce the same types as they did then.

In those days, there still seemed to be hope for all the world. Progress was still inevitable ; for none more than

for university students who expected to see the Bank of
Ireland evicted from College Green. Just as they might
make something of the College, so they might make something of the country. The law school swarmed, as the
National Student said, with students " who were expected
by their parents to become lawyers and by themselves to
become Irish Cabinet Ministers." So a number of them
did ; but not in the kind of government that they expected
in the years before 1914 and only after struggles that would
have then seemed inconceivable. It may be hazarded that
no small amount of Irish politics in 1922 can be traced
back to the L. & H. some years before. But for the moment
all seemed well. Mr. Alec Maguire was election agent for
Mr. McGilligan. In the summer term of 1911 " Mr. J.
Costello wound up a very pleasant night's entertainment
by speaking to the motion, which, indeed, seems to be
self-evident ' That the worst of things must come to an
end.' " From the diary of College events in the *Student*
we learn that at 8 p.m. on Wednesday, January 14th,
1914, Mr. A. Cox was expected to address the Legal and
Economic Society on " The Attorney's Progress."

This too was the period in which clubs multiplied. The
Athletic Union Council came into being in 1910 and took
over the granting of colours—the first grant being to the
Athletic Club (which had already established the pre-
eminence which it has never since lost) after it won the
Inter-University Sports in Cork. The College, it may be
remarked in passing, seems to have been consistently un-
lucky in its choice of colours. Those of the Catholic
University appear to have been brown, green and yellow :
it is perhaps no wonder that the Soccer Club preferred to
appear in black and white. The blue and saffron adopted
for the new College were based, according to tradition, on
a belief that such were the colours of the ancient bards. It
may be so ; but the ancient bards did not wear ties ; and
the creation of a satisfactory combination of blue and
saffron has defeated the devoted efforts of all, except
perhaps the old O.T.C. Blazers were dark blue with a light
blue and saffron edging. They did not wear well and

Most Rev. Dr. William J. Walsh,
Archbishop of Dublin and Chancellor of the National University
of Ireland

were replaced, again under the leadership of the Athletic
Club, by the present light blue in 1930. That too has its
drawbacks ; but dry cleaning has made great progress.

The other clubs made progress and were joined by
fresh creations, the Swimming Club in 1913, the Camog
in the next year (Miss O'Farrelly in the chair) and also
the Tennis Club. The Boat (then the Rowing) Club
appeared in 1917. Many of them, however, laboured under
handicaps of lack of money, lack of grounds, and above
all the decision of many good players to continue with
outside clubs. Even in 1911 the Rugby Club, probably
the hardest hit, protested against " certain parasitic inverte-
brates in the College who, for egoistical motives, still persist
in playing with, and RUNNING, outside clubs." For all
clubs it was the time of slow progress from minor to junior
status and thence at long last to senior, steps marked by the
disappointment of hopes for the season and the need to go
back and start all over again. These are the things told,
in ever-increasing detail as the years go on, after club
dinners to bored young gentlemen who take it for granted
that people will turn up to train, that fixtures will be
honoured and that matches will be won. Only the Gaelic
clubs were free from such heart-breaks—quite free, to judge
from the account of the Sigerson in 1912 :

" On arrival at Galway, the team was met by the
greater number of the people of the city. A procession
was formed, bands in front, followed by three brakes,
conveying the three teams, with a guard of horsemen at
each side. . . . On Sunday night there was a concert,
on Monday a splendid dance was held in the Town Hall,
and on Tuesday the festivities were wound up by a
banquet in the Royal Hotel, followed by a torch-light
procession through the streets."

And at home, playing-grounds were at last found at
Terenure in 1913. Croydon Park and Jones's Road were
abandoned—not without some grumbles at the long tram
journey now necessary. The clubs settled in and soon no
one in the Tennis Club did not know that it was best to
play one's back to the trees along the Tallaght road and

8

to serve if possible when the Blessington tram, belching clouds of smoke, came clattering down the line. Terenure now is a memory with Cecilia Street; yet it was there that so many fixtures were won for the first time, that so many famous Inter-University triumphs occurred. It was there, too, that the Cricket Club found the surroundings so pleasant that it went too rarely on tour.

Societies also flourished. The Engineering Society was founded in 1911. In the next year a Dramatic Society made its appearance and produced " Eleanor's Enterprise " which, rightly or wrongly, seems a long way from T. S. Eliot. In 1914 appeared the English Literature Society and the Commerce which, however, has long abandoned its intention " never to make speeches at its ordinary meetings." Lady students, now sent to lectures in the College itself " in spite of the usual letters over the usual signatures about the dangers of co-education," were seen at dances. In 1911 the Scientific Society, then the College *arbiter elegantiarum*, held the first dance down town, cabs converging from the Green on the Gresham, through what was still known by some as Sackville Street, past the dome of the D.B.C. on one side and a still unregarded Post Office on the other. For the rest, there was a College restaurant but not then, or yet, licensed in spite of optimistic prophecies in the *Student*. But the true College restaurant was the Café Cairo where throughout the year the true work of running the College was discussed in the intervals of talking treason. There too, the successful Auditor of 1912–13 brought all the lady students whose votes he had obtained; there too the Auditor of 1913–14 brought all the plumbers whose votes he had obtained. So runs the legend, at least; what is certainly true is that such powers of persuasion have never since been surpassed and only once rivalled. Tighter rules have seen to that.

The Cairo, not to speak of the Tivoli and the Empire for more robust tastes, might seem sufficient. But one dominant theme in the *Student* of those days, associated with the names of Tom Arkins and Michael Davitt, is the need for a students' union. This was one of the cases in which the delays of authority were insupportable. But it was difficult to know where authority lay in the early days when the Dublin Commissioners were still engaged in the formation of the College. That did not prevent criticism ; and any one who does not believe that the *Student* has become tame in more recent years should look up its issues of forty years ago to see what it said about the Governing Body then. The staff too may be grateful that it has never since taken as much interest in a College appointment as it did in the Chair of Italian and Spanish Literature.

Tensions grew as the years went on. On the façade of the building in Earlsfort Terrace (all that did get built, being only one-quarter of the original plan) appears the date " 1914 "—a bad year in which to start a new enterprise. It was a bad time too for the hopes that had been entertained. The war brought a suspension of inaugurals, of dances, of sports : the impetus that had carried so much into achievement was lost, never perhaps to be regained fully later. The College's part in the events of 1916 and later is told in other pages. Here, it is sufficient to recall the recurring grounds for discontent ; the granting of honorary degrees for war service, the presence of military in the College and other matters, all making a position which was false both for students and for authority. In 1919, there was a transient return to normality. College sports were held, the events being won, as is noted with some acidity, chiefly by the clerics. The *Student* was still keeping alive, although at one time its sale in College was forbidden, but in 1919 it announced its intention of being " definitely not serious." From one point of view it had some scope for humour, with the Terrace cordoned off by military, and the President, cab-less for once, escorted by an armoured car and a platoon of infantry to retrieve the College Roll from his house in Fitzwilliam Square. Not that its seizure greatly helped the King's peace ; it would have taken a good Intelligence Officer to get much out of Dr. Coffey. Later again, the debates on the Treaty were held in the Council Chamber during the Christmas vacation of 1921. Perhaps some symbol might be found in the fact that the Irish Convention of 1917 was held in the senior University and the Treaty debates were held in College. But that gleam of peace passed too and for years afterwards those who came to College passed green hoardings that then substituted for railings and bore the slogans of civil war.

But College generations pass quickly. So quickly that each of them has its private memories and jokes that are incomprehensible to its successors. No use now in trying to explain how the election in 1923 of the first medical Auditor since Michael Davitt was assisted by his rendering of the prologue (" I am the prophet John ") to *The Four Horsemen of the Apocalypse*. No use either to try to explain how Tim O'Hanrahan won the S.R.C. election of 1928 for the Progressive (or was it the Democrat ?) Party by his peroration in the Aula Max of " Stand by your College and your College will repay." In other words, things got back to normal slowly. The Athletic Club entered on its golden age and farmed the Inter-University Sports. The Rugby Club, just beaten in the final by Trinity in 1923, won its first Leinster Senior Cup in the next year. In " 86 " society meetings went on as usual. It was still a shabby " 86 " ; if it comes to that, no one over the age of about thirty feels really at ease among its modern splendours. This, one feels, is not the same place where L. & H. committee-men patrolled the approaches to the gas and water supply ; where harassed Auditors, in spite of such precautions, saw the gas-jets broken and called for Flynn— the most unlikely man in all Dublin to be in " 86 " that time on a Saturday night. Nor is the Aula Max the place where Friday night hops were held, the proprieties guaranteed by Mrs. Greene on one side of the stage and Arthur Clery on the other. Around in the Terrace Dr. Coffey's cab still stood outside while in the Porter's lodge Mick Ryan told stories of the President to all who cared to listen, or re-told them to Jimmy Redmond if there were none such. A placid life, but still enlivened for the young student by the presence of the chronics who blasted the reputations of senior surgeons and physicians and told improbable stories of drinking with the Black and Tans and reminiscences so much older still that their authors seemed to be the Angels of Mons in person. Whatever the G.M.C. or the Americans may say, the chronics were part of a liberal education.

For many, perhaps, one's memories will be of two who died too soon. Some will still think of Arthur Clery's rooms in Pembroke Road or of his tennis at Terenure and self-deprecatory pleasure at being asked to make up a four. Or others will remember the Lucan tram stopping outside the boat-house punctually at twenty past four, in bitter Februarys, the entry into the changing-room, the rubbing of hands and simulation of delighted surprise when asked if one would like a spin in a pair, the stately progress up the river, assisted by two novices who had been promised fixed seats for a fortnight if they paid attention to any remark from the bank.

Others will think of John Ryan striding around the pitches at Terenure and later at Belfield, keeping an eye on the doings of the clubs and a wealth of encouragement to those who he thought deserved it. The test came in the Athletic Union Council where he presided over the allocation of grants, the Athletic Club getting whatever it asked for, the minor clubs playing the balance of power between the Triple Entente of the Gaelic clubs and the Dual Alliance of the Rugby and Tennis. Not much escaped the Doc. With each, we lost a good friend and a good example.

Those were years of transition. First year students were still expected to wear gowns—in some classes at least. Smoking was still forbidden in the Main Hall; not that anybody minded so long as appearances were preserved during the leisurely journeys of the Registrar through the crowds. Crowds there were, for the number of students grew very quickly, taxing still more severely accommodation that had never been adequate. Yet another students' room was opened in an uninviting corner at the back of the Great Hall. An earlier venture of this kind just after the

first war had been described as housing " a few melancholy
clerics and a few inveterate gamblers " ; its successor of the
early thirties was never invaded by the first class of occupant but it provided a liberal and yet practical education
to the second until the slow decay of its furnishings sent
even the most inveterate to other pastures. At the time,
however, the opening was felt to be yet another dawn of
better things. Certainly it was the beginning of a period
in which the S.R.C. rose to fresh heights of performance :
within a couple of years a Students' Union was formed,
students' cards were issued that carried various reductions
from commercial houses in the city, a College diary was
published and for a while the student body was regaled
with two papers at once, the *Cothrom Féinne* of the S.R.C.
and a *National Student* that had been revived under the
aegis of the L. & H. with a wealth of advertisements that
might have supported its predecessors for years. College
journalism was flourishing in those days ; earlier there had
been a short-lived *Atlantis* ; in 1928 the *Chessboard* made its
brief appearance breathing, as it seems now, the last
enchantments of the Roaring Twenties but, as it then
seemed, breathing them so heavily as to produce the direst
apprehensions for the morale and morals of the students.
For some months, by an agreeable coincidence, righteous
journalists divided their space between criticisms of the
staff and of the students.

These were storms in a tea-cup. At long last the Kevin
Barry window was installed and unveiled, thus ending the
Fabian campaigns of so many Governing Bodies. In what
was still an optimistic age, the devotees of the League of
Nations Society met in dusty rooms of " 86 " and discussed
the obligations that the Free State Government had assumed
to resist aggression anywhere in the world, then settled
once and for all by the Treaty of Versailles. No less international, the L. & H. held inter-debates on a scale of
splendour never before dreamed of and, had it not been for
the Depression growing to be something more than a name,
would have extended its patronage from Oxford and
London to the Sorbonne and Louvain. In between such

ceremonial, which all but called for flags and national anthems, it remained firmly true to its past. In three years two auditorial elections were upset with all the pomp of a Commission in each case, affidavits spaciously drafted, witnesses rigorously (and equally spaciously) cross-examined and receipt books carefully perused. Not even the most retiring member of the Chess Club nor the heartiest player on the Ladies' Hockey team was safe from solicitation by auditorial candidates or, later, from inquisition by their opponents.

More important things were happening in the 1930's, but they affected College life only remotely. The *National Student*, with which *Cothrom Feinne* was amalgamated after 1935, referred to the twin evils of depressions and dictatorships but gazed on prosperous tyrants with an markedly undazzled eye. As elsewhere, the Spanish tragedy aroused more passion than anything else in the decade, Blueshirts and oaths of allegiance barely excepted. Students died on both sides in that arid struggle, not the first or last to join in foreign wars in which the Ebro was added to a list that, headed by Gallipoli and the Somme, was soon to be lengthened by unfamiliar names that circled the globe.

The second war perhaps affected student life less than the first. There were no more inter-debates : for a frozen year the clubs were not allowed to travel. Against that, there was all the business of settling into a restored " 86," as complicated a reconciliation of interests as the clubs had found the allocation of pitches in Belfield a decade before. Some of the changes were pure gain : restaurants and reading-rooms bloomed out in a fashion that would have startled the students of thirty years before. For some, the task of resettlement proved more difficult : it is possible to feel that the L. & H. was too venerable an oak to survive transplantation to the Physics Theatre in Earlsfort Terrace unscathed. No one will ever take the door of the new Physics Theatre off its hinges.

But then perhaps no one wants to, nowadays. The post-war burst of activity, following on war-time expansion, has provided clubs and societies to cover most tastes from archaeology to yachting. Two tendencies seem to go together : there are more organisations and their membership seems to be more widely spread throughout the faculties than was the case in the old days. Clubs and societies are no doubt still run by cliques, as inner committees are called by those who do not yet belong to them; but the cliques are less likely than they were to be exclusively composed of arts and law students. Fewer than half of the last twenty auditors of the L. & H. have come from the law school ; a development which will no doubt confirm the deepest, and by no means always unspoken, fears of ex-auditors for the fate of the Society since they left.

When all is said and done, however, the clubs and societies are only the formal expression of student life which is a personal business that is much the same in every generation. The College has changed and Dublin has changed but the terms of life are essentially unaltered. All generations from the fox-hunters of the 1850's and the nation-builders of the 1900's had the same problems, the same delight in new things and at the end the same memories of a few years that remain fresh and vivid and of the friends who shared them—

" I wept as I remembered, how often you and I
    Had tired the sun with talking and sent him down the
        sky."

CELTIC STUDIES IN THE UNIVERSITY AND THE COLLEGE

PROFESSOR GERARD MURPHY

I

ABOUT the middle of the nineteenth century Eugene Curry, son of a West Clare farmer, and John O'Donovan, son of a better-off Kilkenny farmer, were at the height of their powers. Applying their native knowledge of Irish to the study of manuscripts they had, at an early age, each in his own circle, acquired fame as masters of Modern Irish. As a result both had been employed to work at place-names for the Ordnance Survey of Ireland, and at cataloguing for institutions such as the Royal Irish Academy and Trinity College, Dublin. In the course of this work they amassed a wide, though not always accurate, knowledge of the literary Irish of all periods. In 1849, O'Donovan, who was the better educated and the more critical and scholarly of the two, had been appointed to a poorly-paid chair of Celtic in Queen's College, Belfast; and in 1852 they had both been appointed by the government to prepare texts and translations of the ancient laws of Ireland for the Brehon Law Commission.

The Catholic University was opened in 1854. O'Curry[1] tells us in the Preface to his *Lectures on the Manuscript Materials of Ancient Irish History* of his anxieties on this occasion :

" I felt the deepest anxiety as to who the Professor of Irish History should be (if there should be one), well knowing that the only man living who could fill that important office with becoming efficiency as a scholar was already engaged in one of the Queen's Colleges. At this time, however, I can honestly declare that it never entered into my mind that *I* should or ought to be called to fill this important situation, simply because

[1] It was only towards the end of his life he began to insert the O before the English form of his name, but as he is now universally known as Eugene O'Curry he will be so named regularly in this account of him. In Irish he used always to sign himself *Eoghan Ó Comhraidhe*.

121

the course of my studies in Irish History and Antiquities had always been of a silent kind ;—I was engaged, if I may so speak, only in underground work, and the labours in which I had spent my life were such that their results were never intended to be brought separately before the public on my own individual responsibility. No person knows my bitterly felt deficiencies better than myself. Having been self-taught in all the little I know of general letters, and reared to mature years among an uneducated people (though a people both intelligent, and fond of learning when opportunity permits them to apply themselves to it), I always felt the want of early mental training and of early admission to those great fountains of knowledge which can be approached only through the medium of languages which, though once generally cultivated in my native province, had, under sinister influences, ceased to exist in the remote part of the country from which I come, not very long before I was born.[1] And it never occurred to me that I should have been deemed worthy of an honour which, for these reasons, I should not have presumed to seek. To say so much I feel due, not only to myself, but to the exalted and learned personages who, without any solicitation whatever on my part, overlooked my many deficiencies so far as to appoint me to the newly created Chair of Irish History and Archaeology in this National University. The definite idea of such a Professorship is due to the distinguished scholar to whom the first organisation of the University was committed."

Newman, who had chosen O'Curry to fill the chair of Irish history and archaeology because he believed him to be " a man of unique knowledge in Celtic manuscripts," and because he had been told that " he had unknown stores of Celtic learning which would die with him," not alone encouraged him by personal attendance at his lectures, but arranged for their publication in book form. As O'Curry himself has written in the Preface from which we have already quoted :

[1] O'Curry was born in the year 1794, twelve years before John O'Donovan.

" It reflects, surely, no small credit on the infant Catholic University of Ireland, and conveys no light assurance of the national feeling which animated its founders from the beginning, not only that it was the first public establishment in the country spontaneously to erect a Chair of Irish History and Archaeology, but that it has provided with unhesitating liberality for the heavy expense of placing this volume—the first fruits of that Chair, and the first publication undertaken under such auspices—before the public."

After O'Curry's death in 1862, his chair was left vacant for eight years or more. Issues of the Calendar during those years contain, however, the statement that classes would be formed for the Irish language and literature and the comparative grammar of the Celtic tongues. Ultimately, another Clareman, Bryan O'Looney, seems to have been appointed, for a time at least, to succeed O'Curry.[1] O'Looney, who was the editor of several Old, Middle, and Modern Irish texts, died in Dublin in 1901 at the age of seventy-four.

In 1882 all but two of the professors of the Catholic University were appointed Fellows of the recently founded Royal University of Ireland, and the university buildings in St. Stephen's Green became known as University College, Dublin. In 1883 the Jesuits, on the Bishops' invitation, took over responsibility for running University College, Dublin, as a Catholic college preparing students for the Royal University's examinations. It was staffed largely by the Catholic Fellows of the Royal University. Dr. William Delany, S.J., was the president of the re-modelled College, and from his first prospectus, issued in 1883, it was clear that he did not intend to abandon the tradition of fostering Celtic studies which had been initiated by Newman. Three Jesuits are listed in that prospectus for

[1] Calendars from the year 1870 on are not preserved in the National Library of Ireland or the libraries of T.C.D. and U.C.D. D. J. O'Donoghue, *The Poets of Ireland* (1912), and J. S. Crone, *A Concise Dictionary of Irish Biography* (1928), both state that O'Looney was for a time Professor of Irish in the Catholic University, and in 1880, in his introduction to the facsimile of the *Book of Leinster* (p. 13), Atkinson refers to him as " Professor O'Looney."

giving instruction in " Irish Language, History, and Archaeology." Their names were J. J. O'Carroll, Denis Murphy, and Edmund Hogan. Father O'Carroll was interested chiefly in Modern Irish ; Father Murphy studied Middle and Early Modern Irish as a means to understanding historical documents ; Father Hogan, the greatest scholar of the three, probably looked upon himself primarily as a historian ; his published work, however, in addition to English and Latin historical documents, covers every period of the Irish language, though ultimately his main interest clearly lay in the field of Old and Early Middle Irish.

When in 1909, after the dissolution of the Royal University and the founding of the National University of Ireland in its place, University College, Dublin, began its new life as one of the three constituent colleges of the National University, it continued, under the presidency of Dr. D. J. Coffey, the tradition inaugurated by Newman and carried on by Dr. Delany. Chairs of Modern Irish, of Early and Medieval Irish, of Welsh, of Early Irish History, and of Celtic Archaeology were founded in it. The first holders of those chairs were Douglas Hyde, Osborn Bergin, Professor J. Lloyd Jones, John MacNeill and R. A. S. Macalister, all of them scholars of such distinction that from the beginning the College was recognised as the chief centre of Celtic studies in the learned world.

That the link binding the three periods of the life of the College be made more evident to the reader it may be mentioned that MacNeill had been trained by Father Hogan, and that, in the medical faculty of the College, the first professor of Zoology under the new régime was George Sigerson, eminent as a scientist, but famous also as poet, translator, historian and man of letters, who in 1859 had been awarded a prize in Celtic by O'Curry.

By this, the hundredth year since the founding of the Catholic University, and the forty-fifth year of the new life of University College, Dublin, as a constituent college of the National University of Ireland, the Celtic faculty of the College has considerably expanded. The general chair held by O'Curry has been replaced by many particular chairs, including the chair of Irish Folklore held by Professor James H. Delargy, who is also Director of the Irish Folklore Commission, which is run in close co-operation with the College. And to meet the growing needs of the times, lectures, tutorial work, and research in Celtic studies and archaeology are in the care of some twenty professors, lecturers, and assistants, where in Newman's day one professor sufficed.

An adequate account of the work done in the Celtic faculty of the College during the hundred years of its existence would clearly be beyond the scope of a single chapter. Omitting, therefore, all discussion of the work of living persons (such as Dr. Lloyd Jones, now Dean of the Faculty as well as Professor of Welsh), and of the work of the Archaeological department, which tends to exceed purely Celtic limits, we may gain some idea of the contribution made to Celtic studies by the College and its predecessor, the Catholic University, by consideration of the work of Eugene O'Curry, Edmund Hogan, John MacNeill, Douglas Hyde and Osborn Bergin.

II

O'Curry, as has already been mentioned, was born in 1794.[1] When on the 13th March, 1855, he began his first course of lectures in the Catholic University of Ireland, though he had some published work to his credit, he was better known for what he himself has called his " underground work " and for labours which were " never intended to be brought separately before the public on his own individual responsibility."[2] The underground work he refers to would include his vast and informative handwritten catalogue of Irish manuscripts preserved in the

[1] An account of O'Curry's life and a bibliography of his writings may be found in " Síoladóirí .i. Eoghan Ó Comhraidhe agus Seán Ó Donnabháin, Bráthair Críostamhail do sgríobh " (1947).

[2] The only considerable piece of work produced in his own name before the period of his Catholic University activity is The Battle of Magh Léana together with the Courtship of Momera (Celtic Society, 1855). This had apparently been ready for the press by 1853. (See Annual Report of the Celtic Society for 1854, inserted after the text.)

Royal Irish Academy, while the labours " never intended
to be brought before the public on his own individual
responsibility " are in part indicated by frequent acknow-
ledgement of indebtedness for transcripts and translations
of Irish documents to be found in the published works of
scholars such as Todd, Petrie, and Reeves.

Newman wished the talented group of professors whom
he had gathered round him in Dublin to spread abroad
the fruits of their learning, and he made no exception for
his professor of Irish History and Archaeology. Accordingly
in the year 1858, in Volume I of *The Atlantis : a register of
literature and science, conducted by members of the Catholic
University of Ireland,* immediately following an important
theological contribution by Newman himself, we find the
first instalment of an edition by O'Curry, from *Lebor na
hUidre,* of " The Sick-bed of Cuchulainn and the only
Jealousy of Eimer." The concluding instalment of this
edition and translation of a fascinating Old Irish tale
appeared in Volume II, and was followed in succeeding
numbers of *The Atlantis* by similar editions of the Old
Irish " Exile of the Children of Uisliu," and the Early
Modern " Fate of the Children of Lir " and " Fate of the
Children of Tuireann." Of these four important texts,
only one, " The Exile of the Children of Uisliu," had
been previously published, and that in a much less
satisfactory manner.[1]

Besides these four literary texts printed in *The Atlantis,*
the University had, in 1861, published O'Curry's *Lectures
on the Manuscript Materials of Ancient Irish History,* being
the first series of lectures which he delivered under its
auspices ; and later his colleague, W. K. Sullivan, professor of Medical Chemistry in the Catholic University
and afterwards president of Queen's College, Cork, prepared
O'Curry's second series of lectures for the press.[2] This

[1] By Theophilus O'Flanagan, in 1808.

[2] Sullivan, a scholar of distinction in the field of chemistry, has rightly
been disparaged as a Celticist, though superficially his contributions to Celtic
studies may seem more scientific than O'Curry's. Nevertheless, his translations
of papers by Zeuss's continuer, Ebel, published in *The Atlantis,* had the merit
of bringing the scientific work of continental Celticists to the notice of Irish
readers.

second series, *On the Manners and Customs of the Ancient Irish*, appeared in 1873, eleven years after O'Curry's death in July, 1862. Some of O'Curry's work on the laws appeared in Volumes III–V of the *Ancient Laws of Ireland*, which likewise were issued after his death (1869–1901). References to minor posthumously-published papers of O'Curry's may be found in the National Library of Ireland's *Bibliography of Irish Philology and of Printed Irish Literature* [by Dr. R. I. Best] (1913).

O'Curry's " underground work " not alone helped many scholars of his day to understand sources necessary for the advancement of their researches, but is still being constantly used by modern scholars to guide them to the manuscript sources for study of the Irish language and literature preserved in the Royal Irish Academy and elsewhere. It is difficult to assess the value of his published work. Naturally it meant more to people living about O'Curry's own period than it does to scholars to-day. Many readers will be familiar with the tribute paid to it in his essay *On the Study of Celtic Literature* by the great English critic, Matthew Arnold, brother of that Thomas Arnold who was a colleague of O'Curry's on the staff of the Catholic University. Having described the career of Owen Jones, joint editor of the *Myvyrian Archaiology of Wales*, Matthew Arnold continues as follows :

" Even the printed stock of early Welsh literature is, therefore considerable, and the manuscript stock of it is very great indeed. Of Irish literature, the stock, printed and manuscript, is truly vast ; the work of cataloguing and describing this has been admirably performed by another remarkable man, who died only the other day, Mr. Eugene O'Curry. Obscure Scaliger of a despised literature, he deserves some weightier voice to praise him than the voice of an unlearned belletristic trifler like me ; he belongs to the race of the giants in literary research and industry—a race now almost extinct. Without a literary education, and impeded too, it appears, by much trouble of mind and infirmity of body, he has accomplished such a thorough work of classification and description from the chaotic mass of Irish literature, that the student has now half his labour saved, and needs only to use his materials as Eugene O'Curry hands them to him. It was as a professor in the Catholic University in Dublin that O'Curry gave the lectures in which he has done the student this service ; it is touching to find that these lectures, a splendid tribute of devotion to the Celtic cause, had no hearer more attentive, more sympathising, than a man, himself, too, the champion of a cause more interesting than prosperous—one of those causes which please noble spirits, but do not please destiny, which have Cato's adherence, but not Heaven's—Dr. Newman."

Matthew Arnold wrote those words in 1867. In 1873 O'Curry's second series of lectures, *On the Manners and Customs of the Ancient Irish*, was issued posthumously under the editorship of W. K. Sullivan. A year later they were reviewed in Volume II of the *Revue Celtique* (pp. 260–65) by Henri Gaidoz, a distinguished French Celticist. In the first paragraph of his review Gaidoz speaks approvingly of the earlier series, which had aroused Arnold's admiration ; but his approbation is qualified by mention of O'Curry's grave defects in scholarly training. Gaidoz is careful, however, to point out that lectures devoted mainly to indicating the manuscript sources and their contents need not be seriously vitiated by these defects :

"All those [he writes] who have interested themselves in the ancient literature of Ireland remember O'Curry with gratitude for his valuable work on the manuscript materials of that literature (*Lectures on the Manuscript Materials of Ancient Irish History*, Dublin, 1861), a book which is, as it were, a detailed descriptive inventory of the contents of those writings. The nature of that great undertaking by a happy accident served to throw his good qualities into relief and to hide his defects. O'Curry had passed his long life among the many manuscripts of the Irish Middle Ages, reading, collating, copying, translating ; he had so soaked himself in it that this

Father William Delany, S.J.,
President, University College, Dublin,
1883–1888 and 1897–1909

old language had become familiar to him before modern linguistic science in the person of Zeuss had reconstructed its grammar : no one was better acquainted than he with this manuscript literature, though he had hitherto published only a few episodes of it. Unfortunately— we can say it without wronging his memory—he lacked that general education and learning which characterise the scholar, and which cast a light on the more specialised branch of historical studies ; above all he lacked the gift of criticism. For him, everything he found in his beloved Irish manuscripts had really happened, though most of us find no lack of the fabulous element in the annals of ancient Ireland, annals which tell the history of Ireland from before the Deluge ! In France we have long ceased to believe in the existence of Francus, son of Hector, of whom our ancient chronicles speak. In Ireland such treatment of national traditions has not yet become the rule.''

As O'Curry's second series of lectures were known to be more definitely historical in scope than the first, Gaidoz had fears that the defects he had referred to would essentially vitiate them. The concluding part of his review is intended to show that those fears were justified : *Nous craignions que, sorti de ses habitudes de compilateur et d'éditeur où il excellait, il ne sût pas lui-même faire un usage heureux des matériaux qu'il recueillait avec zèle ; l'ouvrage dont nous avons à rendre compte justifie nos appréhensions.*

Of O'Curry's historical work, therefore, only the *Lectures on the Manuscript Materials* need be seriously considered. Not alone did they inform the general reader, such as Matthew Arnold, of the contents of Irish manuscripts, but they served also as a guide to the serious investigator, a guide which has only gradually been superseded. In them O'Curry appears not as an imperfect modern scientific historian, the character he assumes in his *Lectures on the Manners and Customs*, but rather as the last of that series of great native recorders of Irish tradition which includes Keating, Michael O'Clery, and Mac Fir Bhisigh.

In regard to Irish law, O'Curry and his brother-in-law

O'Donovan advanced its study mainly by supplying convenient transcripts for use by future investigators :

"Taken all in all [writes Professor Binchy][1], the seventeen volumes of transcripts and twenty-five of translations which they completed for the Commission represent a gigantic achievement. It is true that their transcription is often inaccurate and their translation often guess-work. Yet no one who has used the materials provided by them can withhold admiration from these two gallant pioneers. Considering the tremendous difficulties that confronted them, the wonder is, not that they made so many mistakes, but that they were so frequently right."

III

To modern eyes O'Curry presents the appearance of a great medieval Irish *ollamh* moving uneasily in the garb of a Victorian scholar. The first holder of a chair in the Celtic department of University College, Dublin, who wore the scholar's robe with ease is undoubtedly Father Edmund Hogan, S.J. Born at Belvelly, near Queenstown, Co. Cork, in 1831, he was the youngest son of a large family, of whom the elder members were native speakers of Irish. Having entered the Society of Jesus at the age of sixteen, he was ordained priest in 1856. Father Hogan was gifted as a linguist, and in addition to learning several modern continental languages was a master of Latin, which he wrote easily and naturally.

Father Hogan's first publications (sources for the history of Ireland in the sixteenth and seventeenth centuries) were historical, and it would seem to have been his work on Latin documents for the life of St. Patrick, begun for the Bollandists about 1880, and continued later, which turned his attention definitely towards the study of related documents in Old Irish. This study resulted, from 1887 on, in a long series of publications in the Irish linguistic field which made him known to Celticists all over Europe.

[1] *The Linguistic and Historical Value of the Irish Law Tracts* (The Sir John Rhys Memorial Lecture, British Academy, 1943), p. 5.

Father Hogan was essentially a collector, classifier, and editor, a worker who understood the scholar's needs and supplied him with material, rather than a great original investigator. His lists of Irish neuter substantives, for instance, appended to the editions of *Cath Ruis na Ríg* and *The Irish Nennius* published by him in 1892 and 1895, provided a mine of useful information for grammarians and lexicographers. To-day his fame above all depends on his *Onomasticon Goedelicum Locorum et Tribuum Hiberniae et Scotiae, An Index, with Identifications, to the Gaelic Names of Places and Tribes*, published in 1910. In spite of certain imperfections this vast compilation will hardly be superseded as a constant guide to the investigator for many years to come.

The *Onomasticon*, Father Hogan's last contribution to Irish studies, was begun in his seventieth year and published by the Royal Irish Academy in his eightieth year. On its title-page the compiler is described as " Edmund Hogan, S.J. ; D.Litt. National University of Ireland ; recently Professor of Irish Language and History in University College, Dublin, and Fellow of the Royal University of Ireland ; sometime Todd Professor of the Celtic Languages, and Member of the Council, Royal Irish Academy ; a Commissioner for the Publication of the Ancient Laws of Ireland ; a Governor of the School of Irish Learning." This list of honours and offices sufficiently indicates the esteem in which Father Hogan was held by his contemporaries. He died in retirement in the year 1917 at the Jesuit house in Lower Leeson Street, Dublin.

IV

In 1890 John MacNeill, a young Antrim man, who was then, at the age of twenty-three, a clerk in the Accountant General's office at the Dublin Four Courts, came to study Irish in his spare time under Father Hogan's direction at University College, Dublin. Already in 1888 he had taken a B.A. degree in Economics, Jurisprudence, and Constitutional History in the Royal University. He had devoted the year 1889 to mastering spoken Irish by means of private study, lessons from a tutor, and a visit to Aran. When he presented himself at University College in 1890, Father Hogan received him genially, and arranged to give him evening instruction :

"After some months [MacNeill himself has written],[1] from being a student I became what might almost be called my professor's apprentice. I was making gradual headway in Middle and Old Irish. Father Hogan always had something in hand for publication and he brought me right into his own work and into almost every part of it. As much as possible, he handed over to me parts of his work to do and threw me on my own resources for the doing of it. Of course, to take it as it came from me or to reshape it in its final stages for publication was reserved for himself, and, after a few months of tuition, all the work on which I was engaged under him was intended for publication. In these tasks I found the greatest pleasure, not more because they were congenial than from being associated with so kindly a teacher and director. He was full of kindness to me. His own natural bent was for history, and a list of his published works in order of date will show clearly that his studies in Irish were at first only accessory to his studies in Irish history. In my case it was just the converse. Coming to him for instruction in Irish, I began to discover how little I knew of the history of my country and how little of its history was to be learned from the books of Irish history that people read."

In 1889, before commencing his studies under Father Hogan, MacNeill had proved his Modern Irish scholarship by notes " On the Irish Infinitive " contributed to the *Gaelic Journal* (IV, 116, 136). In 1892, Father Hogan in his introduction to *Cath Ruis na Ríg* was able to speak of MacNeill's knowledge of the older language in the following words : " With regard to the whole of this volume I have had many helps and hints from Mr. John MacNeill, B.A., who placed at my disposal the treasures of his knowledge

[1] *A Page of Irish History : Story of University College, Dublin*, 1883–1909, compiled by Fathers of the Society of Jesus (1930), 187–8.

of Old, Middle, and Modern Irish. To him, my former pupil and present learned friend, I beg to tender my cordial thanks." Father Hogan next recommended John MacNeill to publish something on his own responsibility.

"At last [writes MacNeill][1] I selected three Middle-Irish poems relating to a common episode. This time Father Hogan left me altogether to my own resources. When I had completed the work, he ' communicated ' it to the Royal Irish Academy, and it was accepted for publication and published in the Academy's *Proceedings* in 1895.[2] Of all my indebtedness to Father Hogan, I count this item the largest. It has led me to recognise that no academic distinction that can be conferred on students is comparable in effect with the publication of suitable original work done by them. Amateurish as it was, the appearance of this essay in scholarship as a booklet seemed to bring me into another world. I had gone out among the giants. It brought me kindly letters of commendation, not without criticism, from some of the Olympians themselves, among them Whitley Stokes and Kuno Meyer. My work in Father Hogan's laboratory had been regulated by no academic programme, tested by no academic test, directed towards no academic distinction, but it had given me knowledge, training, insight, and enterprise, and introduced me to the sacred circle of the learned."

In 1893 MacNeill had co-operated with Douglas Hyde in the foundation of the Gaelic League, and from that year on, in addition to his scholarly pursuits, he bore the burden of public responsibilities, which were ultimately to lead him to take a prominent part in the foundation (in 1913) of the Irish Volunteers, and in the events which culminated in the setting up of the Irish Free State in 1922. Notwithstanding the vicissitudes of his public career MacNeill never lost his interest in Irish history and philology, to which a long series of publications in the *Gaelic Journal*, *Ériu*, *Studies* and the *Proceedings of the Royal Irish Academy*

[1] l.c. 190–1.
[2] It was entitled *Three Poems in Middle Irish, relating to the Battle of Mucrama.*

bears continuous witness. His highly important paper, for instance, "The Irish Law of Dynastic Succession," appeared in *Studies* in 1919, shortly after his election to two parliamentary seats (Derry and the National University); and an illuminating paper on "The Law of Status or Franchise," published in the Academy's *Proceedings* for 1923, was the fruit of a year's seclusion (1920–1921) in Mountjoy prison, where, for recreational reading, he was allowed the first five volumes of *The Ancient Laws of Ireland.*

Confining ourselves here to consideration of that side of his career which was intimately connected with University College, Dublin, we may mention that in 1904, at Father Hogan's instance, MacNeill was invited by Dr. Delany, S.J., then President of the College, to give a special series of lectures on Irish history. These lectures were published in *The New Ireland Review*, which was then the College journal, and much from them has either been incorporated into MacNeill's *Phases of Irish History* (1919) or republished with slight modifications in his *Celtic Ireland* (1921).

In 1909 MacNeill was appointed professor of Early Irish History in University College, Dublin, now a constituent college of the National University of Ireland. In the preceding year he had taken a prominent part in the Gaelic League's efforts to ensure that Irish would be an essential subject for matriculation in the National University of Ireland. But in the famous pamphlet he published on that subject (*Irish in the National University of Ireland*), while demanding that for national reasons Irish should be a school and matriculation subject, he declared that the revival of Irish as a spoken language was not a task for the University :

"Mere instruction in the Irish language is not university work, it is work for primary and secondary schools. . . . The University will teach old and middle Irish, the philology of the Celtic languages, the literature of modern Irish, and the history and archaeology of Ireland. It will teach these subjects more by way of training students to study them for themselves than by supplying readymade facts of knowledge. The student in this department will be as much a specialist as the medical student is when he is engaged on hospital work. . . . (46).

"As a matter of fact, higher Irish studies, associated as they must be with kindred philological, historical, and archaeological subjects, will not impart a national character to the University. The self-same group of studies will be carried on in universities outside of Ireland. . . . (48).

" Doubtless these studies will or ought to command more enthusiasm in the National University than elsewhere because they come nearest to Irishmen, and because Dublin in particular is the most convenient centre for them. . . . But I have argued in vain if it is not already clear that the most eminent learning of this kind, though it must react on national feeling, does not serve the purpose of the living culture of a national language." (50).

Some of MacNeill's future colleagues differed from him in regard to making Irish an essential subject for matriculation in the National University of Ireland. Statements such as those quoted may have reassured them that inside the College MacNeill would not look upon his office as a continuation of the functions of a prominent Gaelic Leaguer. And indeed MacNeill's department in the College soon became famous as a centre of advanced study and research towards which serious students of Celtic studies gravitated.

In his lectures and writings MacNeill approached early Irish history in a new way, neither accepting native sources concerning our origins with the uncritical faith of an O'Curry, nor throwing them aside as undeserving of serious consideration. Rather he studied them carefully, comparing them among themselves, noting their differences and development, and applying common sense and scholarly judgment to their contents. The doctrines taught by the Old Irish " synthetic historians," as he used to call them, were critically considered by him in the light of saga-tradition, the early annals, the history of other countries, and the evidence of the Laws and early genealogies. MacNeill, both as a linguist and a historian, had the gift of being able to group apparently disparate facts into a pattern as when (in a paper published in 1909 in the *Proceedings of the Royal Irish Academy*) he formulated the circumstances which govern the doubling of *n* in words such as *Érenn* (as opposed, e.g., to *Tailten*) in a rule now known as MacNeill's Law, or when in 1919 (in the *Studies* article already mentioned) he showed the pattern into which many references to *fine* and *derbfine* which had puzzled former investigators might be grouped, thus throwing a new light on the " Irish Law of Dynastic Succession." Scholars will differ from MacNeill's conclusions on this or that point ; but no serious worker will abandon the general lines of his method, or deny that with him began a new era in the writing of early and medieval Irish history.

Former students of MacNeill's, many of them now holding important positions in various learned institutions, probably remember him above all as one who stimulated and gave food for thought to all those with whom he came in contact. Even outside his formal professorial work he was endlessly busy with ideas on points of Irish history and culture ; and, as he was a brilliant talker, those ideas were constantly being passed on in stimulating form to students and colleagues. Whether he compared Caesar's information concerning the *clientes obaeratosque* who followed Orgetorix, with Irish laws regulating the amount of stock a *céle* borrowed from his lord, or applied memories of the relations between standard English and Lowland Scots in the glens of Antrim, in his boyhood, to the relations between the Welsh and Irish languages in the days of St. Patrick, John MacNeill could hold his hearers fascinated by the power of his brilliance, geniality, learning and originality combined.

He died in 1945 some years after his retirement from the chair of Early Irish History in University College. His successor in that chair, Dr. John Ryan, S.J., has contributed a biographical sketch of him to *Studies* (1945, pp. 433–48) ; and an account of his connection with the Royal Irish Academy, of which he was for some years President, was published in 1947 in the Academy's *Minutes of Proceedings, Session 1945–46.*

V

John MacNeill had been a student in University College, Dublin, before he became a professor there. Douglas Hyde, a graduate of Trinity College, Dublin, was seven years MacNeill's senior, and had had little or no connection with University College till June, 1895, when its journal, *The New Ireland Review,* began publication of his *Religious Songs of Connacht* in instalments which continued till June, 1905. Hyde was then already famous for several collections of folksongs and folktales and for collaboration in 1893 with John MacNeill in the founding of the Gaelic League, which had rapidly attained phenomenal success. In 1909 Hyde, who some fifteen years earlier had been strangely rejected in favour of the Rev. James E. Murphy when the chair of Irish in Trinity College, Dublin, was being filled,[1] was appointed to be the first holder of the chair in Modern Irish in University College, Dublin, under its new constitution. Famous all over Ireland and America as a magnificent propagandist of the ideals of the Gaelic League, which had largely been moulded by himself, inside the College he was to be known, not as the public speaker capable of inspiring enthusiasm in crowds, but as the genial professor beloved by all, though frowned upon by some of his colleagues for not exacting the severest standard of learning or accuracy from those who presented themselves for degrees.

" 'We must not be purists,' he would say, when it was pointed out that a student mixed his dialects and

[1] In an obituary of the Rev. James E. Murphy, Professor Vendryes has written (*Revue Celtique,* XXXVII, 419) : *Contrairement au Père Edmund Hogan, il parlait l'irlandais de naissance ; mais tandis qu'Edmund Hogan laisse sur la philologie irlandaise une œuvre fort importante, James Murphy n'a jamais publié qu'un ouvrage, une réédition du texte irlandais du Nouveau Testament,* Tiomna Nuadh, *traduit par William O'Donnell (1602) ; il s'était borné à moderniser et à uniformiser l'orthographie. Son enseignement paraît avoir manqué d'éclat. Lorsqu'il brigua la chaire d'irlandais à Trinity College, il eut pour concurrent M. Douglas Hyde, et plus d'un s'étonna du choix qui fut fait entre les deux candidats, protestants tous deux.*

was careless about the rules of aspiration, eclipsis, and grammar in general. 'Keep them amused' was his advice to a young assistant anxious to receive guidance as to how to conduct his classes.

" Serious candidates for the degree in the faculty of Celtic Studies were therefore inclined to specialise in the older phases of their subject, where they were trained by scholars of the calibre of John MacNeill and Osborn Bergin, who had both been prominent with Hyde in the Gaelic League movement. But few even among those students would have denied that it was Hyde who, directly or indirectly, had awakened their interest in Irish. As schoolboys some of them would have come across his collections of folktales, his *Love-songs of Connacht*, his *Religious Songs of Connacht*, or his *Literary History of Ireland*, and realised that in Gaelic-speaking Ireland a treasure was to be found, close to them not alone in place and time, but also by heredity, a treasure which would be for ever beyond their reach if they did not learn Irish. They would know too that, if it were not for Hyde and his colleagues in the Gaelic League, the means of learning Irish in the schools would not have been at their disposal. While Hyde's kindliness and charm of manner won their affection, this knowledge of what he had done for the preservation of something precious that might have been lost ensured their respect and admiration."[1]

In 1932 Hyde, having reached the retiring age, vacated the chair which he had held since 1909. During his tenure of that chair he had added considerably to the number of his publications from Irish oral and manuscript tradition, and from 1926 to 1932 he had edited a journal of Modern Irish studies for the National University under the title *Lia Fáil*. In 1938 he was made the first President of Ireland under the terms of the new Constitution. This appointment was a public mark of recognition of the fact that Hyde's lifework was deemed to have been of national importance. He died on July 12th, 1949.

[1] *Studies*, September, 1949, 279–280.

VI

Osborn Bergin, born in the city of Cork in 1873, was six years younger than John MacNeill and thirteen years younger than Douglas Hyde who, along with Professor J. Lloyd Jones and R. A. S. Macalister, were to be his colleagues in the Celtic faculty of University College, Dublin, from the year 1909 on. Having taken a degree in classics in Queen's College, Cork, Bergin began to learn Irish about the time of the foundation of the Gaelic League, a book of Hyde's being among the first things which attracted him to study and to love it above all other languages : *Sin é, is dócha, an chéad ní do bhrostaigh mé chum na Gaedhilge d'fhoghlaim agus do ghrádhughadh thar aon teangaidh eile dá labharthar nó dár labhradh riamh san domhan mhór.*[1] By the frequentation of Irish-speakers in Cork city and by repeated visits to the Irish-speaking districts of West Cork, and in particular Eyries, where his friend Pádraig Ó Laoghaire had his home, Bergin rapidly became a master of the spoken Irish of West Munster ; and in the year 1897 his knowledge of spoken and literary Modern Irish was so sound that he was appointed lecturer in Celtic in Queen's College, Cork. He held this lectureship till 1904, when, after attending a course in the older phases of the language at the recently-founded School of Irish Learning in Dublin, he went to Germany as a travelling student of the School. In Germany he was awarded the degree of Ph.D. after studies under Zimmer, Thurneysen, and others. Shortly after his return to Ireland he was elected a fellow of the Royal University of Ireland, and in 1907 he succeeded Strachan as Professor in the School of Irish Learning. On the foundation of the National University in 1909 he was appointed Professor of Early Irish in University College, Dublin, regretfully resigning that chair in 1940, when he became first Director of the School of Celtic Studies in the newly-founded Dublin Institute for Advanced Studies.

By his teaching in the College Bergin has left a permanent

[1] D. De Híde, *Mise agus an Connradh*, 175.

mark on the course of Irish studies both in this country and abroad. From him his students absorbed not alone that love of precision and accuracy for which he was famous, but also an understanding of the methods of scientific linguistics and how to apply them to the study of Irish, in which his main interest remained permanently fixed. The majority of the chairs of Celtic studies both in Ireland and abroad are now occupied by former pupils of his.

Bergin's books and his many articles treat of the Irish language at all its stages. Indeed he may be said to have founded the scientific study of Modern Irish, while his knowledge of Old Irish was undoubtedly wider and more accurate than that of any scholar who preceded him. He was also a poet in the Irish language. His *Maidean i mBéarra*, sung to the Londonderry Air, which he himself as a young man used to play on the violin, is regarded as a classic, and several others of his poems are sure of a place in future anthologies. Bergin's greatness as a scholar did not interfere with his lovableness as a man, a sign of which was the intimate friendship which grew up between him and so many of his students.

For a full account of Bergin's contribution to Celtic studies readers must be referred to notices of him published by various former students of his after his death in October, 1950.[1] All of those notices agree in attributing mainly to Bergin the high standard attained in the scientific study of Irish in this country since the foundation of the National University. The following extract from that by Professor D. A. Binchy best defines what is the view of all :

" The death of Osborn Bergin is not merely an irreparable loss to Irish scholarship ; it marks the close of what may be called the heroic age of Celtic studies. More than forty years ago, when the young Bergin had just won his spurs in Germany, Kuno Meyer— no mean judge—said of him : ' He knows more Irish

---

[1] Rev. Prof. F. Shaw, S.J., *The Irish Press*, 7th October, 1950 ; Prof. D. A. Binchy, *The Irish Times*, 7th October, 1950 ; G. Murphy, *Studies*, December, 1950 ; Dr. M. Tierney, *University College, Dublin, Report of the President for the Session 1949–50* (December, 1950), 47–49 ; Prof. Eleanor Knott, *Ériu*, XVI (1952), 1–3.

than all of us,' a remarkable tribute when one remembers that at that time ' all of us ' included such giants as Whitley Stokes, Strachan,Windisch, Zimmer, Thurneysen, Ascoli, and Meyer himself, yet one that proved to be fully justified.

" Ever since, Bergin has been regarded as the supreme authority on Irish linguistics ; no one ever had, and probably no one ever will have, the same comprehensive knowledge of the Irish language in all its stages. His own publications represent but a small fraction of our debt to him. Hardly a single important work dealing with his subject has appeared in our time without a grateful tribute from the author to Bergin's liberal help. To all serious students he gave freely and readily of his vast store, and no scholar was so prodigal in his bounty to others.

" By his work as a teacher he succeeded in establishing a standard of Celtic scholarship in Dublin which could challenge comparison with the most famous continental centres, and his lectures in University College drew students from many foreign countries. It is a measure of his achievement that virtually all the Celtic chairs in existence to-day should be held by former pupils of his—not merely at home in the two Universities and the Dublin Institute, but also in Oxford, Harvard, Edinburgh, Liverpool, Zürich, Amsterdam, and the Scandinavian countries."

Beginning with admiration for his vast erudition, Bergin's pupils, having broken through the barrier of his shyness, which at first they tended to mistake for aloofness and want of sympathy, normally passed to love for the man himself. When he died many of them may have wondered what their tribute to his memory should be. As tribute Bergin himself would doubtless have chosen a resolution on their part to maintain the standard of Irish scholarship in the College at the high level to which he, more than any other Irish scholar, had helped to raise it.

WOMEN IN THE UNIVERSITY AND THE COLLEGE

A STRUGGLE WITHIN A STRUGGLE

Professor Mary M. Macken

I

I write of women under two flags—the Royal University of Ireland 1879–1909 and the National 1909–54. There is no need for us women in this country to go back a full century for our University story. Our sex was well without the walls until, in 1879 the " Royal," following the example of London in the previous year, gave us entry with cap and gown into the citadel. That it was a restricted entry seems to have gone without comment at first. I would not willingly cast aspersions on the Royal, to which I belonged before the National took over. It gave us women our first chance. But I was always, somehow, aware of its Victorian character, other traces of which I myself may have retained as my male colleagues on the Academic Council sometimes laughingly suggested. The particular expressions of that character to which I now refer was the refusal of the Royal to admit women to the Senate or to Convocation with its important rights of election to the Senate, an otherwise government-nominated Body. It was a character that tended, like other things in the sober 80's and the naughty 90's to more exaggerated expression in the vice-regal capital of this outpost of Empire that was Dublin than in London, the Empire's heart.

Whether women were, however striking their qualifications, *legally* disqualified to hold Senior Fellowships seems doubtful. That, when the sex-bar was contested, the question of legality was somehow by-passed is likely. Beyond all doubt they were never appointed ; they lost the fight. Of that there will be more later. The immediate grievance of women students in the Dublin of the 80's when the Royal began to function was, however, that they were being refused admission to the Fellows' lectures in U.C.D. to which College, inaccessible to the sex, fifteen of these Senior Fellows were attached. As Senior Fellows, paid out of University funds, constituted an indirect endowment of the College, it was reasonable to assume that women should benefit equally with their male competitors from their lectures. A pamphlet published in 1888 with the somewhat period title : " The Case of the Catholic Lady Students of the R.U.I. Stated " shows that, over sixty years ago, the author, Margaret Tierney Downes, and her co-signatories were not too ladylike to assert their rights. This they did in a statement as well written as it is well reasoned. The "Appendix " is interesting as a prophetic, if somewhat premature challenge to a Senate that was to withhold Senior Fellowships from women.   It is an extract from the *Weekly Register* noting the appointment of a woman mathematician to a Chair in the University of Stockholm and stressing in the context the fact that Pope Benedict XIV had appointed a woman to the Chair of Mathematics in the University of Bologna.   In Padua, the *Weekly Register* goes on to relate, both the Chair of Mathematics and that of Civil and Canon Law had been held by women in the eighteenth century. The " Ladies' Case " with its copies of memorials sent to Convocation and Senate had thirteen graduate and undergraduate signatories, the list being headed by Mary T. Hayden, M.A.

I salute Mary T. with her 1887 First Honours M.A. laurels still green about her shapely head. Notwithstanding her cropped hair, she was no Amazon ; those in distress could always rely on her motherly heart. I doubt if she ever heard the dictum of the old German clergyman : " Women have long hair, short minds." She would not have been much affected if she had ! Characteristically in fashion's despite and to save time (those were strenuous days for women students) she had once cropped her hair and having found it convenient, it remained cropped to the end. Coming of sturdy, mixed, Co. Tipperary stock— her paternal grandfather was Protestant—she may have inherited the best traits of both denominations ; she kept

always the simple Catholic piety of the child. Her father,
a distinguished Dublin doctor and a Professor of the Catholic
University, was one of the original appointee Senators of
The Royal in 1879. In late Victorian and early Edwardian
Dublin Mary Hayden was a well-known and somewhat
singular figure. I have a distinct picture of her as I first
saw her walk, mannishly, through Grafton Street, then the
favourite promenade of the elegant flaneurs of either sex.
I remember the Gladstone bag gripped, business-like fashion,
in one small hand ; the short stamping step and somewhat
sidling gait (she was an habitual cyclist). In defiance of
the fashion of the time she wore her skirts short and showing
at the front waist-line an "Albert " or heavy gold chain
with a fine seal attached. It had been the property of her
father, whose death in 1881 at the comparatively early age
of fifty-eight was a grievous loss to his gallant daughter
as well as to the brother to whom she was to be father and
mother all her life long. The watch suspended from this
chain she carried in a skirt pocket ; it had, somehow, a
mannish effect !

To return to the argument : I cannot imagine that the
Catholic Lady Students' challenge, if it was one, affected
Father Delany, whose unpleasant task was now and again
to put off awkward claims, of women or others. The
example of Italy would seem irrelevant ; hardly a precedent for Dublin. Mary Hayden's application twice
made, more than a decade later, for a vacant Senior
Fellowship had more actuality ; its challenge was direct.
The applicant was an ex-Junior Fellow who had adequately
discharged a University examiner's duties from 1895 to
1899 when her Fellowship expired. Application was,
however, refused on the ground of a sex-disqualification
and, when that ground was contested, the correspondence
was closed. Equally direct was the challenge, from
graduate student ranks within U.C.D. itself, in F. C. J.
Skeffington's essay : "A Forgotten Aspect of the University
Question," commissioned by the editor of *St. Stephen's* but
subsequently rejected. It was privately printed, together
with another rejected contribution, James A. Joyce's " The

Royal University, Dublin

Day of the Rabblement," as a pamphlet[1] by Gerrard Brothers of 37, St. Stephen's Green. Francis Skeffington was a feminist and already then, perhaps, engaged to Hanna Sheehy, Hons. B.A. and Scholar, who, despite preparation for her M.A. First Honours Degree of 1902, was finding time (and opportunity in the *New Ireland Review*) to controvert the more conservative views of a graduate member of her sex on the question of University women. Francis Skeffington wrote to enforce the claims to be made by University women invited to appear before the Royal Commission of 1901–03. The essay resolved itself ultimately into a strong plea for co-education and a protest equally strong and perhaps pertinent to the plea against the Senate's refusal to appoint women to Senior Fellowships.

Co-education is here seen as an issue ; co-education on University level was the solution proposed to the Robertson Commission by Mary T. Hayden speaking as representative of St. Mary's University College and by Agnes O'Farrelly, M.A., and Miss McElderry as delegates from the newly founded Irish Federation of University Women Graduates. Loreto College, St. Stephen's Green, which had an imposing list of university successes, was not represented by a woman, graduate or other ; and its spokesman was careful to emphasise that he did not give his individual view but that of the community that had briefed him. Their first preference was for recognition for a separate women's College which, adequately equipped and staffed, the University would endow. That the Robertson Commission in its report, full equality of men and women within the University being postulated, expressed the view that both should attend lectures and pass examinations in the same colleges and obtain degrees on the same conditions, is a tribute as much to the excellent documentation of the women's case, to the convincing evidence of the women witnesses and to the cohesive strength of their groups as it is to the statistical tables of academic successes supplied by them.

[1] I wish to acknowledge with thanks the courtesy of Dr. Owen Sheehy-Skeffington, to whom I am indebted for the loan of this pamphlet, now "a collector's piece."

The fear or dislike of co-education, implicit, perhaps, in the evidence on behalf of the Loreto Community, may well have been at the root of Father Delany's refusal to admit women students to full attendance at U.C.D. Senior Fellows' lectures. It may also have influenced his opposition to the appointment of women to Senior Fellowships. Such a fear or dislike was not an exclusively Catholic phenomenon. Miss White, a Newnhamite and, since 1890, Lady Principal of Alexandra, writing to the Senate in 1899 in support of women Senior Fellows, suggested that they might be assigned to St. Mary's and Alexandra; a naïve suggestion and tantamount to the recognition of separate women's Colleges, which our women did *not* want. It is the case that she will make for her College before the Fry Commission on Trinity in 1906–07, two years after women had at last gained admission into Trinity College. Her statement on Alexandra reads rather like an account of one or other of the Oxford or Cambridge women's Colleges on which it was probably modelled and which were then very much in the news in England. She must have impressed the Commissioners and so justified the forebodings of the I.F.U.W.G., who had deputed Miss Hanna of Trinity and Agnes O'Farrelly of St. Mary's to hold a watching brief at a sitting of the Commission. Miss O'Farrelly, dauntless and gate-crashing Trinity under cover, as it were, of Miss Hanna, made her statement against recognition lest it be a precedent for reactionary measures in the long-awaited University reform for Catholics and militate against the only safe solution, co-education on University level. The report of the Fry Commission did, in fact, recommend that the Governing Board of Trinity be empowered to recognise teachers in any Colleges for women in or within a radius of thirty miles from Dublin, So far as I know, that recommendation has remained a dead letter, whilst the recommendation by the Robertson Commission of co-education was fully realised in 1909 in the three constituent colleges of the National University.

For the good end of this struggle within a struggle in the Royal and for its realisation within the National University, women and men students alike are indebted to Mary T. Hayden and Agnes M. O'Farrelly. It was but the barest tribute to their work that the National University Commission nominated them both as members of the first Governing Body of U.C.D., appointing Mary T. Hayden to the first Senate of the National—a fitting tribute to the shade of Dr. Thomas, her father—but, as well, an extra honour for Mary T. herself. That bears out the distinction I would make between these gallant comrades in arms. Both were fighters ; neither was a revolutionary ; both suffragists, neither was a suffragette. They were "characters" ; almost opposites in type yet complementing one another in a way which made their combination effective in a struggle. Both were life-long friends of, among others, George Sigerson, John MacNeill and Patrick Pearse. Both Gaelic enthusiasts ; with the one it seems to me to have been more an intellectual, with the other more a popular impulse that was the urge. Mary Hayden was scholarly and academic ; Agnes O'Farrelly publicist and propagandist as well ; she was skilled in both these arts. Both were socially minded, but from somewhat different angles. I think of Mary T.'s interest in women jurors and women police—an interest so active that it led her to do voluntary police work at night in the Dublin streets. I think as well of her work, so pathetically personal, for Dublin young girls in St. Joan's Club, an organisation which she founded from U.C.D. and where her co-workers were the College women staff and women students ; I recall her personal and practical support of the Women Students' Swimming Club. Agnes O'Farrelly's devotion to the Camogie Club will not easily be forgotten by the generations of U.C.D. women whose favourite sport camogie was. She never missed either the College events or the Inter-Collegiate contests for the Ashbourne Cup, which aroused as much ardour as did the fights for the Sigerson Cup among the "opposite" sex. Agnes had, as well, her Leinster College and Cloughaneely language interests ; her cottage in Donegal was the Mecca of many Gaels, home and foreign. I remember Lord Ashbourne's striking figure, always in

saffron kilts, as he swung along the Donegal roads; I
remember his handsome, leonine head. He was the donor,
through Agnes, of the Camogie Cup. Nor can I forget the
comment of the old Donegal woman who, seeing the kilts
for the first time and, perhaps, through a haze, said to
me as she gazed after him across the half-door of her
kitchen : " Och, the puir mon is in totters surely ! "
Agnes O'Farrelly's encouragement, persevering and loyal,
of Donegal as well as of other home industries is almost
too well known to need mention. She was, too, a social
figure and she liked it ; her hospitality was unbounded,
in Dublin as elsewhere, and she practised largesse on
occasion in and out of College. Mary Hayden had neither
the facilities nor the taste for such entertainments. Agnes
was almost as well known in the Hebrides and in Brittany
as she was at home. When one of her Breton friends
was in evil case after World War II and condemned to
death by a post-Vichy government, she testified for him
and got so many and such impressive signatures of those
who had known him during the Celtic Congresses that her
memorial helped to save his life. While both these U.C.D.
professors were essentially public figures, Mary T. Hayden
was perhaps more strictly professional. It was their tragedy
(private and personal) that they lived to become " Ladies
in Retirement " ; it is ours that neither they nor we realised
the importance of using their late leisure to make, while it
was yet day, a written record of their lives. For theirs
were lives lived to the full through three-quarters of a
century of struggle no whit less strenuous for women than
for men—the two of whom I have the honour to write
would not have wished it otherwise.

Catholic Women's " Colleges " as separate and distinct
from secondary " Schools " were non-existent when the
Royal University admitted women to its degrees in 1879.
They were still so when the *Catholic Lady Students* publicised
their grievances. Alexandra College, on the other hand,
built as a College in the 60's, incorporated in 1887 under
the Educational Endowments Act, well-equipped and well-
staffed, was in a unique position. Though it was Protestant,

its social and its academic prestige in those years attracted
individual Catholic women to its halls and its teachers.
Some of the latter, like Alice Oldham and Mrs. Thompson,
had been among the first to train when the Royal College
of Science opened its doors to women in the 70's. Others,
like Emma Story and Maud Joynt, had headed the early
lists of Royal University Scholars and Bachelors in Arts.
But both the Dominican and the Loreto Orders in Dublin
as well as the Ursulines in Cork were, from 1883 on,
endeavouring to cater, somehow or other, for undergraduate students of their own, in their various schools.
In 1893 a move was made in Dublin.[1] In a fine pioneering
spirit and at much sacrifice, the Dominican St. Mary's
College, accommodated since 1886 in the Eccles Street
Schools, was transferred, under the famous Mother Patrick,
to Merrion Square, receiving in the following year from
His Grace The Archbishop of Dublin, The Most Rev.
Dr. Walsh, a gift of £500 for distribution in prizes etc.
In the same year Loreto decided to concentrate its undergraduates in 53, St. Stephen's Green where a few classrooms were allotted for their sole use. The new College
in Merrion Square soon made academic history, for, in
1895, one bare year after Junior Fellowships were first
opened to competition, Mary T. Hayden won the Fellowship in English and History, and Katherine Murphy that
in Modern Languages. Both gave St. Mary's as their
" College," Mary, however, bracketing St. Mary's and
Private Study with Alexandra.

This double event brought off by two women Catholics
was sensational. Coming in that year from Loreto, Kil-
larney, to Dublin to compete for a Matriculation Scholarship, I felt the thrill of their achievement. My destination
was Loreto, 53, St. Stephen's Green, where Sister Mary
Eucharia was, or was to be, in charge of a very small group

[1] An interesting link with the Catholic University and Dr. Newman was
Sister Stanislaus, daughter of Denis Florence McCarthy, Dr. Newman's
Professor of Poetry. She was co-founder with Mother Patrick in the late
80's of the University Department in Dominican Convent, Eccles St. Her
death in 1897 in her 48th year was a grievous loss. One of her poems in
Songs of Sion, published in 1898, was addressed to the Cardinal on his eightieth
birthday in 1881.

of University girls. I shall always be grateful for the chance—is there such a phenomenon?—that made me as it were " free " of Loreto and Dominican Orders, sending me first as student to " The Green " and in 1903, on my return from Cambridge, as Lecturer to 23, Eccles Street (the transferred St. Mary's) with Sister Gonzales Stone, a distinguished B.A. of the early 90's. With both these religious I worked in absolute harmony. In the anonymity of their cloistered lives I learnt to see one of the secrets of their sweetness and their strength. I owe them not only the opportunities they gave me, each in her different way, of exercising whatever talents I possessed for my own education and that of my students. I owe them as well those many joys of cultured friendship that were, through the years, woven like silver threads into the web of my working life.

Sister Mary Eucharia, who read Latin and Logic with Second Arts in 1896–97, was one of the finest teachers I ever met. Of teaching stock, she had a universal mind with a special love for Philosophy and Ancient Classics. Her personality was many-sided and she had a singular charm of manner combined with an easy grace and dignity which were impressive. She was a keen student of Newman whose *Grammar of Assent* one could almost call her bedside book. Familiar with his history, she had a devotion to his person symbolised perhaps by the fine print of him which used to hang in later years in her small reception room in Loreto Hall. She had, too, a sense of the tradition and the continuity of the Catholic University which she was minded to pass on to her students. I remember her sending me (with a letter of introduction) to call on Monsignor Molloy, then representative in *propria persona* of the Irish Bishops, Trustees of the Catholic University. I remember the trepidation with which I mounted the great staircase of " 86," to be ushered into one of the suite of rooms on the first floor that were the Monsignor's domain. The vast " parlour " that then engulfed me is still called the Bishops' room. I remember his person, impressive despite a pronounced limp ; I remember his fine voice and his friendly kindness to a young nobody.

In my time in " 53 " there were not yet available for
Latin and Science the Junior Fellows, Patrick Semple
and Arthur Conway, who later crossed the Green to tutor
the Loreto women " outlawed " from " 86." P. A. E.
Dowling, B.A., helped us few First Arts—Ada English,
a prospective " Medical," included—to take the compulsory
Mathematics and Science hurdles. He was in the tradition
of the Catholic University by right of his father-in-law
Casey, Newman's Professor of Mathematics, and he smiled
us through the mysteries of " Sine A, Co-Sine B " as he
paced the floor or manoeuvred before the blackboard,
throwing over his shoulders tags from a favourite Gilbert
and Sullivan opera. How we liked him and disliked what
he so successfully taught. I could then proceed to a Modern
Language Scholarship, and Ada could enter upon her
medical studies in Cecilia Street School, in which she was
one of the first women (if not *the* first) to be registered.
Dr. Denis Coffey, Professor in the School, was her sponsor,
the " man in the gap." Ada was later to make national
as well as medical history. She was well known for her
services in " the Troubles " in Western Ireland where
she rose to be Medical Superintendent of Ballinasloe Mental
Hospital. My personal memory of her is clear as I knew her
in that brief year 1895–96 in " 53." I remember her crisp,
blond hair, remarkable blue eyes and fascinating lisp.
She struck me then as being singularly adult. She was, in
fact, some years my senior and tolerant of everything except
incompetence or willingness on our part to put up with it.
For she burned to get at her real work of medicine ; it was
for her as much a vocation as a profession. I always regret
that Ada did not meet Sister Eucharia, absent in that
year through ill health.

Sister Eucharia had two clear periods of office, 1893–95
before I made her acquaintance, and 1896–98 when I
was going through to B.A. In those years in Loreto, the
Modern Language Group, which was later to be such a
favourite in Royal and early National—and not exclusively
with women—had hardly begun to develop. The groups
more usually taken were Mental and Moral Science and

History, Political Economy and Jurisprudence. The first
of these, equally popular with both sexes, was mainly
but by no means always taken as a Pass and the second
as an Honours Degree. I think Mother Eucharia herself
was responsible for the work in the first group; in all
probability she had some external help. The second group
was in charge of James J. Macken, B.A., then and up to
1901 tutoring in U.C.D. He took English also in Loreto.
In the year 1895 he had won the Chancellor's Gold Medal
for English Prose, a distinction that was later won by two
women, one of whom was Mary Byrne, M.A., of St. Mary's.
French was taught by Richard Carson Greer, a remarkable
grinder who died young. For German Sister Eucharia
had secured Maud Joynt, M.A., of Alexandra; she was a
distinguished linguist. Unlike R. C. Greer who never
spoke French, she invariably used the language of her
subject; her German was excellent. In later years the
R.I.A. was to know her as worker on the Irish Dictionary,
for she had become a Gaelic enthusiast. Relaxing occasionally, she translated poems from both languages. I could
never forget her face; small, as she was herself, and lacking
any particular distinction of features, it was full always of
a dreaming quiet. Born in India, she always looked cold;
her heart was very warm. She was reputed a Buddhist.
I glimpsed her in Donegal in 1909 with another Gael, her
friend Miss Scarlett, M.A., also of Alexandra. They were
both " performing the round " with the people of the
district at Doon Well in honour of St. Columcille. U.C.D.
has a memory of her : she gave me shortly before her death
a number of her books for the use of the German Room.

Sister Eucharia encouraged me already in 1896 to
go abroad for language study. She was, like so many of
the Women Teaching Orders who have contacts everywhere with the Continent, an expert in finding suitable
centres in Germany, France or Italy for students otherwise
hard put to it to " arrive." I remember with delight my
first Paris stay at L'École Normale, 39 Rue Jacob, where I
lived *en pension* with an interesting group of women brought
together in that year, as if specially for my benefit, from

various states of Europe and America; waiting for the Armenian " Troubles " to be over. The owners of the École were compulsorily laicised nuns; they wore ordinary dress and went about their business on Left or Right Bank of the Seine like any other Frenchwomen. I remember, not only the Cultural Sights, but a pilgrimage at dawn, on foot and fasting, to Sacré Cœur, Montmartre. I remember a 6 a.m. visit to the " Halles " to lay in stores and a night in the Paris streets, on the 14th July, when the people danced to the Fall of the Bastille. It was a great adventure; one of our compensations for the " inadequacy " of the early " Colleges." The following year it was to be Berlin through the Cork Ursulines and Mary Ryan. Those experiences of mine were not isolated; later Modern Languages " College " women in the truncated Royal system had continental periods for which they are to this day grateful to the Religious who " managed " it for them. A Modern Languages B.A. opened up to us then a whole new world of life and culture.

When Mother Eucharia went in 1901, as Superior of a House of her Order, to Cambridge, I accompanied her, entering Newnham as an " out-student." There was a waiting list of two years for interns and I could not afford that. I stayed at Furness Lodge, where I saw Mother Eucharia attract some of the finer spirits of the University. Frequent visitors were Baron von Hügel; the Anglican Rev. Mr. Conybeare; Canon Scott, the Rector of the Catholic Church and the youthful History Tripos student, Father Williams of Edmond House, later to be Archbishop of Birmingham. The story was continued when she returned to Ireland in 1905, as Superior now of the School *cum* College, 53 St. Stephen's Green. University Reform was then in the air; Women Graduates, conscious of their rights and wrongs, had begun to organise; their forthright evidence at the Robertson Commission had helped to bring in a verdict for co-education; the old R.U.I. order was passing. There was little to be said for it in the new age which it had helped to create; such are the ironies of history. Mother Eucharia's experience had grown in Cambridge as well as in the visit paid from there to Southern Germany where the Houses of her Order are so many and their members so culturally advanced. She was aware of the advantages which women students had in Cambridge, even though titular degrees were as yet denied them. She had seen not only the amenities of Newnham and Girton ; she was also a welcome and frequent visitor to the Secondary Training College for Women in Woolaston Road where some of the Loreto and Dominican graduates had gone for training. Planning now to provide more adequately for her students, she bought, on the death of Sir William Thompson, his house in 54, furnishing it on " College " lines. It was later to be exchanged for 77, a more spacious residence close to University Church. The Dominicans acquired about the same time two houses on the east side, to which they later added the residence of the late Dr. Dargan. Mother Eucharia was the first Head of Loreto as Mother Gonzales was of Dominican Hall. In both these Halls, unable as yet to provide the ideal " room of one's own," they did their best to supply the background of Chapel, Common Room, Library, and Lecture Theatre, as well as facilities and opportunities for those social-cultural activities which help to enliven students' labours. I recall two noteworthy productions in 77 of the *Antigone* of Sophocles—the earlier in an English version and the later in the Irish translation of Monsignor P. Browne. I recall in Dominican Hall interesting Inaugurals with Professor Mary T. Hayden in the chair ; and good talks by, among others, Shane Leslie and Katharine Tynan, both of whom I first met with Mother Gonzales. She had a " genius " for friendships and I was glad she chose me to share some of those friendships with her.

Mother Eucharia died " in harness " in 1928. The Scholarship for Loreto pupils taking Latin or Greek in U.C.D. was the spontaneous tribute to her memory of generations of students and of her many friends. Mother Gonzales, impaired in health, was some years before her death retired from Dominican Hall to the Convent in Muckross Park, Donnybrook. It had been for a few years at the turn of the century the home of St. Mary's University " College " transferred from Merrion Square to be re-transferred to No. 23 Eccles Street. The Donnybrook house is now a Day School with a Hostel attached for nuns attending U.C.D. whose Orders have no Houses of their own available in Dublin. In Royal as in National days neither Dominicans nor Loreto found any difficulty in filling " College " or Hall. My experience of the students of both Houses before 1909 was that, as far as intellectual quality was concerned, honours were easy. I mention two pairs ; neither is any longer concerned with human verdicts, mine or any other's. There were Helena Walsh (Concannon) of Loreto College and Hanna Sheehy (Skeffington) of St. Mary's Dominican ; both opposites and contemporaries ; both University Scholars with the Higher Degree of M.A. ; the one hagiologist and historian ; Hon. D.Litt., N.U.I., Senator and member of the N.U.I. Senate ; the other militant suffragist and potential reformer ; a tragic figure cast in heroic mould ; isolated yet never aloof. Somewhat younger were Eveleen Nicholls, Loreto, deemed the Beatrice of Pearse's Vision ; University Scholar, M.A. and Studentship holder in Celtic Studies, whose heroic and tragic death by drowning off the Blasket Islands in 1909 ended a career of quite unusual promise ; Mary Byrne of St. Mary's, Scholar, M.A. and Studentship holder as well as Chancellor Gold Medallist in English Prose, who, before her premature death, had established a reputation as Celtologist. Her person and her scholastic achievements are commemorated in U.C.D. by the Mary Byrne Medal for Early Irish Studies.

I could add to the St. Mary's list Louise Gavan Duffy on whom the N.U.I. was to confer an honorary doctorate for, among other things, her unique work as foundress-headmistress in 1916 of the Irish-speaking Sgoil Bhrighde, the first experiment of its kind in the New Ireland then in its birth-throes. She was for years one of Professor Corcoran's staff in the Education Department of U.C.D. to which her school, now become " National," was linked as Practising School for Students in Training in the Depart-

ment. Through that Department most of the women
Arts graduates and a number of the men also passed before
leaving U.C.D. to teach. With Louise in her initiation
in St. Ita's (Pearse's school for girls corresponding to
St. Enda's for boys) was at least one other St. Mary's
student, Mary (Maguire) Colum who in her Pulitzer Prize
book *Life and The Dream* gives an account of her " College "
experiences in that formative period in Dublin when Sinn
Féin and The Abbey Theatre, Yeats and Synge and Lady
Gregory were making history. Another contemporary and
a close friend through life of Louise is scientist-mathe-
matician Annie McHugh Blythe who, since the retirement
of her husband from public life in 1932, has been working
with quiet efficiency in the Physics Department in Earlsfort
Terrace. To correspond with these figures in St. Mary's
there would be in Loreto not only the younger Wexford
Ryan group—Mrs. Mulcahy, Mrs. McCullagh and Mrs.
O'Malley of Galway—and the younger Sheehy sisters, Mrs.
Kettle and Mrs. Cruise O'Brien, but as well the two (Wyse)
Power sisters Maura and Aine (Neans). Both of these are
to be Celtologists ; the older belonging as much to the
Royal as to the National, a Studentship Prize-winner ;
dying in 1916. The younger, Aine, entered U.C.D. for her
Primary Degree in Honours Modern Languages and pro-
ceeded to an M.A. with Studentship in Celtic Studies.
Her Ph.D. career in Bonn and later in Berlin as *Chargée
d'Affaires*, long before our Government had made up its
mind to admit Honours Women Graduates to secretarial
status in External Affairs, is a history " in little " of the
N.U.I. woman. The 50's have at last seen a gesture to
University women with a taste and an ability for the
diplomatic career. There have been three women graduate
Secretaries abroad. There is at present a Woman Minister
of the Republic of Ireland at The Hague—Josephine Ahern
McNeill had had considerable experience in London and
" The Park " as wife of the High Commissioner and
Governor General James McNeill.

II

That these Loreto and Dominican institutions are since 1909 no longer University " Colleges " but Halls of Residence may well have been a disappointment to the nuns who, for a decade and a half, had laboured to provide adequate teaching for their students. That in the years between 1909 and 1913 both Orders made efforts to obtain for their Houses at least partial recognition as " Colleges " has now only historical or academic interest. I imagine that as time passed and University College began to expand, the Orders must have come to recognise, if not the undesirability, at least the impracticability, economic and cultural, of separate Colleges for women or indeed for men either. It is certain that what we secular students of the pre-1909 Women's " Colleges " felt most keenly was not the lack of amenities or the restricted freedom for work or play implicit in the School *cum* College system. These we accepted cheerfully, ready " to scorn delights and live laborious days." There were compensations and we were young and light of heart. Our real need, subconscious in some, acutely conscious in others, was for a common centre of student life such as U.C.D. now affords to men and women alike. Everywhere within its boundaries (they have broadened through the years) there are those contacts of mind with mind and that play and interplay of energies and ideas that are the very stuff of University life for the student.

The year 1909 in which U.C.D. as the Dublin Constituent College of the National opened *all doors* to women equally with men was a record year for talent in both sexes. I have still, carefully preserved from the scrap-heap, the R.U.I. Calendar for that year which shows the Royal, barely in its thirties, dying in a blaze of glory in 1908. There is little mourning for the loss ; birth is already here in the death-chamber and the funeral baked meats will bravely furnish forth a new table. I can imagine Dr. Denis Coffey scanning the results, well pleased with the portents for his venture ! Heading the procession at this 1908 " Conferring " is Arthur W. Conway, M.Sc., to receive the

honorary degree of Doctor of Science. He is a marked
man, destined, in the fullness of time, to confer many a
degree in an Earlsfort Terrace risen from Royal ashes.
His future disciples are already blazing a trail through
First and Second Arts ; they are scientists in disguise, for
the Royal was perhaps minded to give prestige, if not
primacy, to the Faculty which was the core of Cardinal
Newman's University. The late Cecilia Street Professor
of Physiology who is President of U.C.D. now will have
known the calibre of his First and Second Medicals ; he
will not be surprised at the brilliant performance of one of
them, heading the lists of 1st Honours B.A. as well as of
his own Medical Examinations. The names of the scientists
in every branch (whose wives, however, will be drawn
mostly from the Arts Section of the College) will appear
later on the Staffs of U.C.D. or of the College of Science,
not yet—but to be—taken over. That transfer will be
of advantage to the " new women," as I shall try to show—
there is at least one indication of their possible quality in
Kathleen Phelan in the 1908 autumn lists. The man who
in 1926 is to manage " the take-over " could hardly as yet
have been suspected by Dr. Coffey, however percipient
he was. He appears as First Hons. man in Greek and in
Latin, with a Latin Verse Prize for good measure. Perhaps
he has already in his sub-conscious mind Law with its
foundation in Ancient Classics. There are to be some
metamorphoses before this northern reaches the Dublin
High Court. In the 1925–27 period of the Governing Body
of U.C.D., it was my privilege as member to witness the
emotion of gratitude which pervaded the President's speech
as he told of the transfer of the College in Merrion Street.
Mr. Patrick McGilligan will, of a certainty, not have been
present to take a bow. Ministers of State did not, as a
rule, when they happened to be members, attend the
sittings.

I do not know if Dr. Coffey was so interested at that stage
in the prospective women students. They would be few
in number—48 to his 488 men—but a fit audience for his
schools. In the rather ramshackle 86 arrangements, his

women staff had the Apollo Room—nothing to complain of ! The women students' rooms were in 82 and adequate for the time. One room on the ground floor was reserved for Signorina Maria Degani and for eventual students of Italian and Spanish. These were slow to come in—they are in better form now. I was later on, in the Earlsfort Terrace period, allowed the use of the house in the evenings for occasional social meetings of the German Society—German had not yet become the Cinderella of the Modern Languages department. As it was taken in most of the leading Girls' Schools and Boys' Colleges, it had become a strong subject in the Royal. There was a German tradition in Blackrock as well as in Clongowes College and Father Delany, S.J., in his evidence before the Fry Commission, made a case for Modern Language studies from which he would hardly have excluded German. Walter Doolin and Jim Magennis, both Honours Languages Undergraduates in the 1909 Calendar Lists, sat, as did Lucius Gwynn, too early dead, on the German benches in the sheds behind 86. They took the subject to a B.A. Honours Degree before starting on their respective careers—so did Jerry Brennan, before going to his death in France in 1914–18. " Dr. Jim " Magennis later spared the German Dramatic Society some of the rare moments of leisure in his overworked consultant-physician's life. Both men and women student performers showed the result of his expertise on Production Nights, which he often attended. These were good days, though arduous. The ordinary meetings of the German Society were in the " Physics Theatre," a ghastly conventicle of an apartment it seemed to me ! We met in the afternoons to allow the attendance of clerical students who could not so easily come in the evenings. I think the " Theatre " was the meeting-place of the famous " L and H," at which women students spoke on occasion and which some of the hardier spirits enjoyed. I remember going to one meeting in the 1916–20 years when discussions were heated. I remember the courage of James Dillon in defence of his father and the tenacity of J. C. Flood ; I do not recall a woman speaker.

Mary K. Ryan, B.A., joined Miss Hayden, Miss O'Farrelly and myself in the Apollo Room in 1911 when she crossed the Irish Sea to assist Professor Cadic and Michael Hayes in the work of the French Department. Strenuous times were ahead for them when in 1913 Professor Cadic fell ill and remained an invalid till his death early in 1914. World War I intervening, the department was to remain without a Professor till it was over. During that time Miss Ryan was in charge and there was the added strain of 1916 when, for a few weeks, she was held prisoner by the British Military Forces. In 1919 she was returned as Member of the Governing Body by the graduates and re-elected in 1921. She did not seek election afterwards. Kate O'Brien, one of our brilliant novelists and one of the group in Loreto Hall whose careers would furnish a book of many pages, calls Mary K. Ryan, in her page and a half of " Memories of U.C.D. long ago," " a cool, alarming scholar." She was a woman of strong character and outstanding ability, quietly determined and of heroic proportions. There never was any doubt of her intellectual powers or of her fine teaching quality. She had during training in Woolaston Road, Cambridge (after her First Hons. Mod. Languages in 1902), made a lasting impression on the Staff of that College. Like other members of her remarkable family, she had much house-wifely skill combined with a decorative Arts and Crafts sense. Her home bore the impress of her personality. With her friend Professor Chauviré and his wife she lived on terms of close intimacy till her death in Bad Nauheim in 1934. She had been for some years the wife of Seán T. O'Kelly and lived after Ranelagh Road in St. Stephen's Green (close to University Church and to 86) until she moved to a modern villa residence in Anglesea Road.

In U.C.D. the women students increased in number from forty-two in 1909–10 to two hundred and sixty-one in 1918–19 when we had already moved into the new buildings in Earlsfort Terrace. Their number is seen to be doubled in 1929–30 when they are in comparative strength in the transferred College of Science. I regard

The Dublin Commissioners, 1908–1911

Left to right—

Back Row : Stephen Gwynn, John P. Boland, Alexander Anderson, Bertram C. A. Windle, Denis J. Coffey.

Front Row : Gen. Sir William F. Butler, Most Rev. William J. Walsh, Rt. Hon. Christopher Palles, Sir John Rhys, Henry Jackson.

that transfer—with its increased facilities for work in a well-equipped department as well as its increasing opportunities for attractive employment in research and teaching —as a factor in the partial transfer of University women students' interest from Arts to the Sciences, natural, mathematical or medical. Scientists are perhaps, like poets, born not made. But I am a believer in opportunity as a stimulus to development. The College of Science opened its doors to women in the 70's when they were outlawed elsewhere. It seems scientific, if not poetic, justice that they should, in another age, not only flock to its student benches but be found now in force in its staff rooms. These have a pair of women Doctors of Science as well as a group of women research workers and teachers, senior and not so senior, among its M.Sc.s and Ph.D.s in the Natural Sciences. In 1952–53 College women students grew in number from the 1929–30 figure of 513 to 747 which, taking an average of the ten previous years, seems fairly stable. That number conceals significant increases in women taking Medicine : a change of figure from one-tenth to one-fifth of the total of College medical students. Occasionally in the N.U.I. Travelling Studentship Lists a woman is seen to capture the lead in Pathology or in Anatomy. That was, also occasionally, the case in the bad days of the Royal. There may be women Medical Doctors or Surgeons of consultant rank in England among the Irish University Graduate groups. They are few in Ireland as yet ; they may be on the way. It is an exacting profession.

In the Arts Faculty, covering roughly half the total of women students in the College and having several subject groups, two of these, considered as groups leading to a Degree, Ancient Classics and Philosophy, are now rarely taken by women. Philosophy has not been taken to M.A. Honours studentship standard since Agnes Cuming, transferring from the Royal, won the Travelling Studentship in 1912. I do not know of more than one woman taking Honours Philosophy since, though the subject was a popular choice in the Royal, especially for women with teaching in

11

view. Maretta Molloy (O'Callaghan) took First Honours in
Loreto College in the period when U.C.D. was partially
open. She attended both Professor Magennis's and Father
Finlay's lectures. I often heard the latter speak in the
highest terms of her ability. She lectured for years in a
London Training College for women. I think Professor
Elizabeth O'Sullivan of Cork was also in her time B.A. and
M.A. in Mental and Moral Science in the Royal. The
only time I remember Ancient Classics being taken in
the N.U.I. by a woman to a higher Degree was when Miss
Heavey of Galway made a record by getting the Travelling
Studentship in 1928. A few women have from time to
time been attracted to the Celtic Studies group. One of
them became and still is Professor of Early Irish in Galway.
She was one of Thurneysen's group of students in Bonn
and staged his 70th birthday celebration when he was
here between the two wars conducting a Seminar in the
Academy. I remember the 70-candle cake and the presentation to Osborn Bergin of the traditional bard's gift
of cows for his dedicatory poem on the occasion. The other
winners of Celtic Studies Studentships are working in the
Institute, in the Academy or elsewhere at their learned
tasks. English Language and Literature is a favourite
choice for students and I should say without verify-
ing that this has a higher percentage of women M.A.
students than any other Arts group. The Continental
Languages, except French which has an everlasting
primacy, are not in good form. French is taken in many
combinations for B.A. and it appears as a winner at
Studentship standard as well. The Professors of French
in University College, Cork, have almost from the beginning
of the National been women. Dr. Mary Ryan, Professor
Emeritus and ex-Junior Fellow of the Royal, is still busy
writing ; she has made a study of Claudel. Dr. Eithne
Byrne (Costigan) who succeeded her got the Travelling
Studentship from U.C.D. in 1926 and won her Doctorate
at the Sorbonne. Spanish and Italian have benefited by
the (partial) separation of the two subjects on the appointment (after the retirement of Professor Degani in 1938)

of a University Lecturer in Spanish and an (overhead) Professor of both subjects. There is now also more liberal staffing : two women assistants in Italian and one in Spanish. German is in a worse position than any of the other modern languages. Presenting more difficulties to the College beginner and having been banished from most of the Secondary Schools it is in evil case. The Schools are, in the times in which we live, very often under the pressure of preparing their pupils —boys or girls—for entry into Services which set little store by continental culture.

Of the other Faculties, Commerce was a favourite choice of students entering without Latin. The women's choice is now perhaps also determined by the prospect of employment under relatively good conditions in Technical Schools. Architecture at the other end of the scale, with its severe discipline and its long expensive course, is a luxury for women. Only the few can afford to wait for the chances of private practice ; a few find posts in architects' offices or in a Government Department. In Music, where the number of graduates is small, the numbers benefiting by the School are large. Women especially qualify with various certificates for teaching posts in schools. The few women graduates there are show a taste for composition and have won Bursaries for study abroad. We may yet see a Dr. Annie Patterson in U.C.D. ! The Musical Society alone would justify the existence of the School, so great is the impetus it must give to the men and women student members. It has a good Executive.

In the continued expansion of U.C.D. during the last quarter-century and in its ready response to national needs it was obvious that its women graduates with their abilities and their resources, academic and other, would find scope not only in the various Faculties but in employment in the College Library with its Library Training School, now presided over by a qualified Librarian—a distinguished Modern Languages M.A. Her staff are chiefly trained women graduates. Another outlet for women has been provided in the Social Sciences School in which the student can proceed now to a B.Soc.Sc. or take a Diploma qualifying for Welfare Supervisor or Almoner posts. The Director of the School is a U.C.D. woman graduate almoner.

For many years after 1909 there was not a woman graduate on the administrative staff. Now, with the expansion and division of offices and with the increase in students to over 3,000 there is room enough for some forty graduates who give their services in all sections to the smooth running of a complicated machine. On the Governing Body, however, there is at present no woman member drawn from the staff of the College or elected by the relevant College Bodies. After the death of Miss O'Farrelly in 1951 there was no longer a woman member. The Government saved the situation by nominating a woman as one of its four members. She is a distinguished graduate of the Royal and extern to the College—a woman of known ability in affairs—Miss Jane Kissane, M.A.

If Margaret Tierney Downes, the stalwart author of the pamphlet " The Case of the Catholic Lady Students Stated " which she and her co-signatories published in 1888, were now to visit Dublin from whatever sphere she inhabits and see Earlsfort Terrace with its many dependencies, I think she would be pleased with the advance women have made in the sixty years' interval. Since I got that very interesting pamphlet from Miss Power and Miss Hogan in the College Library I have made various efforts—most of them in vain—to trace the signatories other than Mary T. Hayden, M.A. I cannot find the author anywhere in any Calendar ! If I could conjure her up, we women of U.C.D. past and present, would entertain her in those 85 and 86 buildings out of bounds for her sex in 1888. Our Lady Deans, B.Sc. and B.A., would " say it with flowers " in the Apollo Room or wherever else our one woman Professor would choose to play hostess. She would be aided in her task by a strong group of women Lecturers from Earlsfort Terrace and Merrion Street : Arts and Science. A woman archaeologist would perhaps plan another day " on the site " in Tara ; a woman member of the Dramatic Society would suggest a visit to the Gate, where a star, a woman member of the Society only a short year ago, is now probably playing lead with the Longford Productions, in which there is always close co-operation between Lord and Lady Longford, an Oxford woman herself. For good measure and if the night is fine a trip to Dunsink Observatory might be suggested. Margaret should meet there our equivalent of her *Signora Caterina Scarpellini*, woman Director of the Rome Observatory sometime in the nineteenth century. Her story Margaret told in 1888 as a climax to the history of women in other countries whose brains could, somehow or sometime, be found equal to men's. Surely women are the theme of the *Appendix* to Margaret's " Case of The Catholic Lady Students Stated "—the *Appendix* itself being just a quotation from the *Weekly Register* dealing with remarkable women in Europe. Dunsink would be reached and we would be received by Mary T. (Conway) Bruck, former Travelling Studentship winner in Experimental Physics (1947) ; then astronomer in her own right in Dunsink and now in permanent partnership with her husband Dr. Herman Bruck, Director of the Observatory. After that experience Margaret Tierney Downes might well think that the *Weekly Register* quotation concerning Signora Caterina Scarpellini was writ in the stars. Dr. Herman Bruck would confirm that view from his reading of the Heavenly Bodies.

THE COLLEGE AND THE NATION

Professor T. D. Williams

University College, Dublin, was opened on 2nd November, 1909, as one of the constituent colleges established under the Irish Universities Act of 1908. The official ceremony was recorded in the newspapers of the time ; and as the establishment of a University College for Catholics had been for a long time an unfulfilled aspiration, the ceremony received considerable publicity in the daily press. It was an enterprise of high moment, and it was one which therefore justified the high hopes expressed in the addresses delivered on the occasion of the opening. In its first year it was a small College by modern standards ; what had been granted was a modest provision for a limited future rather than an expansive or over-generous financial contribution. In many ways the expectations then entertained were less than the reality as it subsequently proved itself. The development of the College was greater and more rapid than anyone antici- pated, and this was to be productive of many of the more difficult problems of the future.

The number of students recorded as attending lectures in the first year was 529. By 1953 the number had risen to 3,153. In 1909–10 the number of degrees awarded was 75, in 1919–20, 217, in 1929–30, 151, in 1939–40, 489, in 1949–50, 689, and in 1953, 682. This bald statement does not indicate the ever-increasingn umber of other services of an educational nature provided by the College in the form of courses for diplomas, evening classes and extra-mural activities, some of which were hardly considered as coming within the function of a university before 1914.

Since 1909 the State has nominally increased its original annual grant by over 700 per cent. ; but only in com- paratively recent years have governments endeavoured to bring their contribution into proportion with the expanding functions exercised by the College. For many years the permanent members of the College staff were accustomed to feel that their difficulties were not realised by the State or its departmental advisers, and that the community as a whole had not been made aware of the services which the Colleges of the National University could give to the nation, if they received adequate financial support. It was widely held in university circles in the early twentieth century that a native government might have been expected to provide at least as much support as an alien administration. In fact, for some time it was to seem that the College would probably have received more if the link with the British university system had been maintained instead of being snapped after 1922.

If high hopes were entertained in the early days of the new Ireland, some of them were therefore soon to be disappointed. A period of comparative lassitude set in which was to affect over many years the College's policy towards its relations with the community as well as towards the special problems with which its staff were increasingly confronted. Progress in ordinary affairs of life is never continuous; and colleges, like other institutions, go ahead by spurts which in turn are followed by periods of relative stability and sometimes relative stagnation. It is only on occasion that special circumstances, or exceptionally vigorous personalities, turn the flood-lights on such institutions, and compel stock-taking and revision of policy. The history of University College has not been an especially exciting chapter in the public life of Ireland. Its successes and its claims have rarely been the object of animated controversy outside its own walls. Instead, the inevitable weaknesses which affect all human organisations have in its case been emphasised. Much current criticism has, in the opinion of many university men, been misdirected and has failed to touch upon the real defects under which the College has laboured, and of which university men have been well aware for many years. What is said in this connection can be repeated with varying degrees of validity for all universities and colleges in the Twenty-Six Counties.

It should, of course, be remembered that if Irish universities might have benefited materially from continued connection with Britain (as has Queen's University, Belfast), that was not the only consideration of which the nation might have been expected to take cognisance. There were to be many claims on the nation's purse after 1922, and if the College's developing needs had been fully satisfied, other interests might have suffered. Dáil Éireann naturally bore chief responsibility for the allocation of limited financial resources among a wide number of interested claimants. It decided that University College required no more than a relatively small increase in its original annual grant of £32,000, at least for the first few years after 1922. The other interests which competed with the university were in many cases, doubtless, very legitimate ones ; and preference was in any event given to them. University College in particular, therefore was to suffer for nearly a generation from its failure to impress its needs on public opinion. Public opinion probably was not then sufficiently convinced of the validity of the university's claims, and possibly it was not even aware of them. For the prevailing indifference towards higher education, the university itself has to share some blame through its failure to bring its case before the public, or at least to make it sufficiently effective. What public opinion cannot do is to justify that omission and, at the same time, criticise the different Colleges for having failed in some respects to attain the same standards as other, more richly-endowed and more ancient institutions. University College, Dublin, was perhaps unduly modest about its own responsibilities and possibilities. Though aware of its potential influence in educating future generations, it rarely spoke its mind out frankly, and often replied to official indifference with privately-expressed grievance and indeed with hopeless abnegation.

It looked to the past and the present, rather than to the future, and it is only in recent times that its governing authorities have tried to capture the vision, which Newman so often called for, of ever-increasing promise and influence.

It is only recently also that this consciousness, both of present defects and of future promise, has been brought home to ordinary responsible men and women in political and cultural life. It is only in the last few years that people have begun to realise the part played by graduates of the College in every sphere of the community's life ; and many of those graduates are themselves beginning to realise the importance to them of higher education, and the necessity of improving it for the benefit of their own children in the future.

Institutions, no less than persons, are partly the product of their environment, and for an understanding of the College's growth and of both its successes and failures, account must be taken of the conditions under which it began and developed. In this connection the question will naturally be raised, what role the College has played in the national life of the community, what services it has in fact given, or ought to have given and in fact did not give. To answer these questions, some remarks may be made initially on the proper function of a university in a national state. Secondly, it will be desirable to review the historical relations of the actual College under consideration with the other institutions which influence the thought and action of all citizens in their ordinary way of life. In particular, connections of the college with the Church, the State and its subordinate departments, the professions and commercial life, are relevant. University men would however insist that what a university should give to the community is by no means always what the community at any given time considers it should give ; that the most important of its duties are precisely those which attract little notice ; and that in the sphere of education, final judgements have to await the passage of time. This means that its success cannot be described in dramatic or sensational terms, but that in the long run, failure or success is sufficiently obvious not to require much controversy or undue emphasis.

Universities, by the nature of their being, envisage the creation of a tradition of ideas and influence ; tradition however requires the passage of time, and it is only in the second or third generation that it becomes possible to assess the contribution made by a new institution to the community out of which it has arisen. It is true that University College goes back to Newman's university; that connection, however, though it may be strong, can only be described as indirect. Times have greatly changed since the establishment of Newman's institution, and the ideals of Newman were not, even in his own time, universally accepted. Since that time the ideas and activities of modern Ireland have altered, on the surface at least; and in the initial stage of the National University, and particularly of its Dublin College, various obstacles lay in the way of any attempt to realise or fulfil deliberately the aims advocated by Newman.

By law the university to which University College, Dublin, belongs is undenominational; it is not a professedly Catholic university, and faculties of theology, for example, cannot be established out of public endowment in any of its constituent Colleges. Professors and statutory lecturers are obliged to make a statutory declaration that in their lectures they will say nothing to offend the religious susceptibilities of any member of their class. Also, University College, Dublin, is, in its constitutional structure at least, comparable to the modern " red-brick " type of college, whose growing influence in England Newman distrusted so much. It is a university established for the people rather than for an élite drawn from a traditional aristocracy. Most of its graduates and undergraduates are very deeply concerned with the practical necessity of earning a living. Special consideration has therefore had to be given to the professional and vocational aspects of education rather than to any exclusively humanistic training. This tendency has steadily increased, and the situation of higher education in Ireland no longer corresponds, if it ever did correspond, to the Oxford ideal which Newman brought with him to Ireland.

Furthermore, University College, Dublin, is part of the National University of Ireland, and though institutions should not be judged merely by their titles, the phrase "National University" indicated to some extent the nature of the motive which had brought it into being against so much opposition, sustained for so long a time. Newman has perhaps been unfairly and ungraciously criticised for his alleged intention of creating in Ireland a university for British (including Irish), Catholic "gentlemen." This interpretation of Newman's purpose was doubtless exaggerated, but he was, like everyone else, naturally influenced by the educational ideals and social background of his youth ; and modern Ireland could fit only with difficulty into any such conception. The Irish Universities Act came into being largely owing to the initiative of the Catholic hierarchy, of British Liberal politicians such as Augustine Birrell, R. B. Haldane and James Bryce ; it was also a response to the long-standing campaign of the Irish Parliamentary Party and to the pressure of a united nationalist public opinion. In the parliamentary debates on the Irish Universities Bill, for example, almost no reference was made to Newman's university ideal, and therefore it is only natural that neither in the intentions of its founders, nor in the historical results, is it very easy to trace a direct, comprehensive connection between Newman's ideal of a University and the reality of University College, Dublin. On the other hand, we have to take into account the different historical environment, and distinguish between statements of principle and their application to new and different circumstances. If we look at University College from this viewpoint, the question which should be asked is "What type of university would Newman have advocated in the twentieth century?" rather than what type of university he actually wanted in 1854. And if we judge by the former standard rather than by the latter, University College, Dublin, is in the process of creating a tradition not inconsistent with the Newman ideal, though it certainly does not coincide entirely with it.

It is of course no less inaccurate to judge University College exclusively by reference to the so-called "liberal charter" of the University than to assess the practical consequences of a university ideal deriving from Newman by the writings in which he expounded his conception of that ideal.

There were two main criticisms of the National University expressed in the early years, one of which derived from Trinity College and from certain English conservative quarters. The bogey of denominationalism was constantly brought out of the cupboard, and many Tory speakers at Westminster declared in their speeches on the Universities Bill that Birrell's measure was only a thinly-disguised effort to introduce religious obscurantism into Irish university life, that the Bill was therefore bare-faced hypocrisy, and that under the guise of a liberal, secular system, Roman Catholicism was receiving, with State support, a firm and dangerous entrenchment. One group was therefore to condemn the Bill as fostering obscurantism, while a second group rejected it as " unduly secular and liberal," because in fact it was not Catholic enough. Prominent among this group were a few bishops who agreed with Cardinal Logue that the National University was merely a " pagan bantling." From an ideal viewpoint, the College did not correspond to the highest conceptions of religious orthodoxy ; in the practical conduct of its affairs it was not in general opinion to lag behind other colleges established under charters more satis-factory to the ecclesiastical authorities. And no judgement on institutions can be complete without taking into account Bishop Dupanloup's distinction between " thesis " and " hypothesis."

The reply to the second type of criticism is that provided by the later history of the College. Its atmosphere has been Catholic but not clerical, scientific but not secular. The provisions made for the religious life of its members have been extensive and pervasive, and they have fostered therefore a Catholic spirituality which has been voluntary and natural rather than imposed and external. There is no single instance of action or of work undertaken by the College to which the religious authorities have taken exception ; and the system as a whole has afforded excellent opportunity for intellectual co-operation between the laity and the clergy. The relations between the clerical and lay members of the staff can thus develop in academic matters on the basis of equal and independent partnership. If that co-operation has not, as yet, resulted in the establishment of a flourishing Catholic intellectual tradition which could claim comparison with some of the older Catholic colleges on the Continent, the fault does not lie with the legal system. The College has been in existence for only a short time, and the period in which it has worked has been a troubled one for the nation as well as for itself.   It has had to struggle with the pressure of financial impoverishment; and the teaching duties to which its staff have been subjected are far greater than those to which members of Trinity College were subjected in its most celebrated age before the twentieth century, or to which members of the ancient or of some modern English universities are, even in our own time, subjected.

One of the most noticeable answers given in 1908 to ultra-Protestant criticism was that of Sir Edward Carson, as representing Dublin University, who spoke in the House of Commons in favour of the Bill. It was one which unfortunately was hardly representative of universal opinion in his own university.   Carson had mentioned the Protestant atmosphere of Trinity College, and added in reference to the proposed new universities (the National University of Ireland and the Queen's University of Belfast) :

" We are frequently told that the setting up of these is a retrograde movement.   It will depend entirely upon themselves whether they are a success or not. If, whether Roman Catholic or Presbyterian, they proceed to conduct their business and frame their curriculum on any narrow basis of sectarian differences, they will be absolute failures.   If they manage their business upon the broad basis of liberty, which can alone gain success in education, they will take their place as great universities among those of the United Kingdom.   I may hold views that do not entirely commend themselves even to many of those who think with me in Ireland ; but I look forward to the day when these great, successful, liberal seats of learning, showing themselves worthy in the great race of science and art, will come forward to say, as I hope Trinity College will : ' Let us join together and make one great National University.' I believe it is the duty of every Irishman, of whatever creed or politics, to wish Godspeed to these universities, and to do his best in a spirit of noble generosity to make them a great success."

There are now two universities in Dublin, but the vision of Carson is apparently no nearer realisation than it was in 1908. University College has now outstripped Trinity College in the number of its students and in the influence which it is exercising over the public life of modern Ireland. This is one of the great changes in Irish higher education, and it is one which is perhaps too often taken for granted. It would never have come about if University College had generally failed in its responsibilities.

Since 1909 the two Colleges have worked largely in isolation from each other, and the official contacts which link University College, Dublin, to its sister Colleges in Cork and Galway are infinitely closer than any existing between it and Trinity College. On the other hand, there is friendly competition in the Royal Irish Academy, and the publication of certain learned journals provides common ground on which members meet and compete in friendly co-operation; and there is no reason why each College should not welcome the development of the other, each possessing a different tradition and background.

A university has three major functions, to teach, to advance knowledge by original research, and to give young people the opportunity, by a mixture of social and intellectual discourse, of " growing up." All of these are necessary and yet none is sufficient in itself. In its achievements regarding research, the College should not be judged too severely, provided there is general realisation of the relative absence of progress in this respect and of the very understandable reasons which explain it. People are sometimes far too apt to compare institutions of mature development and in full stride with those which are as yet only in their infancy. Before members of the College can undertake successful research and thus add to its fame in the international world of learning, they must first of all resolve the problem of teaching. For this purpose, University College has never been over-generously equipped. It commenced its career almost from scratch, as it were, and was immediately thrown back upon the assistance of the State ; it did not and does not enjoy the possession of extensive lands, or of endowments from other sources of a private nature. It was clear from the beginning that the greater part of the annual funds of the College was to come from State endowment. In 1953, after forty-three years of development, the income of the College consisted of government grants and of student fees to the extent of over 90 per cent. of the total ; private endowments were almost nonexistent and the situation was therefore substantially unchanged from that prevailing in the first academic session.

The College therefore has constantly been compelled to seek assistance from the State, and the State, in view of its important liabilities elsewhere, has been mainly concerned to make provision for only the most pressing and limited needs affecting university *teaching*. It has on the whole discharged the obligations which the university authorities would impute to it in this respect honourably and relatively generously. It has not, for example, interfered with the internal autonomy of the College—despite the hold which control over vital funds could have given it. Its annual grants, which rose from £32,000 to £52,000 in 1921, to £147,000 in 1947 and to £231,000 in 1952–53, were made in response chiefly to appeals from the College authorities for provision to face increased expenditure on teaching. Research is, for the State's purposes, a long-distance aim ; it is certainly not the only function of a university, and it has rarely been recognised to be the first one. Any university however which has succeeded in acquiring international reputation has acquired it through the research achievements of its staff. It would be disastrous both for its teaching and for its reputation if, by reason of inadequate financial assistance, the College were permanently limited to the fulfilment of its teaching function.

There is some justification for the view that the Governing Body of the College was until recently, if anything, inclined to underplay its hand in its assessment of future needs. In its financial relations with the State, the College has had to deal with several governments, one of which before 1922 was of course placed in Whitehall. The British government had established the National University of Ireland, and had thus virtually, if not legally, accepted responsibility for the successful development of university education among Catholics. The State provided an annual grant, initially, of £32,000, which was not to be increased for twelve years. In addition the College received an original building and capital grant of £110,000 which, owing to the intervention of the first World War, had to be expanded under the stress of rising prices. The development between 1914 and 1918 of certain scientific departments, such as those of Anatomy, Bacteriology, Physiology, Pharmacology, Botany, Geology and Zoology, as well as of Engineering, could not be provided for out of the original grant. Negotiations for the relief of the College finances which, as from 1917, rapidly ran into an overdraft, were to be continued by Dr. Coffey, the first President, almost throughout the whole of his long tenure of office. The British University Grants Committee, established in 1918, was to recommend further State aid, but all that was done during the next few years was to be largely in the nature of a makeshift.

The College owes for its foundation a great deal to the Irish Parliamentary Party, led by John Redmond and John Dillon ; and it was no secret that the appointment of Dr. Denis Coffey as first President was due in no small way to the intervention of the latter. That Party, while it sought Home Rule, was committed to the imperial connection. Personal opinion and material interests

Dr. Denis J. Coffey,
President, University College, Dublin,
1909—1940

therefore, bound many of the College authorities to policies advocated by the Irish Parliamentary Party, and put them in opposition to the separatist national movement. There is no evidence that politics played any decisive part in the general internal working of the early College, either in its administrative or academic aspects. On its public occasions, however, due attention was given to the official viewpoint, and this is visible in nearly all the public ceremonies and statements of the years 1910 to 1918, and to a lesser extent up to 1921. The College was later criticised for adopting this policy; it would be well if the critics considered the reasons upon which the first President and his friends acted.

The question was formerly often asked, how much University College, as a constituent College of the National University of Ireland, contributed to the struggle for national independence. The function of universities is often misunderstood—in Ireland no less than elsewhere ; the course of learning is primarily international in its aim, and political considerations, even of the highest order, do not form any immediate part of that function. The College commenced its career in troublesome times, and in its first thirty years had to experience many of the difficulties which arose for the community in general out of the first World War, the Anglo-Irish war of Independence, and later the Civil War. The position of the College was rendered especially delicate in view of its dependence for the greater part of its resources upon State support. Before 1922 the State was represented in Ireland by the British Government, and when its authority was challenged, it was naturally concerned to see that opposition to its authority should not be forthcoming from an institution which it had itself called into being. On the other hand, the College was a College of the people of Ireland, and an increasingly large proportion of that people was entering into the struggle against British authority. Where would the College stand ? Was it necessary, or even desirable, that it should take a stand ?

It is not the duty of universities to take the lead in political

12

action, save perhaps in very exceptional circumstances where fundamental principles of justice are obviously called into question either by sections in the community or by its government. Politics is not the whole of human activity, as some seem to think ; life is many sided and there are other ways to salvation ; at one time or another political activity will become more or less important, but it never merits exclusive or full-time attention. And a university has *always* other considerations to bear in mind. Politics is concerned with present problems, and if prevailing political pre-suppositions greatly influence the lecturers' treatment of their subjects, or entirely dominate the interests of students outside the lecture halls, academic interests tend to be endangered. Politics is concerned with giving immediate answers to specific problems, and it is frequently necessary, from a political viewpoint, that decisions be taken, whether they be right or wrong. In many university subjects, practical and immediate answers have not to and cannot be given, and the object of university training is to keep the mind open rather than to close it in either one direction or the other. It is therefore not unnatural that a university should, if anything, appear to be " reactionary," and that it should lag behind rather than precede the community on political issues. In what concerns politics, it is not by means either unusual or unnatural that universities should be in a backwater. On the other hand, it is not the business of a university to oppose new ideas, because in that event it would itself be taking a political view. As far as possible, it should as an institution remain neutral. How far did the original administration of University College succeed in fulfiling its academic duty in the midst of political unrest ? And how far was its attitude dependent upon maintaining friendly relations with opposing parties which were rapidly to drift into conditions of inter-state, and of civil, war ?

In 1911 (July), a royal visit took place to Dublin ; and the opportunity was taken by the Governing Body of the College to offer an address to King George V and Queen Mary on the occasion of their visit. As recorded in

the Presidential Report of 1910–11, King George V was
" graciously pleased " to receive the address of the Governing Body which was presented by a deputation consisting
of the President and Registrar of the College. In the next
year, 1912, an imperial parliamentary conference was
held in Dublin, and the hospitality of the College was
offered to it. All groups with the exception of a very
small minority in Ireland collaborated in these festivities ;
and there is no evidence that at this or any subsequent
time, with one or two exceptions, the College staff did
anything to encourage the type of resistance to the political
status quo which only at a later date was to become, with
some people, a necessary test for citizenship. Between
1909 and 1916, the College in fact was a mirror of the
nation.

It was not until 1914 that the first signs of political
tension, coming partly though not completely from outside,
began to affect the policy of the College in a way
calculated to give rise to criticism from any political group
in the country. The outbreak of the first World War
immediately raised the question as to Ireland's participation
in a struggle in which the British Government and people
were directly involved. The Volunteer movement,
inaugurated by John MacNeill, a Professor on the staff,
was introduced into the College. Though in its Redmondite
form it was criticised in some student circles, it aroused
no more public opposition than it did in the nation in
general. Students and graduates began to volunteer for
the British forces, and the number was constantly to increase
in the following years. There was little doubt in what
direction the President considered the interests of the
College as well as of the Irish people to lie. In his Presidential Report for 1914–15, he referred in high terms to
the gallantry of a large number of graduates and undergraduates who were risking their lives in the war " in
which the interests of Ireland and the Empire are so
profoundly involved." As far as he could ascertain the
number of " patriotic young Irishmen " among the students
of that year was 230 ; and he went on to express the hope

that a permanent memorial, to be erected in the College hall after the return of peace, would indicate the public character of their sacrifice. Owing to intervening circumstances no such memorial was in fact erected.

The year 1916 was a dramatic one in the general history of the community, and there occurs a short reference to the events of Easter week in the Presidential Report for the year 1915–16 :

" There occurred during the Session the sad and tragic events of the rebellion in Dublin. The year has also passed in the convulsion of the Great War in which the interests of Ireland and the Empire are so much involved."—(Presidential Report, 1915–16, p. 6).

Dr. Coffey estimated the number of present and former College members engaged in active service in that year at not less than 450, and a list was issued of those who had either died on active service, or had acquired distinction. The President gave expression to the deep grief of many colleagues over the death of one of the most popular members of the College staff, T. M. Kettle, Professor of National Economics, who fell at Ginchy on 9th September, 1916.

In the same year another member of the staff and an outstanding scholar, Professor John MacNeill, was sentenced to penal servitude for life. He was not re-appointed after the expiration of the statutory seven years to his post as Professor of Early and Medieval Irish History, which he had held since 1909. He was however restored to this position as soon as circumstances allowed.

By the end of the war, over 500 present and past students had served in the British Army and forty-two had been killed. However by 1918, political opinion outside the College and inside among the undergraduates had changed very considerably. From 1918 onwards the students in particular as well as a small but increasing number of the staff began to display signs of intense political activity, and it was not long before many of them were involved in political and military struggles. There is a considerable list of names which might be mentioned of those who, between 1917 and 1921, were active on the side of Sinn Féin.

Whatever their opinions at the time, many of the survivors of that epoch would now agree that it was good that the nation's conflict should have been reflected in the thoughts and actions of members of the College. In the long run, this division was to give a stability to both the College and the new State. Whatever feelings may have been entertained at that time, and in certain quarters even to-day, about the issues of those years, historians will probably say that all parties in their different ways provided a contribution to the solution now universally accepted. And history never sees the exclusive victory of one side or the other ; a middle solution is usually the result of the struggles of competing parties, each sincerely convinced of the rectitude of its aims, but each also unduly blind to the advantages and virtues present in the opposing party.

It would be a mistake to judge the College merely by the standard of its co-operation or lack of it with the nationalist movement. It was not its business to be successful, or even right, in the political conflict ; and Dr. Coffey was mainly concerned with securing firm foundations to develop further a College which had commenced with such weak resources and had, shortly after its inauguration, run into such heavy straits. In any event, the political issues were not clear for many people, and it was only after October, 1918, that it became obvious that the Irish people as a whole were rejecting the thesis of the Irish Parliamentary Party and were prepared to support the struggle for independence from Britain. Dr. Coffey had to take into account, as President of the College, its dependence on the State of the present, which was the British Government. His conception of the College's interests also coincided with his private political convictions. It would have been unwise for him, however, to have discounted any possible State of the future ; and from this viewpoint, he had to play an uneasy but vitally necessary game in manoeuvring between a party which was growing weaker, which was the one he privately would have supported, and one which was destined to grow stronger and finally to become the native government with which the College had to deal over the burning question of increased financial grants.

Authority came into conflict with the students on one issue in 1918, which also had a political background. A proposal was made that Honorary War B.Sc.'s be conferred on Second Medical students who had been on active service in the war for at least nine months. The Council of the S.R.C. issued a protest which met with the strong disapproval of the President. In similar political matters, the S.R.C. gradually became more active. Unanimous resolutions of protest were passed against the wearing of British Army uniforms by at least two Professors when in the precincts of the College; votes of sympathy were expressed with the " Korean Revolutionaries "; and fraternal greetings transmitted to Egyptian students in Cairo and elsewhere. There were also difficulties in regard to a subscription for a Kevin Barry Fund. In retrospect this much may be said, that it was inevitable that there should have been students who were more politically advanced than their conservative elders. It was also fortunate that authority was able to steer the ship between dangerous rocks.

From 1918 onwards, the President displayed great impartiality in his official attitudes. He was ever kind in personal relations—this was one of his greatest virtues— with all students, irrespective of their political views. And there was no instance, after 1918, of College authority being used to assist the British forces in Ireland in their attempt to suppress the national movement. On at least one occasion the College was raided by security forces, and it was known quite widely that members of the republican army (Richard Mulcahy was one of them) were sheltering in the College rooms and laboratories.

The College certainly therefore did not lead in the national struggle ; it tried to avoid it, and on the whole, did so successfully without giving too great offence to either party. Dr. Coffey was profoundly conservative in his beliefs ; he would not have understood the virtue of revolution, though he never was deliberately unkind to revolutionaries. He was not a man of obvious heroic stamp, and he sincerely would have found it difficult to see how a revolutionary attitude had any normal relevance for the difficult job he had been asked to undertake. He was, at the same time, a realist, and though prepared to support losing causes, would never have committed himself to a lost one. Under his administration therefore, the College came " round the corner." If it only narrowly survived, it did in fact survive.

The political struggle was, however, merely one problem out of many which the College authorities had to face. Ordinary academic life went on uninterrupted throughout the whole period. The main task of building was undertaken between 1912 and 1917, and the costs originally envisaged for the buildings in Earlsfort Terrace rapidly mounted. Those buildings were finished in 1919, and from that date practically all the College's work has been performed on its present site. In that year the President submitted a statement at a meeting of all the universities of the United Kingdom convened at the request of the President of the Board of Education and of the Chancellor of the Exchequer. Those universities also found themselves in a similarly difficult situation after 1918 because current, as well as capital, expenditure had moved suddenly upwards. In a section of the Report issued by a University Committee established by the British Government after 1922, it was stated :

" We have to face the unwelcome fact that the cost of providing University education has increased, is increasing and cannot be diminished ; and that for some years ahead all that can be expected from the State, from local authorities, and from private benefactors will be barely enough to keep the Universities we now possess on a reasonable scale."

The report then went on to note that since the War practically every item of a university's expenditure had increased, and although all their sources of income had risen by well over 100 per cent., there was little margin over for the many fresh developments that were needed. A strong passage followed :

" In our report four years ago we suggested that ' even the smaller multi-Faculty institutions of full university rank (by which we meant those providing Faculties of Arts, Pure Science, Medicine and Technology), need an income of not far short of £100,000 per annum, *if only pre-war activities are to be maintained.*' The experience which we have gained since the date of report has shown us that this was an under-statement. The capacity of organisations whose essence is spiritual cannot, of course, be satisfactorily measured by money standards . . . but if it is unwise to underestimate the power of genius to overcome limitations of equipment, it is no less foolish to ignore the extent to which, under modern conditions, material factors normally control the progress of university work ; and we think it should be recognised that if a university of the modern civic type with moderate-sized Faculties of Arts, Pure Science, Medicine and Technology is to be maintained at the level of efficiency demanded by the requirements of the present day, it will need an income of at least £150,000 a year."

Negotiations of the College (now separated from contact with British universities) with the Free State Government were not particularly satisfactory ; and instead of what (with the addition of fees) would make up the £150,000 a year mentioned in the British report as required for " moderate sized " universities, the total annual state endowment amounted to £52,000, an increase of £20,000. The President gave voice to his bitter disappointment in his Report for the year 1923.

The Irish Free State of course had to discharge its own heavy liabilities elsewhere ; and the problems arising out of the Civil War and the consequential damage rendered unlikely any over-generous treatment. The question was raised however by the College authorities whether the grant actually given was, in fact, sufficient to carry on even a modest programme. Before 1926 it was rarely possible to add new members to the staff. This was precisely the period of expansion in universities outside Ireland, where the departments of science were to receive considerable favour, and where allowance was also to be made for lessening of the teaching burdens upon members of all faculties, so as to enable them to give more time to research.

It is possible that financial considerations were not the only ones which determined the attitude of the State. The College at that time was not as popular as could have been desired, and the community was not sufficiently aware of the benefits it could give, and in fact was unobtrusively giving, to the new nation. It had not and has not yet become an *alma mater* in the minds of many of those who have been in it, and subsequently left it, although there were, and are, noticeable exceptions. In the first twenty years of the new State, College men were to contribute in no small degree to the building up of a new Ireland, and it is only in recent times that people have become aware of those services. One need only mention here, for example, a few of many cases : the Shannon Scheme, the Electricity Supply Board, the Turf Development Board, the various departments of the Civil Service, the judiciary, the bar, politics and, to a much lesser extent, commercial life. It would be only honest to admit that many of those who were educated in the College felt no sense of compelling responsibility towards the institution they had left behind ; and unlike comparable institutions in America or in Great Britain, the College has never received noteworthy assistance from successful men in commerce.

On the other hand, it would be wrong to expect private enterprise to solve all its problems ; for expenditure on the modern university can, in the last resort, be satisfactorily provided only by the community acting through the State. In any event, the chapter of service rendered to the nation in every form of life has been very considerable. And of course, if that service has not yet been universally recognised, the fault may not lie entirely with the outside world. University people, like others, are not notable for seeing the mote in their own eye. The failure of the College to develop a tradition extending to those who were formerly linked with it professionally is partly due to defects, some of which have been inherent and others perhaps not so unavoidable. On the other hand, its critics inclined to ignore, in the period under discussion, the obstacles which it had to face. Nothing succeeds like success, and a young College could hardly compete successfully with other colleges enjoying extensive endowments and a long tradition. Its demands and complaints were often to meet with cynical indifference. A great deal of this was due to the lack of personal intercourse between professors and lecturers on the one hand, and students on the other, and also to the absence of suitable accommodation in the form of a students' union, or of a College club, such as is possessed by many other modern and ancient universities.

At length however, in 1926, the Free State, by an act of imaginative generosity, introduced the Agriculture and Dairy Science (University Education) Act by which the College of Science and the Albert Agricultural College with their staffs were transferred to the College. The Act of 1926 established a new Faculty of General Agriculture, which continued mainly to operate on the farms and buildings at Glasnevin. The permanent income was now fixed at £82,000 a year, an addition of £30,000; and a further special grant of £25,000 was made in the same year to discharge a debt on the cost of College buildings erected during the war. By 1931, the total income had risen to £109,346, of which students' fees consisted of between one-fourth and one-fifth. The transfer of the College of Science buildings allowed for a considerable growth of student numbers which, though it did not immediately make itself felt, became very pressing after 1932. A period of transition occurred therefore between 1926 and 1930, and in that year, according to the President's Report, expenditure on teaching and maintenance had attained a definite character. It seemed as if the College was now once more satisfied with the provision made for it by the community. The estimate however was unduly optimistic ; for it had left out one important factor, namely the unexpected subsequent growth in the number of students, all of whom required a considerable subsidy from sources of revenue which the College itself could not provide.

After 1926, the political temper abated somewhat, and the relations between the government and the College were cordial until 1932. It was true however that fundamentally the same problem which had arisen between 1916 and 1922 was still present, namely the necessity of remaining on understanding terms, not merely with the State of the present, but also with any State or government which might arise to-morrow. The passion of civil war had divided the country ; it had not divided the College in the same way. Many College men had worked successfully with the government of 1922, and only a very small minority of senior College members sympathised with the opposition. The Chancellor of the university, however, Mr. Eamon de Valera, was the highest authority in the university. His election had taken place during the Truce in 1921, before the Treaty and the subsequent " split." It was no secret that certain members of the opposition resented what seemed to them to have been a one-sided political attitude on the part of the overwhelming majority of the staff between 1922 and 1932. Such a charge if based solely on the private political opinions of College administrators and teachers would be an absurd one ; the majority of the electorate were, after all, in favour of the pro-Treaty parties until 1932.

Mr. de Valera and his colleagues were perhaps not entirely indifferent to the fact that in the elections to Dáil Éireann for the Constituency of the National University, a majority of the voters favoured Cumann na nGaedheal ; and with the introduction of the new Constitution in 1937, university representation in the Dáil, abolished in 1934, was transferred to the Seanad, a legislative body possessing much less authority. The case against university representation has of course been accepted in other countries, and the Conservative government in Britain, for example, has not seen fit to repeal the Act abolishing university seats in the House of Commons. It is true that theoretical arguments may be advanced against the privileged position of universities in this respect; but College men felt, and possibly rightly so, that the previous record of the College (and the university) and the interpretation placed upon it by Fianna Fáil influenced to some extent at least that decision. It was one which affected Cork and Galway no less than Dublin; but its significance for University College, Dublin, was no less on that account. In some ways, perhaps, the College may have benefited; if it has lost a forum, it is now less involved in controversial struggles in that House where they might be most dangerous. And furthermore any resentment which was felt by Mr. de Valera's administration was modified in the course of time, and there is no doubt that University College is very appreciative of the favour and attention which his government—despite past history—was to give to its needs since the end of the war.

After the transfer of the College of Science in 1926, there ensued a long period of transition, which was to last until the end of the second World War, when the College found itself in an unsatisfactory position similar to that in which it had found itself between 1918 and 1922. As in the case of the first World War, numbers steadily increased during and after the second World War; by the session 1946–47 the total had reached 3,362. At the same time, expenditure on equipment and staffing had also grown, and the College finances had run into desperate straits. The annual deficit was becoming insupportable. Mr. de Valera's government responded to the appeal of the College and in 1947 agreed to pay off the outstanding deficit of £85,000 and also made an increase in the annual grant to cover additional expenditure on salaries which were then restored to something like their pre-war value. The annual endowment from the State had risen from £82,000 to £124,524 in 1948. This was in addition to the special annual endowment to the department of modern Irish.

These were considered to be only half measures ; they remedied immediate pressures, but did nothing to solve the long-term needs of an ever-expanding College, which had now become, in extent of its undertakings and in the number of its students and staff, far greater than any other College in the whole of Ireland. It was at this stage therefore, which coincided with the advent of Mr. Costello's government in 1948, that an approach was made by the College for a general solution of its long-term requirements. The question of future buildings and the provision of a much greater capital grant than ever before was raised. This also raised the new and revolutionary proposal of virtually a new College to be erected outside the city area ; and this in turn has stimulated speculation on the future relations of such a College with the other constituent members of the National University.

An interesting aspect of recent developments in the history of the College has been the introduction of extra-mural courses. These were founded in January, 1949, beginning with a course in social and economic studies, lasting two years, in which the following subjects were taken : social theory and social ethics, political theory, economic studies, national economics, public speaking and procedure at meetings, trade union history, local government, and general commercial studies. These classes are important in two respects : first, in that they attempt to give some of the benefits of higher education to people hitherto excluded from university courses ; and secondly in that they bring the College indirectly into contact with the trade unions which originally encouraged this idea. These courses were extended to the country, and provincial centres have been established in various localities such as Dundalk, Drogheda, Athlone, Mullingar, Carlow, Kilkenny and Wexford. Not all University men are equally enthusiastic about this new enterprise ; but then there is never agreement concerning important innovations. There are dangers, which do not require to be stressed here ; but every new venture is on its trial until it proves itself.

Furthermore, the part played by evening students in

degree courses has recently expanded greatly; and as a result of alterations in College policy, much greater facilities are being accorded to evening students to participate in higher education. Their commencement dates back to 1931 but they have been greatly extended since 1952. A different type of student from the day student is now entering the College, and teachers and civil servants in particular, who before the inauguration and development of evening B.A. classes had little opportunity to concern themselves with higher education, are now making use of precious opportunities. A few of the most prominent of University teachers and researchers in the English-speaking world have been evening class products; half-measures are rarely profitable and once undertaken the evening classes are likely to be developed as far as staffing permits. In this event the College may benefit from the presence of evening students as much as they will from contact with the College.

These developments affect the relationship of the College with the nation; they are developments also which have been almost universally accepted in British and American universities. Formerly colleges were the preserve of the aristocratic or the middle classes; they are now partly opening their gates to the working and poorer groups in society. This re-orientation is one which has been welcomed as an ideal; it remains to be seen if those who are pessimistic about the practice will be justified. In the opinion of the present writer, if the College is assisted by the nation in regard to buildings and staffing, extension and evening teaching may prove to be revolutionary steps in preparing the nation, and public opinion in all strata of society, to confront the complex social and intellectual problems of an age which, in itself, is more revolutionary than most of its predecessors.

One further point needs to be stressed, and that is the increasing awareness in commercial and trade circles of the advantages of contact with university and college education. In contrast with circumstances prevailing in Britain, business life and the College have rarely had close relations. There has been a distrust of College men on the part of the business community ; there is little personal and social contact between the College as a whole and distinguished servants of the State and society in other spheres. The benefits which academic and professional men can acquire from intercourse with each other are rarely recognised, and it is all the more to be welcomed therefore that, largely owing to the efforts of Mr. Lemass, Mr. Seán Leydon, Sir Charles Harvey and Professor George O'Brien, the Institute of Management was founded in 1952. This venture is one which, if successful, will substantially extend the benefits of university and academic education : it will also be of use to the College itself.

The recent report of an American medical inspection committee has emphasised the necessity of considerable expenditure on equipment and staff, if the country is to receive the medical service it needs, and if its sons and daughters who become doctors wish to receive employment overseas. What holds for the medical school, holds in some degree for most other departments. The whole business will be an expensive undertaking, and may have a serious bearing on the future finances of the State. It is a question however which cannot be ignored, if one wishes to have a university which maintains comparable standards with other universities. A price has to be paid for everything, and education is not, any more than anything else, to be bought cheaply. Ireland is not a country of great natural resources ; it cannot hope to compete with others in industrial enterprise, and one of the few fields in which it could give services of international value is that of education. And in this development, University College, Dublin, can certainly play a large part. What it needs from the community is not merely a need felt by itself alone ; the other constituent colleges of the National University also require proportionate, if smaller, relief. There is a common interest binding all the colleges and universities in Ireland on this question ; the community on the other hand, if it wishes to make use of its opportunities, will have to understand that need, and the State, acting as the agent of the community, bears a heavy responsibility for the initial action which would give the universities and colleges the opportunity to do what they should do. Only after they have been given that opportunity can they be legitimately criticised.

Professor Eoin MacNeill

PROSPECT FOR THE FUTURE

Professor George O'Brien

In the last hundred years, University College has undergone several transformations. It started as the Catholic University, passed through the period of association with the Royal University, and, finally became a Constituent College of the National University. Its new beginning in 1909 should be described as a reincarnation rather than a birth. It is to be hoped that in this reincarnation the spirit of the old bodies passed into the new one, and that the College of to-day possesses the merits and the virtues of its heroic ancestors. After a century of change, a position of stability appears to be reached. I shall assume, therefore, that the College will retain its identity and independence and will survive in its present form. I shall refrain from discussing its relations with other centres of higher education. I shall assume that two Universities will continue to exist in Dublin, working in friendly rivalry, but not, I hope, in cut-throat competition. I shall also assume that the National University will retain its present federal position in relation to the College. I shall discuss the future of the College as it is to-day ; not of any reincarnation that might follow its dissolution.

My connection with University College extends back over forty years. When I was an undergraduate, in the years 1910–12, the College was in its old home, 86 St. Stephen's Green. It had just emerged from the days of its Jesuit control. To students of my generation, it is easy to recapture the atmosphere depicted by James Joyce in his *Portrait of the Artist* and *Stephen Hero*. I had a number of professors who were all distinguished in their own way—Father Finlay, Tom Kettle, J. G. Swift-McNeill, Arthur Clery and James Murnaghan. The Literary and Historical Society was as vigorous in those days as it is now. Its members included many students who played an important part in the foundation and fortunes of the new independent Ireland. Its more sedate sister, the Legal and Economic Society, was, in some respects, an even greater nest of talent and nursery of statesmen. My active participation in the affairs of these societies taught me something about debating, more about politics and more still about human nature.

After a short career at the Bar, which was brought to a premature end by illness, I returned to the College as a professor. I owe my appointment to the great kindness of my friends, Dr. Coffey and Father Finlay, to whom I here wish to pay a tribute of gratitude and admiration. These were two of the leading personalities who moulded the College in its early days. Their influence was all for good. The College had by then moved to its present home in Earlsfort Terrace, which, though a notable monument to its gifted architect, Professor Butler, has never possessed for me the sentimental association and nostalgic atmosphere of " 86." I am always proud to have received my education in " Father Finlay's Tin University."

I owe a great deal of what I possess in life to my connection with University College. As a student, it gave me my professional and liberal education, and prepared me, by lectures, reading and debating, to fight the battle of life. As a professor, it has given me an income, a status and an entry into an inconspicuous but agreeable political career. But what I value more than any of these is the large number of friends of all ages that I have made in the College. The outstanding value of university education, the intercourse of ideas between people of different generations, is essentially a two-way traffic. I may not have taught my students very much of value, but I have certainly learned a great deal of value in return. I would like to take this opportunity of putting on record my high regard for the students of the College. In my long teaching career I cannot recollect ever having experienced a single example of studied bad manners or deliberate misconduct. I am conscious of not having given an adequate return to the College for all my indebtedness. But, however short

I may have fallen in service, I have never been deficient in loyalty or in gratitude.

In the last forty years the College has grown at an extraordinary rate. The growth of accommodation has been obviously entirely disproportionate to the number of students. At the present time, the College is short of classrooms, laboratories, hostels, libraries, amenities and every sort of accommodation. Overcrowding is its great problem.

Although the percentage of the Irish population receiving university education is less than that in many other countries, it seems reasonable to assume that the period of rapid expansion is coming to an end. It is not necessary to discuss the interesting question whether there is an optimum level of university education in a country. This discussion would involve many difficult problems. What should determine the optimum number of students ? Should it be decided by the numbers who could pay for university education out of their own resources ? This would lead to the waste of considerable ability. Or should it be decided by the number of young people who could pass a competitive entrance examination ? This would give rise to difficult questions of selection in the schools. Or should it be decided by considering how many people could benefit from higher education ? This would involve even more difficult problems of selection. Should the criterion be the estimated future demand for graduates in the professions and other walks of life ? This problem is complicated by the growing professionalisation of many activities, the spread of the field in which graduates are employed, and the large number of graduates who are inevitably exported.

It might further be queried whether the decision regarding the numbers in the universities should be decided by the universities, who have the responsibility of teaching the students, or by the government, which has part of the responsibility of paying for their education. These are far-reaching political problems which it is unnecessary to discuss in the present context. The fact is that the number of students in University College will depend in

the future, as in the past, on the inter-play of the forces of
demand and supply for higher education, moulded partly
on the pattern of income distribution, partly on the opportunities for finding employment, and partly on changes in
government policy.

Looking to the future, it seems safe to predict that the
growth of the College cannot continue at the same rate
as in the past. The population of the country is stationary
and the proportion enjoying whole-time university
education has probably reached its maximum, or at least
its normal level. Any increase in numbers will take the
form of additional evening and extra-mural students, who
do not put such pressure on accommodation as day students.
This gives the College authorities a breathing space to
take stock of their present and future needs. The first
thing is to overtake arrears and to provide the essential
minimum of service for the present student body. The most
pressing and urgent need is an increase in the teaching
staff. The great increase in the numbers of morning and
evening students, and of students seeking diplomas of new
types, has imposed a very heavy burden on the existing
staff. Not only is there a need for more professors and
lecturers, but also for more tutors.

The successful recruitment of additional staff will not
be possible unless salaries are raised to a satisfactory level.
At present the competition of industrial and commercial
employment is tempting some of the best graduates away
from academic life. This is a process which will have
cumulative adverse reactions on the whole standard of
university education if it is allowed to proceed uncorrected.
Inadequate levels of pay injure the efficiency of the College,
not only by failing to attract some of the most desirable
applicants for posts, but by distracting the attention of
teachers from study and research by financial worries
and by driving them to seek supplementary sources of
income. Parsimony in university salaries can prove a
very expensive false economy to the whole community.

A longer view of the future opens the prospect of a great
building programme. That the College requires additional

buildings is common ground amongst all political parties. In a recent debate in Dáil Éireann, this principle received unanimous agreement from all parties in the House. It may, therefore, be assumed that, whatever site is chosen for the new buildings, a great programme of construction will be embarked on in the not too distant future. It is to be hoped that the best traditions of Irish architecture and building will be followed on this unique occasion ; and that the great example of the rulers of Ireland in the eighteenth century will be worthily followed. A noble building will not only adorn the city, but will inspire pride and high ideals in future generations of students.

The building of the necessary accommodation for the College will be a lengthy operation. Even if the new College is situated beyond Donnybrook, the move from the present buildings will be gradual and spread over many years. It is to be hoped that the houses in Stephen's Green will never be abandoned. They contain the historic roots of the College and have many associations of great traditional value. There will always remain a need for some premises in the centre of the city, for extra-mural courses for example. Newman House would make a magnificent Graduates' Club if it was no longer required for its present use. Moreover, it is overwhelmingly desirable, on grounds of sentiment and historical continuity, that some link should bind the College with Newman's beautiful church.

Whatever building programme is attempted, the first concern of the College authorities must be with the nature of the education provided. A great university depends on the quality of its students and its professors more than on its buildings. The College has itself been a remarkable illustration of the triumph of mind over matter. It is much more important to provide good education in bad buildings than bad education in good ones. In discussing what the aims of education in the future should be, the College should never forget the teaching and example of Newman, whose spirit should always inspire its teachers and their disciples. To strike a personal note, my own

life has been influenced by Newman more than by any
other writer or thinker. He has coloured my outlook on
religion, on teaching, on social affairs, on literature and
on art. I have always felt that his spirit has haunted the
precincts of Newman House. His beautiful bust in
University Church is symbolic of his tutorship and care
over the College. If he could return to the scene of his
labour, he would be gratified to find so noble a tree sprung
from the delicate roots which he tended with such anxiety,
such disappointment, such hope and such love.

Even if the background of university life to-day renders
inapplicable some of Newman's practical suggestions, the
spirit of his approach to education should be cherished
and preserved. The very stress of professionalism to-day
makes it all the more urgent that we should live up to the
great classical tradition of liberal culture which he constantly preached. We should always regard it as our aim
to give a good general education rather than to produce
experts. The primary function of the College is to impart
a liberal education to its students. It is less concerned
with the production of technically trained graduates than
with that of men whose minds are so developed and flexible
that they will readily adapt themselves to the needs of
any specialised career. Even in the professional faculties
a liberal bias must be given to education. The aim of the
College is not to provide more technicians but to turn out
highly educated men with expert qualifications in different
professions. University education should be directed to
produce, not narrow specialists or pedants, but men of
affairs possessing special knowledge in particular fields.
The characteristic product of the best university education
is an attitude of mind, a point of view, an outlook on
life.

We should never lose sight of the fact that the duty of
the College is to raise moral and aesthetic standards as
well as to impart mere intellectual erudition. In this
matter, the role of the societies, clubs and other places
where students meet and discuss matters with one another
is very important. Education is largely a matter of con-

versation between students and professors and between students themselves. Newman's motto " Cor ad cor loquitur " should be ever borne in mind. University College has always suffered from the lack of residential facilities. This is one aspect of its acute shortage of accommodation in general. It is the intention that the new College, wherever it is situated, will contain halls of residence where the students can live, dine, and converse. This will help to realise Newman's idea of the College as distinct from the University, as the place where morals and manners are taught to the younger generation. It is probable that the religious Orders will be invited to erect hostels on sites provided by the College. The present hostels in the city have done excellent work and have proved of the greatest service to the students living in them. There is no reason why this precedent should not continue to be followed in the future.

The preoccupation with examinations and the intensity of competition for honours contain dangers for Newman's conception of university education. It is too much to hope for a return of the leisured conditions of the past, but at least the ideal of an all-round, cultivated, intellectual and moral development should be kept in mind in a period of growing pressure on time and resources. One new feature that has come into College life gives rise to some apprehension. The practice of students taking outside work during their vacation has an adverse effect on their examination work. With the rising standards in all examinations, the time during the vacation is essential for reading and study. The popular notion that vacations are synonymous with holidays and are therefore a time for idleness is entirely unwarranted. Both the staffs and the students of universities do very valuable work in the intervals between terms which are too much occupied with lectures and other activities to permit of continuous study. A student's university career should be regarded as a continuous whole, divided into periods of lectures and periods of reading.

If the financial pressure of modern times drives students

to supplement their income by working at non-academic tasks during the vacation, some effort should be made to increase grants to enable them to avoid this distraction. If the public subvention given to poor students is insufficient to provide them with leisure during their vacation, it is fulfilling only part of its function. Modern university education is causing many psychological problems owing to the high competitive standard of examinations. Students require all their physical and nervous energy for academic work. Work during the vacation induces fatigue, which greatly undermines the student's working capacity during the remainder of the year. This new custom, if not remedied by higher scholarship grants, will result in a lowering of standards and a waste of potential ability. Of course, the ideal of a general, liberal education, based on reading, thought and conversation, will utterly perish.

Many of the proposals which have been made above require the expenditure of more money. University education, like everything else, is becoming more expensive. The additional funds required to make it efficient cannot be expected to come from the students or their parents. It is perhaps not too much to hope that graduates may provide some financial assistance for the College, as is done on a large scale in the United States. But the greater part of the money required must be provided by the government. The case for the public endowment of higher education is universally recognised to-day. Its justification is not the benefit enjoyed by the students who receive degrees, but the benefit enjoyed by the country as a whole which needs professional and technical experts and still more, educated leaders of public opinion. Without our professional schools, Ireland could not have progressed as it has done in the last thirty years. All the learned professions, the civil service and many of the new public bodies have been recruited from the ranks of our graduates. The education of this professional class will still remain an important function of the College. Indeed, many pursuits are now becoming professionalised and are employing university-trained men. Examples are primary and secondary education.

The shortage of trained and qualified teachers in the primary schools is a matter of concern to-day. These schools require smaller classes and larger staffs. Many experts in education are of opinion that the present method of training teachers in training colleges requires revision and that university graduates would be better teachers. The whole question of the training of primary teachers is due for consideration. It should probably combine university and professional training. Meanwhile, it appears foolish that the schools should be short of teachers, while well-educated graduates are short of employment. Where no trained teacher is available, graduates might be experimentally employed in primary schools. This step would kill two birds with one stone : it would make up the deficiency in teachers and would provide employment for some graduates. The presence of graduates in the primary schools might succeed in spreading the climate of university thought among school-children and thereby diffusing liberal education over a very wide area. The influence of University College need not be confined to its own students. It could colour and inform the intellectual outlook of the whole community.

In other countries, a great many university graduates are employed in business. With so many more able children going to the universities than in the past, the fund of talent available outside the universities is narrowing. Keen business men are therefore seeking ability where it may be expected to be found. Irish business, while employing more graduates than it did, is comparatively backward in this respect. A new science of business administration has grown up in recent years. The Irish Management Institute is actively exploring the possibility of co-operation between Irish business and the universities. University College has taken an active part in the affairs of this Institute since its foundation. The College has provided accommodation for the meetings of the Institute and has also invited lecturers to deliver public lectures on business subjects. The curriculum in the Commerce Faculty is being moulded with conscious regard to the requirements of business in the modern age. While the technical education of businessmen is not a matter for the university, the education of men apt and suitable for the higher levels of business is clearly within its scope. A distinction has been drawn between the education of managers and education for management. The latter, not the former, has been conceived as the proper province of the Faculty of Commerce. It is right to state that the College has received much encouragement and co-operation from the leaders of Irish businesses and public utilities since the incorporation of the Institute. The prospects in this field are distinctly bright.

At the same time much remains to be done to enlighten employers about the value of higher education. If businessmen applied as much study to the selection of their staffs as they do to the sale of their products they would reap a rich reward. It is one of the duties of the Appointments Bureau connected with the College to build up a new demand for graduates by providing enlightenment on this subject. The College could also provide a certain amount of vocational guidance for under-graduates. At present many students go through their College career without a clear notion of where it is taking them. The older professions are becoming overcrowded and may become even more overcrowded in the future. It is a matter of urgent importance to divert undergraduates away from the falling markets into the rising markets and untilled fields. At the same time it must be emphasised that the College is not a labour-exchange or an employment bureau. Its primary function is to teach its students, not to find careers for them. In this matter, graduates could do much to help each other. It is to be hoped that the organisation of graduates now being formed will act as a means of opening new careers to its members. Another method of helping in this matter would be the formation of a Graduates' Club, which might become a centre of great influence.

When everything has been done to satisfy the needs of the Irish market for graduates, the College may still find itself producing an export surplus. The question whether our graduates should seek employment abroad has received considerable attention in recent years. This question is part of the general problem of the effects of emigration. Everybody is familiar to-day with the argument about the evil effects of investing large sums in the education of people who will add nothing to the national income of the country. This argument has a special application to university graduates, because their education is more expensive than that of other classes of the community. It must be conceded that the home employment of our graduates is much to be preferred to their export. But, at the same time, a certain amount of export may be a necessary condition for the successful supply of the home demand. Furthermore, the reputation of the College has been greatly enhanced by the valuable work done by its graduates in other countries. The Irish people have at all times performed a certain missionary task. The cosmopolitan associations resulting from the emigration of our graduates should strengthen rather than weaken the national tone of the College. A narrow isolationist outlook is inconsistent with the liberal tradition of university education. The far-flung connections arising from the export of our graduates has enormously increased the influence and reputation of the College in the world.

The fact that a number of our graduates emigrate is sometimes used as an argument against the provision of public money for the College. The same argument could, if correct, be used against the provision of public money for primary and secondary education. A large number of children from all sections of the population are fated to go abroad. If it is correct to argue that such children should not be educated at the public expense, the case for the present expenditure on primary and secondary education would be considerably weakened. Indeed, the argument might be pushed further. The expenditure of money on children's allowances, maternity hospitals, school meals and all the public health services could be impugned on the ground that part of it is subsidising emigration. In other words, the question of the emigration of university graduates is one aspect of the general question of emigration. It is impossible to argue that the College should be deprived of its public grants on this account, without advocating a similar deprivation for maternity and children's hospitals and primary schools. In both cases, the proper line of approach is to attempt to build up employment at home. In the case of graduates, this involves a widening of the field of the professions and the acceptance of the principle that graduates are a very good investment in businesses of all kinds. The establishment of this principle rests largely on the reputation of the graduates already employed, who, therefore, have a heavy load of responsibility on their shoulders. Every graduate who lowers the reputation of university education is narrowing the market for younger graduates and is encouraging their emigration through their failure to find employment in Ireland.

It has also been argued that the presence of foreign students reduces the justification for the expenditure of public money on university education. The number of students in the College whose domiciliary origin is outside Ireland is a very small fraction of the whole, far less than that of the British universities. Moreover, many of these students are the descendants of Irish emigrants of the first or second generation. In fact, a certain distinction is made between Irish and foreign students, with the object of ensuring that, as far as possible, foreigners receive less public assistance than natives. But this distinction could not be carried to the extent of completely excluding foreigners. The spirit of university education is essentially cosmopolitan. The great medieval universities used to draw their students from all over Europe. A spirit of isolationism is fatal to liberal education. Our students derive great advantage from associating with students from other countries, who bring new ideas and fresh points of view into debates and discussions. In my own experience,

I have seen the good effects on my students of the presence in their midst of young foreigners with a different background and outlook. Newman's ideal for the Catholic University was that it should provide a meeting-ground for English-speaking Catholics from all parts of the world. This remains a more worthy ideal of policy than the narrow nationalistic ideal of restricting our education to Irish citizens.

These questions of public policy in regard to university education have become more urgent with the growth of university grants in recent years. The proportion of the total income of universities in all other countries to-day coming from public sources is continuously increasing. This is a sign of the times. Art, culture and learning are coming to depend less and less on private patrons and more and more on the public purse. The high direct taxation, the policy of equalising wealth and the provision of subsidised university education, are all factors operating in this direction. At the same time, the cost of running the College is rapidly rising. The recent American report on Irish medical schools has drawn attention to the very expensive requirements of modern medical education. This is equally true of all the natural sciences. In physics, chemistry and the allied subjects, considerable expenditure is needed on equipment and raw materials, if teaching and research are to conform to modern requirements. In every faculty, salaries are increasing to keep abreast of rising levels in other professions. The cost of buildings, upkeep, administration and labour are all rising. Universities, like everybody else, are finding it hard to make ends meet.

Students are becoming less self-supporting than in earlier times. The field from which they are drawn has greatly widened. Education is no longer the privilege of the rich. In University College a proportion of students receive assistance from county councils and other public bodies. In 1952–53, 223 students were county scholars, subsidised by 31 county councils. The extra-mural courses are partly paid for by trade unions. This widening of the scope of university education is strictly in accordance with the tradition of the great medieval universities. It is also in sympathy with Newman's ideal. The Catholic University attempted to give many extension lectures to working men. The diffusion of culture and science over large numbers, even in a weak solution, must raise the respect for learning in the community and will act as a stabilising influence in an unsettled age. But these facilities all cost money, and, in an age when rich patrons are no longer to be found, the public purse is the only source of the necessary expenditure. The time is approaching when the universities will be regarded as part of the social services to be provided for in the Budget.

When so much public money is being spent on university education, it is a matter of urgent importance that expenditure should be as beneficial to the community as possible. It is essential that the very best type of student should receive whatever public money is available for subsidising whole-time higher education. Whether the present method of selection gives the best results is doubtful. Researches recently carried on in other countries have shown that universities are better judges of suitable candidates for scholarships than public authorities. The time has arrived for an inquiry whether the present system of selection by local authorities is the best in modern Irish conditions. There is no reason to believe that ability is spread evenly throughout the population or that different counties possess the same proportion of children calculated to profit by subsidised higher education. Without prejudging the issue, it may be suggested that the central government should provide the necessary funds for free places in the universities and that the universities should choose the beneficiaries. This would probably ensure a greater national benefit than the present method of selection.

The justification for this public expenditure is very easy to make. University education benefits not only the students who receive it but the nation as a whole. Our greatest natural resource is the ability of our people. The Irish people, in particular, have always shown an aptitude and a taste for learning. The development of their great native ability is the best investment possible for public money. On the lowest material plane, such investment will pay a rich dividend ; but society will gain many indirect benefits, in the social, moral, political and cultural spheres, from the spread of university education. The development of such education, however, requires great expenditure to-day. The College has, from the beginning, been under-endowed. Its early years have coincided with a period of great political disturbance at home and abroad. It has never had the experience of living in normal or stable times. In comparison with other countries, for example Great Britain, the amount spent in Ireland on university education is remarkably small. There is an unanswerable case for a great increase in university endowments.

An increase in the sums devoted to university education would assist scientific and technical progress, and ultimately the efficiency of agriculture and industry. The most progressive countries have been those that have provided the greatest amount of financial assistance for their universities. The first function and duty of universities is teaching. But the line between teaching and research is not very clear-cut and defined. The two activities are frequently inextricably connected and are, indeed, complementary. The endowment of universities can, therefore, be justified on the ground that it encourages not only teaching but also research. The possibility of conducting research may enable the universities to play their proper part in important national work of economic and social development. The successful pursuit of such activities depends upon the capacity to take long views. It would be desirable if the provision of university endowments could be put on a permanent basis and removed from the annual estimates. Fruitful research requires considerable investment in equipment and staff that needs financial security over a prolonged period.

A great many Irish problems have suffered from a lack of organised research in the past. This is largely the result of historical reasons, into which it is unnecessary to enter.

There is no excuse for the lack of facilities for such research to-day. At present, public money is being spent on institutions outside the universities, to endow research into cultural and scientific matters which could be as competently and more cheaply conducted inside the universities. The line between pure and applied research is hard to draw—if, indeed, it exists. The great technical advances of recent years have had their roots in pure research in university laboratories, of which the practical applications were not foreseen. The advance of technical improvements can be safely entrusted to the initiative of progressive industries. But scientific research, not calculated to produce any direct industrial gain, must be conducted in academic institutions. The most suitable academic institutions are the universities.

The provision of public money for research in the universities would link up research and teaching, whereas at present these two naturally related functions are to some extent divorced. The endowment of research in the universities would enable some members of the staffs to enjoy greater leisure from teaching duties than they do at present, with benefit to themselves, their students and their subject. One development greatly to be desired is the publication of a learned scientific periodical under the auspices of the College. The establishment of a University Press is long overdue. The prestige of the College would be greatly enhanced by the existence of such a Journal and such a Press, which would encourage research by facilitating publication.

Before governments can increase university endowments, public opinion must, in a democratic age, be convinced of their utility. The creation of this public opinion is, to some extent, within our own powers. Reference has already been made to the part played by our graduates in the professions and public services. It is to be regretted that more of them do not take part in political life, in the framing rather than the administration of policy. University College possesses a great responsibility towards the Irish nation. It represents the confluence of two great struggles

Dr. A. W. Conway
President, University College, Dublin
1940–1947

—the struggle for political freedom and the struggle for the higher education of Catholics. Now that these two struggles are successfully over, at least for the greater part of Ireland, the College must make use of its position to help the nation. It must attempt to permeate public opinion with correct values on political affairs. In order to do so, its graduates must mix freely in public life. The presence of three representatives in the Senate, while a recognition of the national importance of the University, is not an adequate representation of higher education in the legislature. It is to be hoped that graduates will be encouraged to play a larger part in the future than they have done in the past in politics and in the newspaper and broadcasting worlds. Irish political leaders, editors and Radio Éireann have a duty to the University and to the public in this respect. It is through channels such as these that the College can play its full and proper part in the public life of the country.

The growing dependence of universities on public funds has in other countries begun to threaten the principle of academic freedom. It is only right to state that in Ireland this principle has been scrupulously respected by all governments since the Treaty. At the same time, there is a strong argument in favour of the appointment of a University Grants Committee on the British model, which would take the finance of university education completely out of party politics. However, there has been so far, no threat to our freedom. Any invasion of our independence must be strenuously resisted. Even such apparently harmless innovations as grants earmarked for special types of teaching or research must be viewed with vigilant suspicion. Our limited experience of earmarked grants has not increased our desire for this type of endowment. No more Trojan horses must be allowed to enter our gates.

On our side, that freedom must not be abused. Academic freedom will not survive unless public opinion supports it ; and public opinion will not support it unless the universities deserve that support. Universities have duties as well as rights. They must live up to their principles of unbiassed

14

search for truth and disinterested love of knowledge. It
is the duty of professors to refrain from using their position
to advance the cause of any political party, clique, or sect.
Universities should preserve an attitude of neutrality on
political controversies unless fundamental moral issues
are at stake. The climate or tone of lectures must be
calculated not to wound or offend any sections of the
audience. It must be remembered that the students of
the College are drawn from every class, creed and party.
It would be a gross abuse of academic freedom to tread
on the corns of any student. The professor's duty is to
teach his students to think along right lines. If he conveys
the correct premises, his students can be trusted to arrive
at the correct conclusion. A great deal can be done by
suggestion. A large number of assumptions can be taken
for granted. On matters of ultimate values, all the students
in the College may be assumed to be in agreement. Words
are generally understood in the same sense by the teachers
and students, who, in essentials, speak the same language.
It must never be forgotten that education is not confined
to the lecture room and the examination hall. Professors
can influence their students to a large extent by good
example in such matters as toleration, punctuality and
good manners.

The College must face the future with pride in its own
achievement. It has made remarkable progress in a short
period, in spite of inadequate endowments, buildings and
staff. We must never allow ourselves to develop an
inferiority complex. We are not a provincial, but a national
College. We draw our students from every county in
Ireland and from many Irish families living in other parts
of the world. We are not sectarian, intolerant or narrow.
We derive our tradition from the Catholic liberal outlook
of Newman, whose ambition it was to provide higher
education in Dublin for Catholics from all nations. We
have our roots in the perennial Irish love of learning and
in the desire of the Irish people to possess a university of
their own not copied from alien models or animated by
antipathetic ideals. We must make use of our newly

found freedom to foster that combination of Catholic
culture and democratic liberalism which is the peculiar
contribution of Ireland to politics in the world to-day.
The College should attempt to reflect what is best in the
nation and to enrich it in its reflection.

APPENDIX

THE NEWMAN HERITAGE

The Catholic University of Ireland, 1854–1883 [1]

This year we commemorate the opening, exactly a century ago, of the Catholic University of Ireland. The particular moment was fixed, as we shall see, almost by accident; but it was an inevitable necessity that brought the University into being. In their struggle towards equality with their Protestant fellow-countrymen, Irish Catholics had a long way to go. If we take the medical profession in Dublin at this date, we find that of 111 doctors in situations of trust and authority, 99 were Protestant and only 12 Catholic. Catholics had to gain access to the education that would fit them for leadership. If the State did not found a university suitable for them, they must sooner or later try to found one themselves.

Ireland already had one university, Trinity College, ancient and illustrious. Catholics had for long been excluded from it. They were now allowed to enter and graduate, and a few did so. But as the need of university education for Catholics became greater, it could not be met by a College Protestant in constitution and atmosphere, in which Catholics could hold neither scholarship nor office.

Clearly, there must be another university. But it was not yet our most pressing need. Nothing might have been done about it for a long time if Sir R. Peel had not come forward in 1845 with the offer of a university to Ireland. It was to be a new kind of university, the first trial of the secular and utilitarian theory of education. The Queen's University, with Colleges in Belfast, Cork, and Galway, was undenominational, and it was closely controlled by the State, the Professors being in effect Civil Servants. The country hesitated; the terms were peculiar, but a great deal was offered. Young Irelanders welcomed a scheme that would bring together Irishmen of all religions. O'Connell was hostile. In 1850 the new Colleges were condemned by the Church. Would these Colleges, if they had been accepted, have taken on a local character as the undenominational Colleges of the National University did later? Certainly they would not have done this quickly; perhaps only very slowly and very partially. For the Queen's Colleges were not autonomous. They had not Governing Bodies with local representation. They must be as Dublin Castle determined; and it was significant that among the 60 Professors nominated there were only 7 Catholics. Hardly thus would educational ascendancy be terminated.

[1] A broadcast talk from Radio Éireann on 25th April, 1954.

Condemned by the Church, the Cork and Galway Colleges failed miserably; while that in Belfast, scarcely more successful at first, eventually prospered.

The Queen's University was the immediate cause of the foundation of the Catholic University. Forbidding their people to use the new Colleges, the Bishops desired to offer an alternative. There was an encouraging example before them. Belgian Catholics had founded their University of Louvain in 1835, and already it was successful and marked for permanency. The idea of doing the same here may have originated in Rome, perhaps with Pope Pius IX himself. Certain it is that Rome and Ireland were at one on the matter. Planning began in 1850. And then occurred something very striking. Against the sombre, perplexed background of our mid-nineteenth-century history we witness, and its effect is enhanced by the contrast, a bold and brilliant decision. Our Bishops invited an Englishman, unconnected with Ireland, and not long a Catholic, to lead the enterprise. Not less bold and generous was John Henry Newman's acceptance; his readiness to bestow some of his best years on a backward country, to which he owed nothing. But there was a great link between the parties—their Catholicism, and their concern for Catholic education.

Newman's opening move was to settle in his own mind and convey to the Irish public the *idea* of the university he hoped to found. People were puzzled about these matters, and Irish Catholics were more puzzled than anyone else; they had never had a university and now they were offered two at the same time. Some leaders of contemporary opinion held that universities went out of date at the invention of printing. Others said that universities were required, but they must be strictly modern and useful, schools of science and technology. Others thought that the ancient ways of Oxford and Cambridge were the right ways and needed no reform; a university meant classical literature and a pleasant social life. Some stood for the new London idea; no social life, no teaching even, but good stiff examinations and degrees for all who passed them. Who was right?

Newman set forth his philosophy and programme of university education in the *Discourses*, of which five were delivered in the Rotunda in 1852, and in the *Sketches* written later for his *University Gazette*. These treatises, large, luminous, cogent, summed up the great traditions of European learning, making them available first for our Dublin venture and then for anyone in any country who has to legislate for a university. Newman held that the prime function of a university was to train the intellect. The medium should be literature, including poetry, philosophy, and history. The method should be oral and social, the close and vital contact of the student with men of mature intellect. He found most but not all of what was required in his own Oxford; other features he took from Louvain. Oxford, he thought, had overdone the tutorial system, in which the teacher descends to the learner's level, and neglected the professorial method, in which a master expounds his subject at the highest level, to which his audience must try to rise. Newman insisted on having professors in Dublin, adding tutors as he could afford them. In other ways, Oxford had become superstitiously conservative. Newman, though rejecting modern notions of a university as a treadmill or a technical school, wanted his university to be modern, believing that the way to preserve the great tradition was to adapt it to present use. He set up Chairs of modern literature, English, French, Italian, Spanish. Seeing the importance of science, he had Chairs of Physics and Chemistry. Further, though he held the Arts to be the core of the university, and designed a two years' Arts course for all students, he believed that a university must prepare students for the learned professions—not only of Medicine and Law, but also of Engineering and Architecture.

A vital question of course was, in what way was the University to be Catholic ? Newman did not wish it to be a seminary. To train men for the world, the University must put before them, fully and frankly, the world's image in literature. The Church, he thought, should exert her influence on the University chiefly in two ways. First by insisting on the presence and primacy, among the sciences taught, of Theology ; and secondly, by attending to the moral and religious life of the students in residential halls and colleges. It went without saying that the professors in a Catholic University should be Catholics. Except for the theological chairs, Newman selected all laymen.

From early in 1854 until the end of 1857—three and a half years— Newman was here continuously, working out his programme. He was installed as Rector on 4th June 1854, and on 3rd November lectures began in 86 St. Stephen's Green.

Meanwhile, he had picked his staff—26 professors and lecturers, 20 being Irish, 4 English, 2 continental. Let us glance at some of these. For Greek and Latin there were Englishmen, James Stewart and Robert Ornsby. These two, like all Newman's Englishmen, fitted in well with their Irish colleagues ; they remained here all their lives, becoming eventually Fellows of the Royal. A later comer was Thomas Arnold, brother of Matthew Arnold the poet and critic. He was a notable pioneer of English as a university subject—mapping out its vast, untamed field for undergraduate study. Our elders remember him and call him Tommy Arnold—for having left Dublin and the Church he returned to both, and was a professor in the old University College. Remarkable too was Pollen, Professor of Architecture, and architect of the University Church.

Of the Irish, the most outstanding were W. K. Sullivan and Eugene O'Curry. Sullivan, a Young Irelander, was Professor of Chemistry. He was a man of great ability. Newman owed him much, especially in the vital undertaking of the Medical School : " his views were large and bold," says Newman, " and I cordially embraced them." Eugene O'Curry had been a copyist, cataloguer, and servant of other men's scholarly labours when Newman—and this alone would prove his quality as a university administrator—made him a professor. Newman did more for him. He persuaded the humble man that he really could lecture, and attended the lectures himself; and had a fount of Irish type cut for the University to publish the lectures—the famous *Lectures on the Manuscript Materials of Irish History*—in worthy form. This was the first Chair of Irish Antiquities ever set up in a university.

I cannot name the whole staff. All were good. It was a real university staff. With such men forming a society and publicly expounding their subjects, though other things might be lacking and students be few, it could be said that the University was in being. " We *have* a Catholic University," declares the *Gazette* in one of its early numbers. There would be no going back; and as the University was good in itself and necessary to the country, students would eventually come.

It should be said that, at first, Newman had thought of the University as one that could hardly have lacked students—a university seated in Dublin, but designed for the whole Catholic English-speaking world. He had suggested Wiseman and Manning as Chancellor and Vice-Chancellor. There were many distinguished men among the English Catholics who might have come over as professors. And there were at that time more potential students for the University in England than here. If it had been so organised, a good deal of English wealth might have come to its aid. Newman never thought of the University as a purely or even mainly English institution planted on Irish soil. But he did think that his own people might have a larger part in it than they eventually had. When it became clear that the Bishops were not prepared to take greater risks for a greater possible success, and that the University must be almost wholly Irish, Newman did not complain.

An Irish Catholic University could not at that time expect large numbers. Peel's action had obliged the Bishops to move too early. Our schools had not so developed that they could provide the students; not yet had they taken the tonic of the Intermediate system. The Catholic middle class had hardly begun to see the meaning and value of higher education; and as the University could not give degrees a material incentive was lacking.

But Newman saw that the hesitation was temporary. Ireland needed the University, though she was slow to make use of it. As things were, he said " the supply must come before the demand, though not before the need." He saw that a social revolution was in progress, in which the University had a part to play. " The old names of the Irish race," he said, " are mounting up into status and power." " We consider the Catholic University to be the event of the day in this gradual majestic resurrection of the nation and its religion." Dimly, he seems to foretell the mass movement of students to the Colleges of the National University which heralded the formation of the Ireland we now live in.

The Catholic University opened on 3rd November 1854. On Sunday 5th the Rector gave a *soirée* to introduce the students to their academical career. There were fifteen of them. The Rector addressed them, telling them—as our President now tells seventy times as many—what they had come to a university for : to prepare for various professions and pursuits, but also for something more important—to become educated men, capable of self-dependence, and valuable to society. Their fewness, he said, did not dismay him ; it would contrast happily with the magnitude of the future. He recalled Shakespeare's Henry V, declaring on the eve of battle that he wished his soldiers fewer rather than more :

> " The fewer men, the greater share of honour.
> God's will ! I pray thee, wish not one man more.
> Rather proclaim it, Westmoreland, through our host,
> That he which hath no stomach to this fight
> Let him depart ; . . .
> He that shall live this day, and see old age,
> Will yearly on the vigil feast his neighbours . . .
> . . . we shall be remembered,
> We few, we happy few, we band of brothers."

After the Rector's " beautiful and moving address," says the *Gazette*, " the youthful academics separated, highly delighted with their first evening in College."—Alas, the great future was distant indeed ; any of the little band who were to see the University well established must live to a ripe old age.—But I should not have left the " youthful academics " without giving the outline of the routine upon which they had entered. " The course of an Intern Student's day," the *Gazette* tells us, " is as follows : Morning Prayer ; breakfast ; professors' lectures ; exercise and dinner ; presence indoors at dusk ; and sometimes lectures in the evening. He attends the University Mass on Sundays and other days of obligation, and such devotions as the Dean of his House appoints for him ; and is expected to frequent the Sacraments."

The Arts students soon rose to 50 or 60, and, except in one year of which I shall be speaking, never got much beyond that. The Evening students rose to 179, from which they slowly declined. Science never got going, except as part of the Medical course ; neither did Engineering ; nor did Law, for the courses of an unrecognised university were of no help towards a professional qualification. The solid success was Medicine. Here the lack of degrees hardly mattered, as some of the chartered bodies accepted our courses. Medical numbers rose steadily year by year.

I have not touched on the question how the University was financed, but it is important. Not out of public funds, of course ; not out of the donations of wealthy benefactors ; not out of fees, which brought in little. The University was paid for by the shillings and pence of the poor. Irish exiles in America and England gave valuable help, especially at first. But most of the money was collected at the church doors, annually on the third Sunday of November ; the amount varied between £5,000 and £10,000. It is a thing of strange contrasts, this Catholic University. On one side you have the eloquence of Newman, the fine flower of English aristocratic culture, setting forth the perfect idea of a university ; on the other you have the devotion and self-sacrifice of a people struggling out of misery, and scarcely knowing what a university was. It is hard to say which was the more sublime.

Newman left us for good in November 1858. He had given the University such a start as no other man could ; a magnificent plan and a working model of that plan, though on a small scale. He could hardly have done much more by staying longer ; and the seven years he had promised us were concluded.

People read of the Catholic University in Newman's biographies, where its later history is not told. He covered it with brilliant light for a few years ; then it seems to sink into darkness. The biographers even suggest that it petered out in total failure. But what really replaced the transcendent illumination of Newman was not darkness, it was the drab, uncertain dawnlight of the Irish nineteenth century. And his beautiful, dexterous mastery of plan and execution were replaced, not by inertia, but by the uncertain, clumsy, yet persistent advance of our national revival.

Newman's departure was a definite check. The University continued, but people wondered for how long. The Bishops hesitated, and did not fill the rectorship for two and a half years. The cost to the people of an institution that gave little immediate return was a serious consideration. At the start, the Bishops must have hoped that success would fairly soon lighten the load. When the University proved itself, the State would surely grant an endowment, or at least the power of giving degrees ; even that would bring in more students, and more money. There was danger of being led into a vicious circle by the consideration that nothing succeeds like success ; more money, raised from the people, would improve the University, and so increase the chance of State aid ; but if such a gamble failed the people would be left shouldering a heavier burden. The prudent decision eventually taken was to keep the University going on its original scale, until the State should do its duty. So it held out for nearly thirty years. It was a rear-guard action ; but for most of those years the University was probably capable of going over to the attack, if an opportunity had arisen.

In 1862 there seemed to be such an opportunity. Then, when Newman's initial impulse was spent, our native energies attempted a second spring forward. Dr. Bartholomew Woodlock—an able man, and, next after Newman, the hero of the whole undertaking—had become Rector. He determined to try to get more students, to ask the people for more money, to seek a Charter from Lord Palmerston—and lastly, to quit what in his optimism he decried as " the " the Pro-University on Stephen's Green " for a fine new building, to be erected on a site in Drumcondra. As for the Charter, Lord Palmerston curtly refused it, and perhaps that should have been the end. But they went on.

On Sunday 20th July, 1862, took place the solemn ceremony of laying the foundation stone of the Catholic University. No second stone was ever laid on that foundation, and the whole thing might seem comic in its futility, but that it expressed the determination of our people to have a great university of their own; a determination which, in the long run, nothing could stop them from achieving.

Let us look back at that famous day. Newman's publicity had taken the form of the luminous discourse to a select audience; Dr. Woodlock chose to revive a well-tried Irish method of agitation, the monster meeting. Almost the whole of Dublin lined the route or walked in the procession; trains came in all the previous day and night with deputations from the provinces.

In the morning, staff and students walked from Stephen's Green to the Pro-Cathedral for Pontifical High Mass. There were four Archbishops, two Irish, one English, one American; and 22 Irish Bishops, 9 American and Canadian, 1 English. Robed deputations from seven municipalities were there, and " a large and most respectable congregation." The procession started at half-past one. It was headed by 2,500 schoolboys; then came 20,000 representatives of the trades, with banners; then the students, in academic dress—among them, probably, one who was to be a professor in our College fifty years later, George Sigerson. Then walked the professors, Arnold, O'Curry, Hayden, Sullivan and the rest, and the Rector; then the clergy; the corporations; the prelates—these in carriages. So they made their slow way to Drumcondra. It was six o'clock when all were in their places on the field.

The Archbishop of Armagh, Dr. Dixon, blessed the stone and put it in place. Mr. McCarthy, Professor of Architecture, assisted him; we still have his drawing of this castle in the air—and a castle it is, an enormous *château* in the style of the French Renaissance. Speeches were made, and the great crowd dispersed; while the principals went on to a well-deserved University Banquet in All Hallows. There there were more speeches, and toasts of the Pope, the Queen, and the memory of Daniel O'Connell.

May I tell of one more ceremony? These ceremonies were important, because the University was a great idea and a small reality; and the ceremonies were intended so to impress the idea on the world that it might become a great reality.

This was the Commencement of the session 1862–63. It was held in the University Church. The altar was screened, and on the screen was a portrait of Pius IX; below, on a dais, were the Rector and staff. On platforms at either side were the prelates. In the front of the church sat the young men who had passed their final examinations. Behind was the public, including " a numerous and brilliant assemblage of ladies." The Rector, as was customary, spoke of the University and its prospects.

"The gentlemen," he went on, "whose names will be announced here to-day, have been judged worthy respectively of the degrees of Bachelor of Arts, and Bachelor of Science. I ought to be in a position actually to confer these degrees on them. A truly paternal government would, ere this, have granted us the power of doing so." The young men were called up and presented by the Dean to the Rector as worthy of their degrees ; and they went down again empty-handed. A fine sense of ceremonial, I think, was shown in these "maiméd rites." Perhaps hardly less fine was the action, long afterwards, of the National University ; having resolved to give no honorary degrees in its first decade, it made an exception in favour of the survivors of the Catholic University, who had earned degrees and been denied them.—But I return to the 1862 Commencement. The Rector, having explained his inability to award degrees in Arts, declared that he was about to confer the Licentiate and Doctorate of Theology, being empowered to do so by the Pope ; and these degrees were then conferred on the successful candidates.

The session 1862–63, thus bravely opened, was the peak year of the University. Students in Arts rose from under 60 to about 90. Medicine reached 108. There were 110 in the evening class. But the effort failed at once—undermined probably at the start by the denial of the Charter. Next year the numbers were down, the collection fell, the building site was sold. One feels for Dr. Woodlock, that hopeful spirit whose expectations were dashed. But he was not beaten. For sixteen years he fought on, keeping the University useful within its narrow sphere, and ever watchful for a chance to magnify it.[1]

When he resigned in 1879, things were in a pretty bad way. Funds were shrinking ; many of the professors appointed twenty-five years before were getting too old for work ; students, outside of Medicine, were growing fewer.

But in the previous year, 1878, something happened which would soon provide plenty of students—the Intermediate Education Act, with its advantages to Catholic schools. And in 1879 came the chance of direct help in the Royal University Act. The Royal degrees would be open to the students ; and a Catholic institution in Dublin was promised an indirect endowment by way of Fellowships. To make the best use of these benefits, the Bishops decided to turn the University House and its staff—the Arts portion of the Catholic University—into a College, *University College, Dublin,* and to invite the Jesuit Order to

[1] No sketch of the history of the University after 1863 was possible within the limits of a broadcast. Dr. Woodlock sought to improve the "feeding" of the University by affiliating and inspecting schools, and even by founding a school. The Catholic University School was opened in 1864, the Professor of Classics being its headmaster until after a couple of years it was put in the charge of the Marist Fathers. So late as 1878 the building of the large *Aula Maxima* suggests that the University's outlook was not one of despair.

manage it and supplement the elderly staff with younger men. So, under the presidency of Dr. Delany, began the distinguished and fruitful Jesuit epoch of our institution, extending from 1883 to 1909, of which Mr. C. P. Curran will be speaking next Sunday.

The Medical School went on independently, keeping up the name of the Catholic University; in 1909 it was re-united with the Arts College in our present institution.

To take leave of the gallant venture attempted against such odds, but not in vain, by Newman, Woodlock, and other splendid men, and by the Irish people, may I quote some prophetic words of Newman's own? "I see," he said, "a flourishing University, which for a while had to struggle with fortune, but which, when its first founders and servants were dead and gone, had successes far exceeding their anxieties."

J. J. HOGAN.

MEMORIES OF UNIVERSITY COLLEGE, DUBLIN
THE JESUIT TENURE. 1883–1908 [1]

THE ROYAL UNIVERSITY represented the first capitulation of the English Government in our long university struggle. It made a ramshackle, yet workable bridge between the Catholic University and the University College about which I propose to speak. The Act creating it dissolved the Queen's University but preserved its three amply endowed Colleges which were now to work in loose association with University College, Dublin. University College won little other advantage save access to the new Royal degrees and an understanding that a certain number of salaried Fellows of the Royal should teach in the College. The Royal University itself had no teaching function. It was an examining body which maintained in Earlsfort Terrace an Examination Hall in premises which it took over from the Dublin Exhibition of 1864. The Hall continued to be used for many other purposes including Signor Esposito's orchestral concerts. Many of my listeners will remember the story of Oliver Gogarty knocking at the great door and asking Peter the Porter : " Was this the Royal University ? " Peter, red-faced and irate, and knowing his man, said, " You know right well it is." " I don't know," said Gogarty, " last time I passed this way it was a flower show." This was the institution which for thirty years degraded the idea of a university.

The management of University College was entrusted to the Jesuit Fathers in 1883. For this transfer the credit is due to two men, Dr. Walsh, the Archbishop of Dublin, and Father Delany—men so different in temperament, in their political opinions, in their methods, as might deserve the pen of a Plutarch or a Lytton Strachey.

[1] A broadcast talk from Radio Éireann on 2nd May, 1954.

The Archbishop was certainly one of Plutarch's men. His tenacity, his clear vision in practical politics, his sledge-hammer blows in controversy transformed the educational field. Day in, day out, from 1880 to 1908, he kept every aspect of the University grievance before eyes not always as clear-sighted as his own. If Father Delany's views were more accommodating and his approaches more indirect and more *suaviter in modo*, his grasp of essentials was no less firm and he brought into the academic arena great experience in the practical work of education.

Their platform appearance stood in the same contrast. Both men were small in stature. There was something monolithic in the great Archbishop's massive head and stocky figure which went with his blunt, resolute speech. He was no orator. He preferred facts to phrases and his eloquence was that of the chartered accountant, fired by the sense of a just balance. Father Delany's address was equally logical but more graceful. His spare figure easily assumed the stance of the orator, his hand holding his gown as the folds of a toga. His speech had substance and point, and he used to full advantage the resources of a well-modulated voice ; but he relied for his effect not on its charm but on his complete, persuasive lucidity.

It was into his hands that the flickering torch of the Catholic University was passed. If the torch had been wholly extinguished—as it was not—in this land

> " Where to fail is more than to conquer
> And victory less than defeat "

the Catholic University would still have been remembered as an inspiring effort, just as Sparta holds no finer memory than Thermopylae. But when Father Delany laid down his office in 1908 he could point to university distinctions, won by the College in his last year, almost three times greater than the combined achievements of the three fully endowed and equipped Queen's Colleges. The College had no direct endowment and throughout this whole period he had to contend with yearly deficits. A varying number—from two to six—of his Jesuit colleagues were Fellows of the Royal University receiving £400 a year each for their work in that capacity. These sums they devoted to the maintenance of the College, the President himself drawing no remuneration. Well manned as the College was in point of personal ability it was almost destitute in material equipment. The labs. were rudimentary and there was no library ; in effect the National Library was the College Library and T. W. Lyster, its librarian, will long be remembered for the paternal guidance he so freely afforded the students.

In reviving the memory of Father Delany's first staff, I must necessarily rely on tradition, but curiously enough, my own recollection goes back to one who was in the original group appointed by Newman himself, and yet was one of my own examiners. I mean, of course, Thomas

Arnold. Tommy Arnold, as we all called him, was Matthew Arnold's brother and held the first chair in English Literature. He was a man of seventy-six or seven when I knew him and had for some years given up regular class work, but I heard him once in the Aula Maxima and, though I have forgotten what he said of Beowulf and Cynewulf, I am not alone in remembering his clear but thin utterance with its slight stammer, his tall figure stooped at the reading desk, clear-cut features with wide mouth and the fringe of the side whiskers which he wore in the fashion of men of his generation like the old Chief Baron. Looking down on the Green from the windows of our English Literature class we used to see him pass every Saturday morning coming from his house in Leeson Street to the University Church, and we watched with affectionate respect this old gentleman of varied religious experience who, at Grasmere, had seen Wordsworth called to order at a meeting held to protest against the introduction of railways to the Lake District, and in the poet's own house had heard him read a sonnet he had just written.

Two others of the old Catholic University staff I would mention if only because I knew them. Dr. Sigerson and Monsignor Molloy were both scientists. Sigerson had the chair of Biology, Molloy of Physics, but apart from science, they had little else in common except their wide—and if you like—their old-fashioned culture. My dear friend, Dr. Sigerson, who touched and adorned every aspect of Irish life, is now part of our history and literature, and I dare not venture to summarise his achievement. He came to the College, the pupil and colleague of Claude Bernard and Charcot and master of the new learning of Nancy and the Salpêtrière. He was the friend of Gambetta and Mommsen, but also of Mitchell and Kickham and John O'Leary. Acton wrote of him as " the best Irishman I have known." Lines from his own *Saga of King Lir* could well be applied to his appearance :

> " Magnificent he stood : his red-brown locks
> From ample brow and kingly head flowed down
> A lambent flame . . ."

When Birrell, as Chief Secretary, paid his first visit to the College on the eve of his University Bill he saw with amazement this splendid Viking apparition and enquired who he was. " Such a monument, he said, " must certainly have a university to hold it."

One thought of Monsignor Molloy in a different way. Belonging to the extinct race of Castle Catholics, none of us cared for his politics and this perhaps still colours our opinion of him unfairly. He was a tall, courtly figure walking with a limp and a stick. I used to think Talleyrand must have looked like him. He had an unequalled talent in expounding in a popular way the most recent discoveries in physics and was in great demand as a lecturer, drawing large and fashionable audiences. He enjoyed a special prestige by reason of his association with Marconi in exploring the aether, and gadgets such as I am using at this moment. As students, we loved his performance, as he bent tentatively and most carefully over his bag of tricks. Invariably after two unsuccessful attempts he produced the waves he wanted and sent them to ring a bell at the end of the long table where his assistant, George, stood to receive them and the applause of his audience. We weren't the less enthusiastic because we knew that George had the poorest opinion of a lecturer who brought off his experiment at the first go-off. The *houp-là* always came with the third.

The President brought over Father Gerard Manley Hopkins in 1884 from Balliol and Stonyhurst to fill the classical chair and Hopkins taught in the College until his death five years later. His pupils understood he was a poet but none else except very few intimates. He had published little and that little obscurely and was remembered amongst us only as a shy, sensitive recluse. Katie Tynan spoke of him in association with Lionel Johnson, another poet-scholar, and not only, she said, because each had the stature of a child and the brows of wisdom. Both made the same appeal to her feminine tenderness, but I used to hear also how Hopkins was mercilessly chaffed for his Englishness by his colleague, Père Mallac, a French lawyer and freethinker who became Catholic and Jesuit and belonged to the philosophy faculty in the College. These were days of Anglo-French tension, even before Fashoda, but I imagine that behind the chaffing, more than politics, there lay the eternal feud between Platonist and Aristotelian. Hopkins leaned towards Plato and Duns Scotus, but the black-avised Mallac stood fiercely for the Stagyrite. Anyway the poet had a good friend in Father Darlington and when Gerard Hopkins wrote at that date of " his third remove to Ireland " it was to speak of it as a place where

> " . . . he can
> Kind love both give and get."

I scarcely heard his name mentioned in the College of my day and it was not until Robert Bridges brought out his poems in 1918 that people realised that a major poet had lived and died in their midst.

Father Delany made another interesting, half-forgotten appointment, this time to the department of Irish studies. Father Denis Murphy is still remembered for his edition of O'Clery's *Life of Aodh Ruadh O'Donnell*, for his *Cromwell in Ireland* and his studies in the Irish Martyrs. The same cannot be said of his more unusual and perhaps more scholarly successor, Father John O'Carroll. Father O'Carroll was the last direct descendant of the Princes of Ely. He was a quite amazing linguist, speaking seventeen languages fluently and the complete master of their literatures. He could speak eight others and read in still eight or nine more. He ranged freely from Icelandic to Hungarian, but his strong line seems to have been in Russian and in those Slavonic tongues and dialects in eleven of which, in happier days, on the Orient Express, you were exhorted not to spit. He wrote much in Father Finlay's *Lyceum* on Pushkin, Gogol and Dostoievsky long before the days of Garnett and

Maurice Baring. He knew Middle Irish; wrote much also in the *Gaelic Journal*; worked in the old Society for the Preservation of the Irish Language and the Gaelic Union which followed it, and in the early 'nineties conducted a class in modern Irish in the College as Pearse did later.

In this field of Irish studies Father Edmond Hogan of the *Onomasticon* is much better remembered. He came well down into my day and though I was not his pupil, I saw him more than once, in his bed-sitting-writing-room. Being then something of a valetudinarian, he worked in front of a famous folding-screen, its surface pasted with old *Weekly Freeman* cartoons, and for the good of his health he kept a box of pills in his bedroom slippers. In those days he had for his pupils the late Dr. Seamus O'Kelly and Seamus Clandillon and George Clancy who, as Mayor of Limerick, was shot by the Black and Tans. It was to Dr. Hogan that John MacNeill served his scholar's apprenticeship, doing under him the spade work of *Cath Ruis na Riogh*. John MacNeill who was later invited by Father Delany to lecture on Early Irish History in the College has written finely on this old Bollandist, the link between the old and the new tradition of Irish scholarship and the last of a long line who used Latin easily and naturally as the language of communication between the learned.

It goes against my grain to pass over with bare mention the brilliant group of scientists who, if they were not so picturesque as some of their literary colleagues, made a strong bony structure for the College: Harry McWeeney and Conway in Mathematics, McClelland and Preston in Physics, with Huston Stewart who lectured in the old Physics Theatre to a conjoint mob of us—First Arts and First Medicals. The curious in these matters may glimpse that class at a disrespectful moment in the *Portrait of the Artist*.

Father Delany's quality as an educationist comes out in the choice of these men and in his capacity to work with them, on the whole, smoothly. In the later years of his term as President he set up and shared the government of the College with a Council of six professors—five of them were laymen in my time—who were elected every three years by and from the professorial body. The second significant advance made at the same period was the admission of women students to the College lectures, or at least to those principal lectures delivered in the Aula Maxima. These were fundamental changes, but otherwise the President's personal influence on the students was small compared with others on the staff as, for example Father Finlay, Father Darlington and William Magennis. Father Finlay's name is indissolubly linked with the economics of our agriculture, but his influence on successive generations of students went far beyond that. This Cavan son of a Scotch engineer had a closer knowledge of the Irish character and a larger grasp of public affairs than anyone else in the College. His early training had been in France and he came back a formidable logician gifted with style. Teaching in turn philosophy, political economy, and political

15

science, he was master of what he professed, and what he had to say he said with authority, precision, and a mordant wit. Walter Bagehot, his fellow economist, once classified men dentally—he divided them into molars and incisors. Father Tom was one of the incisors. His was the way of sharp definition and analysis. Popular slogans and the easy phrases of the platform shrivelled under his cool, humorous dissection, curled up and died. But he was far from being the negative, corrosive-academic type. Whenever possible he directed the activities of his students into writing and public affairs and one way of judging the intellectual temper of the College is by reference to the monthlies he founded and edited : *The Lyceum* and *The New Ireland Review*, predecessors of *Studies*.

Then there was Father Darlington who as Dean of the College knew all the students and was untiring for their comfort. His mannerism have become legendary—the brisk rubbing of hands and quick assentations—as when W. P. Coyne told him of his intended marriage. "Just the very thing, Mr. Coyne, just the very thing. I was about to do the same myself." But these mannerisms hid nothing of his deep and kindly understanding. In my time as well as being Dean he held the English Chair and passed from it after a year or two into the Philosophy Faculty. His teaching of each subject profited from his experience of the other. Perhaps he was not so very distinguished as a philosopher, but his approach to Hamlet through Aristotle and Aquinas had a particular savour for one student bored with the solemnities of Dowden and Bradley. This Aristotelian under-current emerged whenever the Dean spoke, as he often did, at the College Societies, and indeed it fits in with what Father Delany used to say, that the Faculty of Philosophy should be the heart of any university. Tom Kettle, John Marcus O'Sullivan, John O'Byrne followed Finlay's and Magennis's classes for their degree, but students from other faculties put in occasional appearances, and, in fact, it was not so easy for any student to escape some tincture of divine philosophy.

My name was entered on the College Books in Michaelmas 1899, and when the new undergraduate had shaken hands with the Bursar he shyly passed from his presence up the staircase of No. 85. He had no acquaintance amongst the students but this dereliction did not long endure. He was intercepted on the first landing by a senior student, bearded and in knickerbockers, quick-firing in speech, of businesslike address but adroitly courteous. Frank Skeffington enormously flattered the newcomer by knowing his name and mentioning an examination distinction he had just won. But he swiftly followed up his advantage by pointing out the plain duty which lay on me to join the Literary and Historical, of which he was Secretary. Obediently, I entered my name on this second roll and in that Society, as a dumb observer, I watched the behaviour of many of my later friends. Frank Skeffington was the cat-fish in that far from stagnant tank. He was a radical and democrat, blending the English tradition of John Stuart Mill and W. T. Stead with the Irish and international outlook of Michael Davitt. All the seeds of his later development were stirring. He was already a pacifist and a militant feminist and, acutely conscious of every social problem, had linked his Home Rule with labour sympathies. He loved argument and had a net opinion on every point of human behaviour. At an age when students are usually content to hold many opinions in loose solution, his were all armed *cap à pie* and ready for battle. His every opinion was a principle for which he was ready to die. He had, for example, certain fixed opinions on rational dress and as auditor of the Literary and Historical he had occasion to discuss his auditorial address and the general protocol of the meeting with the President. The discussion proceeded towards a friendly close. But Skeffington was wearing his knickerbockers as usual and Father Delany ventured to say that the Auditor should wear the evening attire proper to gentlemen on such an occasion. In his staccato Ulster accent Skeffington said, " I'll come as I am or not at all." And, accordingly, the whole function was abandoned. Later he resigned from the Society after he had unsuccessfully disputed its constitutional right to subscribe to the Irish Language Fund. He was, I repeat, the Socratic cat-fish in our tank. No one agreed with him, but we all loved him for his courage, his Cato-like intransigence, and his unquenchable good humour.

Tom Kettle entered the College in 1897. The ill-health which shadowed his whole life compelled him to retire, now to his father's farm at St. Margaret's, and again to Innsbruck, but even at a distance his magnetism drew us towards him and his intellectual ascendancy remained unquestioned. Son of Andrew Kettle, farmer, Land Leaguer, and staunch Parnellite, Tom drew from the land the farmer's realist sense of politics and like his friend, Willie Dawson, he grew up steeped in the *minutiae* of Parnellite lore. In College he followed the philosophy course except for a year at Innsbruck where he read history as well as philosophy under a formidable team of Teutonic professors. Tom Kettle, however, lost nothing there of his native distinction or sense of style. However much his mind moved under Hegel and Schopenhauer, the cloud was stabbed with wit and glowed with the warmest humanity. His was the most brilliant intelligence of his generation and he had the most widely stretched and vigorously exercised mind in our student group. All his studies were focused on contemporary politics and they covered a great field—sociology, history, law and literature. They provided rich, sudden reinforcement to his passionate eloquence and a weight of metal that lent singular driving power to the shafts of his epigrams.

Tom Kettle and James Joyce were the two men of genius in my period. Joyce came to the College a year before I did and I have already described over this radio how I first saw him. It was at my first lecture ; the class was in English Literature ; the lecturer was Father Darlington, and his first words were from Aristotle's *Poetics*. Towards the end of the lecture he had occasion to mention Stephen

Phillips, a lesser poet of the 'nineties who had just written his *Paolo and Francesca*. He asked if anyone in the class had read it, and then " Have you read it, Mr. Joyce ? " and a voice answered indifferently " Yes." I looked round and saw my first poet.

He was then seventeen, and, though he had not yet published any of his *Chamber Music*, his article on Ibsen's latest play *When we Dead Awaken* appeared in the *Fortnightly Review* only six months later. Earlier in the same year he read his paper on *Drama and Life* to the Literary and Historical. It was an assault on the romantic theatre and a vindication of Ibsen, but unfortunately nothing of it survives. His other address to the Society on Clarence Mangan was published in the College magazine, *St. Stephen's*, when Hugh Kennedy, later our first Chief Justice, was its editor. Joyce's delivery of that address remains in my memory—his voice metallic in its clearness and very deliberate as if coming from some cold and distant oracle.

He was working for a Modern Literature degree in Italian, French, and English, but his reading was a good deal off the course. I suspect there were few young men in these islands at that date so equally interested in Guido Cavalcanti and the Scandinavians, in Dante and Arthur Rimbaud. What distinguished him most was not the exceptional character of his reading, or the maturity of his own mind, but his complete absorption in the art and function of literature and his defiant assertion of the conclusions at which he had arrived. He stood jealously in defence of his own integrity. He was wholly indifferent to questions which excited the general body of the students and this lent him a false appearance of arrogance. He had the liveliest sense of the absurd but though he could be grotesquely funny at times, he was not gregarious as most students are and in conversation he preferred to talk with one friend at a time. He stood apart from those interminable discussions which kept the rest of us, after closing hours, at the National Library, swinging backwards and forwards between our lodgings, loath to separate, unwilling to conclude anything. Joyce's conclusions were oracular, cryptic, and admitted of little debate, but his aloofness implied no discourtesy or personal antagonism. There was, on the contrary, a great deal of mutual respect.

I will mention but one other name. When Arthur Clery was Auditor of the Society he seemed to me to be groomed for an inevitable, conventional professional success. His mind was formed on the classics, his manner graceful and suave, his speech polished in the temper of his favourite eighteenth century. His sentences fell in impeccable cadence and he had a pleasing gift of epigram. Then something happened. The Gaelic bug bit him, and this change was typical of what was happening in the College when we had all gone Irish Ireland and were growing very tired of the stuffed shirts. Let me recall an Inaugural of that date, a formal occasion and one of some importance since the platform was graced with the presence of Mr. Birrell. It was Birrell's first public appearance as Chief Secretary, and he was to speak on the University Question. He made his statement with his usual expressions of sympathy and promises with which we were only too familiar. On this occasion, as events proved, there was more reality than usual in the politician's pledge, but it availed Mr. Birrell nothing. Some servile speech followed from some Whig and then Arthur Clery spoke as no one since J. F. Taylor had spoken on a university platform. The ferocity of his speech was enhanced by a shaggy beard which, for a brief period, Arthur chose to wear. He rent, flayed, tore and tattered that well-meaning Chief Secretary. He spat on his promises, derided his non-conformist conscience and guyed all his Liberal Gods. He made that platform look like some arena where a bewildered bull lay staring, uncomprehending, under the rain of many darts. Yes, with his undergraduate's gown Arthur had put aside the things of English culture, scrapped his formal eloquence and received ideas ; scrapped, too, what looked like a career and become a new man. He exchanged Horace for à Kempis, gave me his vellum-bound Petronius— I hate to ask myself why—and of the eighteenth century kept only its wit and love of epigram. From that on he lived an Irish Aristides— entirely unworldly, living ont he point of honour, as some would say quixotically, but in the dangerous days he was a Supreme Court Judge in the early Republican Courts.

The growing unrest in the student body ran parallel with the growth of new ideas outside and a corresponding turbulence in the streets. Following a pinchbeck Jubilee, the incidents of the Boer War, a succession of Royal Visits and a provocative conferring of an Honorary Degree on Joseph Chamberlain led to street demonstrations in some of which our students joined the Cecilia Street medicals, led by the stalwart Tom Madden of Kiltimagh, himself a Surgeon's man. Internal College politics grew more acute and student restiveness came to a head with some injudicious assertion of authority by Father Delany who was fearful of offending some in high places. A series of angry demonstrations against him and against the Senate of the Royal culminated in the Organ Row led by Cruise O'Brien. It led to the resignation of the Chancellor, and to the flight after much cackle of the senatorial geese from the Capitol. In 1908 the Royal fell.

Looking back, we seem a small company—no more than 80 or 100 artsmen—but our numbers ensured a liberal ratio of professors to students and brought us into close comradeship with each other and into fruitful contact with our elders. I sometimes think—when my friend Lennox Robinson does not spare me that trouble—that the ideal University class should seat no more than a dining table. No more walked with Plato in the grove of the Academy or sat with Zeno in the Porch.

There was a week in my time when on two successive Sundays we walked in two funerals, Father O'Growney's and Charles Gavan Duffy's. As we marched we heard a woman say from the sidewalk : " Them's a fine body of young men. Who are they ? " And her friend replied :

" They are," said she, " Them's the grocers' curates." I think she
was partly right. They *were* fine, these young men : Skeffington and
Kettle, Joyce and John Marcus O'Sullivan ; Arthur Clery, George
Clancy, and Tom Madden. They all worked for the faith in them and
died on one barricade or another. From the sidewalk I salute them.

C. P. CURRAN.

THE NEW COLLEGE, 1908-1954 [1]

IT is now almost forty-three years since I entered University College
as a rather younger than average student in the Faculty of Arts. When
I came up from St. Joseph's College, Ballinasloe, to sit for an Entrance
Scholarship, the College was just entering upon its third year under
Dr. Coffey's administration. I was of course much too young and
unconcerned with such matters to have any inkling of the significance
of Dr. Coffey's appointment. He had been Dean and Registrar of
the Medical School of the Catholic University which had continued
to function in Cecilia Street all during the years while the College in
St. Stephen's Green was receiving its Jesuit stamp. His appointment
in one sense marked the re-emergence of Newman's institution and its
junction once more with the broad stream of the College's progress.

Although I was afterwards of course to have many medical students
among my friends, I seem to remember that in 1911 their doings in
Cecilia Street were still remote enough from our small world at 86,
St. Stephen's Green. There were 254 of them out of a total of 530
students. Last year there were 641 of them out of a total of 3,324,
so that it can hardly be said that their numbers have increased in a
manner by any means out of proportion to the general increase.
Probably because my own work seldom or never brought me to Cecilia
Street, my first impression of the College was that of a still strongly
Jesuit institution. Dr. Delany, it is true, was only a name to my
generation, and even in after times I did not often meet him. Father
Darlington, whose personality had so dominated in the College almost
from the beginning of its Jesuit period, was to me only a shadow.

The Jesuit Father with whom I had most contact was inevitably
Father Henry Browne, Professor of Greek. He had come from Oxford
to succeed Father Gerard Manley Hopkins in 1890, and there can
seldom have been a greater contrast than that between him and his
distinguished predecessor. Where Hopkins had been an introvert and
a sufferer, Browne was a crusader, utterly unselfconscious and entirely
devoted to whatever work he had in hands. My first recollection of
him remains very vivid. It is of the bewilderment with which, fresh
from Ballinasloe, I faced for the first time the Oxford accent and
manner at his oral examination for the Entrance Scholarship. I can

[1] A broadcast talk from Radio Éireann on 9th May, 1954.

still hear his voice asking me for " any mention of Dorians in Homer."
He afterwards became my beloved master and kind friend. Father
Browne was not the only person to administer.such linguistic shocks.
My first term in the College was largely spent in the company of a
group of boys from St. Columb's College, Derry—one of them now
Bishop of that See—and I remember vividly how hard it was to under-
stand them.

The last years of the College under Father Delany had been years
of much student liveliness, the embers of which still smouldered a
little under Dr. Coffey. What kept this liveliness going was in part, I
think, the fact that many of the student leaders in the new College had
actually been in residence in the old. The influence of this small
group on the heterogeneous body who entered the College after 1909
was out of all proportion to its numbers. Whether because of their
common experience of life in the residential Jesuit College or by reason
of their own gifts, those who had shared in the last phase of the Jesuit
period were the natural leaders of the new generation. Some of them after
1909 had already become members of the staff, and of these I think it
will be universally agreed no one contributed more to the creation of
the spirit which the new and larger College needed than Arthur Clery.
It is indeed hard for anyone of my generation to realise that this wonderful man with his strange and entirely individual combination of learning
and wit, cynicism and simplicity, high seriousness and gaiety, has been
gone from us now for twenty-two years.

With an institution so Irish as the College has been and is, it is
probably inevitable that some day someone will write its history in
the form of a series of anecdotes. The central figure in such a history
will inevitably be the President himself. When I succeeded to his
office a few years ago our Head Porter delighted me one day by telling
me that Dr. Coffey used to diffuse his personality throughout the room
where I was working. The diffusion was by no means confined to the
four walls of a room. No head of an institution ever knew all the
details of its working more thoroughly than Dr. Coffey knew his College.
Tireless devotion and never-ending sympathy were perhaps his two
outstanding qualities. Even at the end of his term of office, when
numbers were beginning to become rather overwhelming, he was still
reputed to know the history of every student. His sympathy, while
perhaps it took somewhat different forms, was quite as legendary in
its own way as Father Darlington's fabulous capacity for putting himself in the place of the person he was talking to. It was by no means
confined to the more distinguished or even the more respectable among
the student body, and there are many legends illustrating his capacity
to assist " border-liners " at Examination Board meetings and to give
a helping hand, often under peculiar circumstances and in devious
ways, to the less successful of those under his charge. This capacity
for sympathy was accompanied by a very effective, if quiet, dignity of
manner. Partly owing to his low voice he was not effective as a speaker,

though here again the warmth of his heart often lent him a moving kind of eloquence. In matters of College business and administration he relied heavily on patience, and the proceedings at meetings over which he presided were apt to be devious. The complaint was often humorously made that he got important matters through under the heading of "Other Business."

Next to the President the most important men in the College were of course the Registrar, A. W. Conway, and the Secretary and Bursar, John W. Bacon. Dr. Conway's bulky frame and somewhat lethargic manner concealed one of the most penetrating intelligences in Ireland and a wit of remarkable keenness. During Dr. Coffey's presidency it was inevitable that a man of Dr. Conway's easy temperament should play a comparatively small part in the administration of the College. His quality in this respect only got a chance to show itself when he succeeded the older man as President, and he was by then sixty-three years of age. His seven years as Head of the College were years of quite extraordinary difficulty, coinciding as they did with the worst phase of the Second World War. Nevertheless he succeeded both in focusing attention on the College's almost desperate financial straits and also, by devolving to the Faculties much of the business which Dr. Coffey had kept in his own hands, in restoring an academic balance which after thirty years of almost one-man rule had come to be badly needed.

John W. Bacon, though also a man of quiet and equable temperament, was by no means lethargic. Distinguished as an English scholar before his appointment to the Secretaryship, he had a great gift for order and a disciplined energy which was to prove of very special value as the College's numbers grew. A slightly stern manner hid in his case a sort of wry and humorous kindness which came to the assistance, often unexpectedly, of many a hard-pressed student.

During his whole administration Dr. Coffey was plagued by the inadequacy of the financial provision that had been made for the new College in the Act of 1908. The new College took over from the Jesuit Fathers the houses from number 82 to 86 St. Stephen's Green, which the Jesuit Fathers in their turn had inherited from the Catholic University. It also took over the old premises in Cecilia Street where the Medical School had first opened under Newman in 1855. In 1892 the sum of £3,000 had been spent in repairing the School, but I doubt if it received a single coat of paint during the next forty years. In addition to these very inadequate and widely scattered buildings, the College had transferred to it the offices in Earlsfort Terrace formerly occupied by the Royal University. These buildings, which had been erected about forty years earlier to house an exhibition, were as unsuitable for the work of a teaching institution as any building could very well be. The total sum available for new buildings was £110,000. The outbreak of war in 1914 caused an enormous increase in the cost of building, which had to be met for the most part out of income. As a result, only a small part of the building originally planned could be erected. A decent front hid the wreckage that was left of the Royal University buildings, and desperation led the College even to use portions of this wreckage as class-rooms and laboratories. To this day, however, nearly one-third of the old building stands as a useless and dangerous ruin right behind Butler's elegant façade, while the College Library, instead of having a separate building, is housed in scattered halls and corridors. Amalgamation with the College of Science in 1926 gave much-needed space for Chemistry, Biology, and Engineering, but this provision was followed by a new influx of students for whom the space very soon became once more inadequate. Cecilia Street, which for some years had been used only for Anatomy, was not finally abandoned until 1931. It is not unfair to say that Dr. Coffey, during the last years of his term of office, felt himself to be defeated by the magnitude of a task which had increased rather than diminished for all his efforts to deal with it.

Great wealth, as is well known, brings many moral dangers in its train, and perhaps University College is fortunate in having escaped the risks that dog the footsteps of over-endowed youth. I do not think however that the Irish public is at all sufficiently aware how wide is the margin by which that escape has been achieved. The national struggle from 1916 to 1921, the Civil War which followed, and its aftermath in bitter party division, all helped in various ways to divert attention from the desirability, indeed the urgency, of developing and utilising the national asset which the College unquestionably represented. It should not be thought that Dr. Coffey's colleagues at this time, who must often have discussed such matters with him, were intellectual nonentities or devoid of practical common sense. They included men of the calibre of Douglas Hyde, John MacNeill, Father Tom Finlay, Father Timothy Corcoran and John Marcus O'Sullivan, all of whom had a wide experience of public life and of the ways of governments.

Material stagnation very fortunately had nothing to correspond with it on the intellectual and spiritual side of the College's life. Although the increase in numbers of students so fantastically outran the growth of the staff, great work both in teaching and research was accomplished in every part of the College during Dr. Coffey's and Dr. Conway's years. The Medical School had already a great tradition behind it in the work of Ambrose Birmingham, of Dr. Coffey himself, of Alexander Blayney and of that fabulous figure Surgeon M'Ardle. Their successors are fortunately for the most part still with us, but the recent lamented deaths of James N. Meenan, Henry Meade and Henry Moore enable me to pay some tribute to their shining ability and their great devotion both to the cause of the College and to their own art. In Chemistry and Physics, Hugh Ryan and John A. McClelland were spared to direct new and enlarged Departments and to train remarkable successors, now, alas ! gone in their turn. T. J. Nolan and J. J. Nolan were already bright stars of research and scholarship when I came to the College. Both died in harness and each left a flourishing School where the spirit of research is very much alive and where all that is needed is endowment. In the new science of Biochemistry, as in Mathematical Physics, the College took and held a place on the highest international level. A flourishing School of Civil Engineering was created almost out of nothing by the ability and energy of a single Professor, happily still with us. With its sister Departments of Mechanical and Electrical Engineering, developed since 1926, it supplies graduates in adequate numbers who are doing indispensable work at home and have made their name in every English-speaking country. The School of Architecture, founded by Scott, developed under Butler to something approaching its present strenuous activity. The new School of Agriculture, again helped by the Act of 1926, has not only turned out large numbers of highly trained experts ; the work of its research departments in plant breeding, plant pathology, animal nutrition, soil science, horticulture and forestry has become an essential basis for further progress. The Arts Faculty and its sister Faculties of Law, Commerce, Philosophy, and Celtic Studies, have supplied the great majority of its higher Civil Servants to the Irish State as well as taking an enormous share in the development of the two great legal professions and in the Judiciary. A very large proportion of the country's secondary teachers, lay and clerical, have passed through the College, and it has made itself felt in the work of the Primary Schools. In spite of the secular character imposed upon it by the Act of 1908 and by its Charter, the College has never forfeited, but rather confirmed, its claim to be *the* University for Irish Catholics.

But perhaps it is in the field of Irish studies—where Newman's appointment of Eugene O'Curry set such a splendid precedent—that the College has made its greatest contribution to the welfare of the nation. Already in 1907 Dr. Delany, perhaps consciously following Newman's footsteps, had appointed John MacNeill Professor of Early Irish History in the Jesuit College. Historians have still to assess the full range of MacNeill's many-sided work. As founder both of the Gaelic League and of the Irish Volunteers, he played a part second to none in the Irish revival. As Professor of Early Irish History he was the first to apply modern scientific and critical methods to a subject which, before him, had been given over to legend. It was typical of the man and his stormy yet immensely fruitful career that his greatest work was first given to the public in the form of a series of lectures delivered outside the College in order to support his family when he had temporarily lost his Chair after being condemned to penal servitude for life on the suppression of the Rising of 1916. MacNeill was reappointed very soon after his release and was of course to serve more than one other term in prison. During his absence the work of his Chair was nobly and loyally carried on by the late R. A. S. Macalister, Professor of Celtic Archaeology, who, like MacNeill, was a pioneer in his subject and of whom it may be said that all Irish archaeologists of to-day are directly or indirectly his pupils. Similar help was given by Mary Hayden, Professor of Modern Irish History, herself a daughter of one of Newman's Professors, a pioneer in the struggle for women's rights in education and one of the best beloved members of Dr. Coffey's original staff. The two Professors of Irish were men of outstanding quality in their different ways. Dr. Douglas Hyde came to the College already enjoying an immense reputation as co-founder and President of the Gaelic League. He was perhaps more a poet and an artist than a scholar, and certainly he was a character to have known whom was an education in itself. His career fittingly crowned by his election as first President of Ireland, he remained to the end the same gay, charming, affectionate mixture of simplicity and subtlety that he had been during his quarter of a century in the College. Like Hyde and Macalister, Osborn Bergin was a Protestant. A marvel of linguistic attainment, he could compose verses with equal facility in Sanskrit, Greek, Latin, Ancient and Modern Irish, and of course English. He had been taught Greek and Latin in Cork by the formidable Sir William Ridgeway, and was afterwards a pupil of Wilhelm Schulze in Berlin. He was " the master of those who know " in matters relating to the Irish language, and all Irish scholarship in the future will build upon the foundations he laid.

It would take many talks to give a full description of the varied personalities who worked during those thirty years under Denis J. Coffey, and the effect of whose work is visible in every aspect of the new Ireland. Only a few of them can be mentioned on this occasion. In 1909 John Marcus O'Sullivan was fresh home from Heidelberg where he had gained great distinction with his Doctorate in Philosophy. Appointed to the Chair of Modern History, he established himself at once not only as a profound thinker and inspiring teacher but as a charming and indeed alluring personality. He reminded one of the great Professors of ancient times so graphically described by Newman who drew crowds by their eloquence and by the variety of their knowledge. It is a great pity that he never found time to prepare for publication even one of the three famous courses which he gave in different years—on Machiavelli, Luther, and Rousseau. From 1927 until 1932 he won fresh distinction as Minister for Education, but his greatest monument will be the live and flourishing School of History which, in spite of all difficulties and distractions, he left behind him in the College. Of a much older man, whose dominance in his own sphere had been established long before the Act of 1908, it would be almost an offence not to speak in such a commemoration as this. William Magennis, Professor of Metaphysics, played many distinguished parts during his long life-time, and it was never settled in which sphere he was more fascinating and impressive as a teacher, Philosophy or English Literature. As a lecturer John Marcus O'Sullivan used to say that he excelled the great Platonist, Windelband. A dialectician of endless subtlety and resource, he had immense charm and authority, if only he had learned to prune his periods. His long and colourful political career brought him I think but little satisfaction for the reason that he was so much a whole party in himself. Yet the political and intellectual life of Dublin and of Ireland would have been very different and much poorer without him. The peculiar qualities of both men are brightly illuminated for those who knew them by the fact that Arthur Clery used to boast that he never missed a single one of Magennis's lectures on Metaphysics for twenty-five years, while he himself was Professor of Law. Perhaps it may be no harm to say that the compliment, so far as I am aware, was not returned. Father Timothy Corcoran came to the College from Clongowes, where his prowess as a teacher of Latin and Greek was legendary, and by 1909 he had already won a high reputation as a writer on educational history. Appointed to the newly created Chair of Education, he made his mark at once, and very soon his work in training candidates for secondary teaching extended his influence throughout all the schools of Ireland. Father Corcoran was a man of strong opinions on all of the many subjects that interested him. His nationalism was particularly deep-rooted and strongly held and his extensive researches into Irish educational records found an outlet in a series of remarkable works of documentation. One of his many services to the country was his work as a co-founder of the Irish Manuscripts Commission which has done so much for historical research.

It is notorious that there are those among the Dons in the older English Universities who openly express their belief that the best College is one which is all Dons and no students. Statistics, as I have suggested, are sufficient to demonstrate that University College, Dublin, has not been measurable by this austere standard. Indeed the list of its students might easily be made to sound like a muster roll of the whole Irish people. Pearse, MacDonagh and Plunkett were all graduates of the Royal University who had been taught in the Jesuit College, and MacDonagh, during the years before the Rising, was a genial and popular Assistant in English. Ginger O'Connell, who came back from New York in 1914 to become the trainer of the Volunteers, was an M.A. in Mental and Moral Science. The names of Kevin Barry and Frank Flood will always be venerated in the College. They were singled out by a tragic fate from a large number who put their lives at stake during the years from 1918 to 1921. Among those of earlier date Thomas Arkins in particular will not be forgotten if only because he was the first champion of the idea of a Students' Representative Council. *The National Student*, founded in 1910, reached its height under the Editorship of Eimar O'Duffy just before the Rising. Kevin O'Higgins and Patrick Hogan were already outstanding in the student world in those years. As with all things human the annals of student life have had many ups and downs since 1909 ; but two things can be asserted of the students of University College without fear of contradiction. They contain among them most of Ireland's ablest young intellect, whose quality is such that it may well strain the capacity of any teaching staff; and their standards of conduct and discipline have always been such as one might expect from the Catholic Irish homes from which the great majority of them come.

I think enough has been said in these talks to show that the story of the development of Newman's Catholic University into the modern University College, Dublin, is one of the most complex and fascinating chapters in the history of modern Ireland. At every stage the work of the College has been intimately linked with the slow but inexorable recovery of the national strength. Critics of the College have sometimes suggested that because its first founder was an Englishman there is something questionable about its credentials. I would ask such critics to acquaint themselves fully with the history of its origin and development before delivering judgement. Newman came to Ireland not only as an Englishman but as one of the greatest of the Church's converts, and he came at the joint request of the Irish Hierarchy and the Holy See to found a University primarily for Irish Catholics on the model of Louvain. If he tried to mingle Louvain with Oxford he also understood better than anyone else that the Catholic University of Ireland must respond to the historic needs of the Irish people. The work of O'Curry and his successors has proved that Newman's vision has never been repudiated. With the prospect of a new estate, new buildings, and a greatly increased endowment, the right policy for the College is surely to continue walking in Newman's footsteps. There is no reason why such an institution, fortified by such traditions, should not remain intensely Irish and make its primary task the doing of Ireland's work, while at the same time, as Newman intended, drawing to itself " as to a sacred soil . . . students from east, west and south." The College faces its second century with its faith and pride in its founder undiminished and with courage derived from the record of those who, " when he was dead and gone, had successes far exceeding his anxieties."

MICHAEL TIERNEY.